The Spiritual Soul

The Spiritual Soul

New Pentecostal Insights on the Human Being

Matthew J. Churchouse

PICKWICK Publications · Eugene, Oregon

THE SPIRITUAL SOUL
New Pentecostal Insights on the Human Being

Copyright © 2024 Matthew J. Churchouse. All rights reserved. Except for brief quotations in critical publications or reviews, no part of this book may be reproduced in any manner without prior written permission from the publisher. Write: Permissions, Wipf and Stock Publishers, 199 W. 8th Ave., Suite 3, Eugene, OR 97401.

Pickwick Publications
An Imprint of Wipf and Stock Publishers
199 W. 8th Ave., Suite 3
Eugene, OR 97401

www.wipfandstock.com

PAPERBACK ISBN: 978-1-6667-8137-3
HARDCOVER ISBN: 978-1-6667-8138-0
EBOOK ISBN: 978-1-6667-8139-7

Cataloguing-in-Publication data:

Names: Churchouse, Matthew J. [author].

Title: The spiritual soul : new Pentecostal insights on the human being / Matthew J. Churchouse.

Description: Eugene, OR: Pickwick Publications, 2024 | Includes bibliographical references and index.

Identifiers: ISBN 978-1-6667-8137-3 (paperback) | ISBN 978-1-6667-8138-0 (hardcover) | ISBN 978-1-6667-8139-7 (ebook)

Subjects: LCSH: Theological anthropology—Christianity. | Holy Spirit. | Theological anthropology. | Yong, Amos. | Kärkkäinen, Veli-Matti. | Pentecostal churches—Doctrines.

Classification: BT701.3 C48 2024 (paperback) | BT701.3 (ebook)

VERSION NUMBER 04/12/24

[Scripture quotations are from] New Revised Standard Version Bible, copyright © 1989, 1995 National Council of the Churches of Christ in the United States of America. Used by permission. All rights reserved worldwide.

Dedicated to
my loving and beloved wife Anna,

whose beauty in body and soul
inspires and points me beyond
to its divine and radiant author
and his gift of glory eternal.

Contents

Preface | ix

Acknowledgments | xiii

Introduction | 1

Part I: Setting the Scene

1. The Doctrine of Human Constitution in Western Pentecostal Theological History | 19

Part II: The Contemporary Pentecostal Anthropology of Yong and Kärkkäinen

2. Yong and Kärkkäinen's Doctrine of Human Constitution | 49
3. A Critique of Yong and Kärkkäinen's Doctrine of Human Constitution | 80

Excursus: Platonist and Classic Cartesian Dualisms | 117

Part III: Towards an Enhanced Pentecostal Philosophical-Theological Model of Human Constitution

4. Biblical Holistic Dualism in Light of a Pentecostal Spirit-Filled World | 131

5   Advancing a Contemporary (Holistic) Substance Dualism | 162

**Part IV: A Pentecostal Enspirited Proposal for
Enhancing the Doctrine of Human Constitution**

6   The (Theological) Spiritual Soul and an
    Enspiritable Holistic Dualism | 197

Conclusion | 225

Epilogue | 239
Bibliography | 241
Subject Index | 255
Author Index | 263
Scripture Index | 265

Preface

THE TOPIC OF PENTECOSTALISM and of what it means to be human have further grown in their significance in the contemporary era of history.

Pentecostalism has continued to spread throughout the world to the point of now being the fastest-growing spirituality—specifically, spirituality-of-*renewal*—to be occurring on the face of the earth, with the lives of millions of people having been renewed by this transformative spirituality. The related anthropological question—of what it means to be human—is likewise displaying its impact, being the question that underlies the pertinent matters of human identity, future, and purpose being felt in the contemporary climate by people and cultures worldwide.

These interrelated topics gained my particular attention and passion during my years of doctoral study at the University of Birmingham. My interest in Pentecostalism had already been enlivened through worship and participation in churches of a Pentecostal/Charismatic persuasion—engendering a desire to explore Pentecostalism to a deeper and further degree. The related topic of anthropological interest then arose in that ensuing period of research due to a developing intrigue in the philosophy of mind and its questions concerning the mind-body relation. These two correlative topics joined together in my doctoral focus resulting in a PhD on the subject of Pentecostal (/Charismatic) theology and the human body and soul relation.

This book is some of the out-workings of those years of research and writing; yet the ideas have been widened and deepened due to the time and events that have transpired in the years since that project's completion. For me, personally, those events have included the excitement of developing relationship and the subsequent joy of marriage, the fulfilment of ordination and then ministry in the heart of the city of Birmingham, the lament of the season of Covid and the loss of physical relation, and the gladness of becoming a parent with all its challenge, potential, and wonder—all occurring in the six years that followed the PhD's completion; such experiences have brought further thought and deeper reflection on the topics of spirituality and anthropology. As a result, whilst based on my previous research, the book *The Spiritual Soul* is a distance beyond that doctoral project with its ideas having been honed and developed in the years that followed the PhD's conclusion.

Due to the book's background and conceptual focus, it is written in the language of the academy, written primarily for Pentecostal scholars and theological students. Yet, in the interest of widening its usefulness and accessibility to the non-scholarly-but-interested reader, a few signposts might be of help for engaging with the book's content and thought.

First, the book's introduction and conclusion contain as much of the argument as possible; these bookends are intended to give a clear overview of the book—its focus and direction of travel—and are deliberately written in a manner generally accessible to the popular reader, whilst maintaining a style appropriate for the theological academy.

Second, a brief outline of the book might (here) be helpful. The book's earlier chapters are of review and analytical critique; the reader interested in historical views of the human, or Pentecostal views of such in the present, might be drawn to these opening chapters. The latter chapters of the book are more of theological construction; those interested in the teaching of Scripture and the relation of the soul to the body might be more drawn to these subsequent chapters. The pinnacle of that constructive work appears in the sixth and ultimate chapter, which expounds the nature of the spiritual soul and its relationship to the Holy Spirit; those interested in the Divine-human encounter at the core of Pentecostal spirituality might be drawn to this final chapter.

Third, regarding the shape of the chapters, (as with the introduction and conclusion) each chapter introduces and finishes with a summary of the chapter's content—intending to make the book's overall argument clear for all readers. Once the content of each chapter begins to engage with its respective dialogue-partners, it becomes albeit denser, drawing fully upon terminology, language, and concepts more familiar to the theological academy; so, for the benefit of the non-scholarly reader who is interested but less familiar with the technical language (and also for the benefit of the busy scholar), these opening and closing paragraphs are intended to serve as summaries of each chapter's content, giving a sense of the flow of the argument that runs through the course of the book.

Such reading will give an understanding of the book's overall argument(s), while contained within the denser material of the chapters are discussions of specifics and noteworthy matters. For instance, belief in the spiritual soul in relation to contemporary neuroscience, the bearing that is had on the soul by the reality and nature of angels, a person's character and its spiritual growth, what is happening inside/to a person when encountering the Holy Spirit—these are a handful of the pertinent topics that arise in the fuller material.[1]

So, whilst written primarily as a work to contribute to the scholarly discipline of Pentecostal theology, it is hoped that the above selection of signposts will enable the non-academic reader to interact with the book, as well as the scholar and theological student; indeed, for *all* who engage with the work, my hope is that its themes will be of insight and benefit, offering holistic and spiritual stimuli to each of its interested readers—to everyone willing and seeking to attend to *The Spiritual Soul*.

---

1. For those interested in such topics but not keen to read all the book's content, the index provides further pointers as to where this material can be found.

Acknowledgments

In the process of writing *The Spiritual Soul*, I have been deeply appreciative of the encouragement, provision, and care of certain companions alongside on the journey. It is with warm and heartfelt thanks that I reflect on these faithful companions—whose support has been integral to the book's being authored and published.

Thanks are due, first, to Jeremy Allcock—my "training incumbent"/ministry mentor during my years as a curate at St. Martin's Church in the Bullring. Jeremy both was and continues to be a role model of character and care, who, from the earliest days of my curacy, was glad to recognize my passions and interests; I am thankful to him for his example and for giving me time during my years at St. Martin's to pursue a variety of academic ventures, particularly the writing of this book.

The publishing of *The Spiritual Soul* came about through encouraging discussions with Michael Thomson at Wipf and Stock Publishers, and then with valuable help and advice from Robin Parry and Stephanie Hough—my editors at Pickwick. The publishing model of Pickwick is one that I have been particularly glad of and drawn to, appreciating their ethos and style, in bringing this book to publication.

I am grateful to Mike Blaber, Rachel Tweeddale, Philip Miti, Ben Forbes, Juliette Farrell, Phil Davies, and my parents—Paul and Jan Churchouse—who have been very kind in proof-reading drafts of various chapters; (whilst I take full responsibility for any faults that remain in the text) I am particularly appreciative to them all for their time, effort, and commitment in their checking these chapters for errors, and for their thoughts, suggestions, and comments to help refine the book's content and style.

A huge debt of thanks is owed to my loving and beloved wife Anna. My spouse, companion, and cheer-leader, and also the full-time mother of Benjamin—taking a beautiful lead in his care—she has been golden through the time that I have known her, and her character, friendship, and love have been invaluable throughout the course of writing this book; the book's dedication on its opening pages can only be a small token of my gratitude to and love for her.

And ultimately, I am beholden to the Spirit of Christ, the Lord the giver of life. It has been the prayer of Anna and I that he might be the wind in my sails when writing—and indeed the wind in the sails of our lives. His animating and encouragement in life, and specifically throughout the process of writing, have been what have vitalized *The Spiritual Soul*, giving energy and life to the work from its origin to point of completion.

Introduction

Defining Pentecostalism

PENTECOSTALISM, AT ITS CORE, is a renewal spirituality that emphasizes a human's (on-going) transformative encounter(s) with God, by the Holy Spirit of Christ, in ways that are (more) spontaneous, unexpected, and dramatic, as well as those (more) calm, expected, and formal.[1] This definition of Pentecostalism as a *spirituality* is somewhat different to the more popular understanding which tends to view Pentecostalism doctrinally as a denomination which emphasizes subsequent Spirit baptism and the miraculous gifts as its defining features. This latter more popular definition might be fairly close to how *Classical* Pentecostals have traditionally defined themselves, however the consensus that has arisen in Pentecostal *scholarship* defines Pentecostalism as a *spirituality* as opposed to a set of doctrines, and a spirituality which "plugs in to," or (like a river) "runs through," many Christian denominations bringing a Spirit-enlivening renewal to their worship and indeed to their worshipful living.[2]

---

1. Cf. Warrington, *Pentecostal Theology*, 20; Cartledge, *Encountering the Spirit*, 19, 25, 27; Yong, *Spirit-Word-Community*, 119–49, 160; Yong with Anderson, *Renewing Christian Theology*, 14; Smith, *Thinking in Tongues*, 26–27; Vondey, *Beyond Pentecostalism*, 8.

2. See Hollenweger, *Pentecostals*; Land, *Pentecostal Spirituality*; Cartledge, *Encountering*, 133.

Such a spirituality has actually been present throughout church history,[3] but particularly had a renaissance since the turn of the twentieth century. Allan Anderson argues that, since that turn of the century, the best taxonomy for Pentecostals is to categorize them into Classical Pentecostals, Older Independent/Spirit Pentecostals, Charismatic Mainline denominations, and Neo-Pentecostals/Neo-Charismatics[4]—this suggesting that the terms "Pentecostal" or "Pentecostalism" can be used to refer to any of these groupings that practice the spirituality.[5] This idea is further underlined by Mark Cartledge, who has demonstrated that the term "Charismatic" can be happily interchanged for the term "Pentecostal,"[6] or, as Amos Yong prefers, "Renewal" can also be used synonymously;[7] indeed Hannah Mathers has gone on to speak of the "Renewal Tradition," by which she means a tradition of Christians that "emphasize and accentuate the Spirit's role . . . [with] a degree of reference to the Spirit that is missing in other streams of Christianity."[8] All these contemporary thinkers recognize that the term "Pentecostal" is better employed as an *adjective* than a noun, to describe believers in a range of denominations who experience and practice this type of spirituality—a spirituality that plugs into an already existing tradition.[9] The terms "Pentecostal,"

3. See Cartledge, *Encountering the Spirit*, chapter 2.

4. Assemblies of God, Foursquare, Elim, Church of God being examples of Classical Pentecostal churches; The True Jesus Church in China, Zion/Spirit-type churches of Africa would classify as examples of the Older Independent churches; Charismatic/Renewed Anglican and Catholic churches being examples of the third category; and Vineyard, the house church movements, the New Wine network coming under the neo-pentecostal grouping.

5. Anderson, "Varieties, Taxonomies, and Definitions," 13–29. Anderson's is an extension of Hollenweger's work (the father of Pentecostal scholarship) who originally categorized Pentecostals into three groups (due to his writing in 1972 before the arising of the neo-pentecostals): Classical, Pentecostal-like Independent churches, and mainline renewal Pentecostals (Hollenweger, *Pentecostals*, 1). Both scholars recognize the second group as controversial and these do not term themselves Pentecostal, but Anderson contends that these "Spirit/Independent" churches might also be included under the general banner "Pentecostal" as those that show markers of the Pentecostal "family resemblance" (17)—those "concerned primarily with the *experience* of the working of the Holy Spirit and the *practice* of spiritual gifts" (citing R. M. Anderson's [more sociological] definition of the spirituality, *Vision of the Disinherited*, 4 [emphasis A. Anderson's]). For a fuller theological definition of the spirituality, see the definition in the main text above (and the theologians in the footnotes below).

6. Cartledge, *Encountering*.

7. Yong with Anderson, *Renewing Christian Theology*.

8. Mathers, *Interpreting Spirit*, 4.

9. Cartledge confirming in a personal conversation that the Classical Pentecostals

"Charismatic," and "Renewal" could hence be used synonymously to refer to any Christian believer who practices such a spirituality,[10] but for simplicity, this book will employ the single term "Pentecostal," the one most commonly used in the scholarly literature.[11]

Scholarly Pentecostal Theology

As the Pentecostal movement was burgeoning in its renaissance at the start of the twentieth century, Pentecostals were originally reluctant to engage with academic theological thinking, considering it as dry and irrelevant for everyday Christian living. But as the century progressed, such an attitude changed, and Pentecostals have steadily developed a corpus of theological work through that time, covering a range of topics.

By the turn of the twenty-first century Pentecostal theology had developed to a notable level—Pentecostal scholarship emerging as a specific strand of the Christian theological academy, recognizable from its scholarly journals, conferences, monographs, and other academic work. However, as Pentecostal theology has developed into a scholarly discipline, Pentecostals have wanted to consider what is *distinctive* about their theologizing, and how their theology could be specifically described as *Pentecostal*. In particular, the more popular Pentecostal theology of the last century shows very little difference from Evangelical theology, from which Pentecostals traditionally borrowed a lot of their approach and theological thinking. Indeed, with possibly slightly more emphasis on being filled with the Spirit and on miraculous gifts, Pentecostal theology often drew heavily upon Evangelical theology, which is partly what has given rise to the common perception that Pentecostals are basically

---

could quite easily be termed "Charismatic/Pentecostal Holiness believers," the spirituality enlivening the already existent strand of Methodism around the turn of the twentieth century.

10. The term "renewal" is not capitalised in the book to allow for its wider and less specific usage.

11. Pentecostal scholarship has tended to use "pentecostal"—with a lowercase "p"—when referring to this encompassing grouping, with "Pentecostal"—with an uppercase "P"—being used to refer to the first group of Anderson's taxonomy. However, with the term often being used at the outset of a sentence, it can sometimes be difficult to adopt this usage, so the term "Pentecostal" will be used in the book—in the comprehensive sense designated above—and when referring to believers in the first of Anderson's categories, it will refer to that grouping specifically as "Classical Pentecostals."

"Evangelicals plus Spirit baptism and practice of Spiritual gifts."[12] But since the time of Steven Land's pioneering *Pentecostal Spirituality*,[13] what is distinctly Pentecostal about Pentecostal theology has been a question that Pentecostals have been seeking to address.

Whilst the question is still being considered, a consensus among Pentecostal scholars is that Pentecostal theology is that which *begins* from participation in the Pentecostal spirituality. Like all Pentecostals historically, contemporary Pentecostal scholars *ground* theology in the final authority of Scripture but the spirituality is the contextual framework from and within which they operate when constructing their (Pentecostal) theology.[14] J. K. A. Smith and Amos Yong speak of the Pentecostal "social imaginary" or "pneumatological imagination" (respectively) as a (pre-cognitive) framework or worldview given rise to by participating in such a spirituality; this "imagination" then supplies the pre-suppositions that Pentecostals assume and bring to their Pentecostal theology.[15] Put in differing words, through participating in the practices of Pentecostal worship (and its wider "lived experience of faith")—with its emphasis on experiencing the Spirit (as described in the section above)—Pentecostals form a pre-cognitive lens through which they interpret the world. Entailing a "radical openness" to the Spirit,[16] this pre-cognitive lens results in Pentecostals viewing the world as suffused with the Holy Spirit, expecting to find signs of the Spirit's working throughout this Spirit-suffused world.

The pre-cognitive lens, therefore, with its radical openness to the Spirit, is the contextual framework and start-point that informs

---

12. In inter-denominational Evangelical movements, this perception is common. Pentecostal scholars, particularly in the 1990s and early 2000s, recognized this, and typically articles such as Cross, "Rich Feast of Theology," 7–47 set out to address the question.

13. Land, *Pentecostal Spirituality*.

14. Cf. Vondey who, in application of this insight to Pentecostal theological method, comments, "The move to theological reflection is born from this emphasis on the Spirit of Christ, and although theological articulation can begin with doctrine (or other starting points), the development of Pentecostal doctrine always passes through a personal encounter with Christ through the Holy Spirit. In this Christo-pneumatological sense, Pentecostal theology *begins* as spirituality." (Vondey, "Presentation," 2 [emphasis his]).

15. Cf. Smith, *Thinking in Tongues*; and Yong, *Spirit-Word-Community*. In effect, the difference between Pentecostal and Evangelical theology is one of theological *approach*. Acknowledging that difference, and employing the Pentecostal approach in their writings, both scholars cited are also content to describe themselves as Evangelical (as well as Pentecostal).

16. Smith, *Thinking in Tongues*, 33. See also Albrecht and Howard, "Pentecostal Spirituality," 241.

Pentecostal theological thinking—Pentecostals operating from and within their spirituality, with the associated pneumatological worldview, when carrying out their theological work. This makes (contemporary) Pentecostal theology distinctive as a theology that is grounded in Scripture as the final basis of authority but interpreted through the lens of the Pentecostal worldview, one given rise to by the Pentecostal spirituality and experience of the Spirit.[17]

Pentecostal Theological Emphases

Given the spirituality as the starting point of Pentecostal theology, and the importance of the experience of the Spirit, Pentecostalism is well known for its resultant theological emphasis on the renewing work of the Holy Spirit. Whilst the center of the spirituality is Jesus Christ—the focus of the Pentecostal "Full Gospel"[18]—the Spirit's personhood and work of renewal, in bringing people into encounter with Jesus Christ, is gladly accentuated and pronounced by Pentecostals in their spirituality and

17. Although being a distinct Pentecostal method, this interestingly appears to have the potential to be employed alongside and within (so Pneumatically enriching) Kevin Vanhoozer's advanced Evangelical theological method—his "canonical linguistic" approach. (See Vanhoozer, *Drama of Doctrine*.) Though Vondey has argued that the cognitive-poetic imagination that Vanhoozer designates may be too limited an imagination to capture the fullness of the pneumatic imagination Pentecostals begin with (Vondey, *Beyond Pentecostalism*, 37–40), my personal view is that Vanhoozer's cognitive-poetic imagination, shaped and formed by the polyphonic genres and speech-acts of Scripture—but of course so by the Holy Spirit who breathed them—could be a helpful pneumatic focussing lens for Pentecostals, who at times have wanted to see the Spirit at work in all things without (biblical) limitation.

On the specific question of the Spirit in the world, see further the work of J. K. A. Smith drawn upon in chapters 4 and 6 of this book.

18. The "Full Gospel" of Pentecostalism centers on Jesus Christ—Christ being the savior, Spirit baptizer, healer, (sanctifier,) and coming king. There is some debate among Pentecostals as to whether the "full gospel" should be designated as fivefold (as per the "Cleveland" [Pentecostal seminary] school of thought)—including, in the full gospel, Jesus as "sanctifier"—or whether it should be fourfold, leaving out Jesus as the "sanctifier" (as per the view of Aimee Semple McPherson). This is, in some ways, more of a historical debate than one of a more contemporary nature. Given that the term "healing" in Pentecostal theology has expanded to now include physical, mental, spiritual, social (etc.)—healing of every kind—the word "healing" has, in effect, become synonymous with the term "wholeness." As such, because sanctification (/holiness) is included under this expanded definition of healing, whether one gives a separate category for Jesus being the sanctifier, or whether that is included under "healer," appears to be a distinction that is now very slight—more a distinction of terminology and history, carrying little implication for the modern-day worshipping practice of Pentecostal spirituality and theology.

hence theology.[19] But there are certain other theological emphases that then flow from the experience of the Spirit and this distinctive renewal pneumatology—emphases that are commonly more pronounced in the Pentecostal tradition (than they are in other Christian traditions).

As an instance of another *of* those Pentecostal emphases, indeed one that flows from the experience and emphasis above—esteeming the Spirit's outpouring as having occurred in *the last days* (Acts 2:17 [cf. Joel 2:28])—Pentecostals put a particular accent on the *eschatological* kingdom of God.[20] In their biblical understanding, this eschatological kingdom was inaugurated by the ministry of Christ, who (post-resurrection and ascension) poured out his Holy Spirit to empower his people for witness in the "now" of the eschatological kingdom whilst awaiting its promised consummation (the "not yet" of the eschatological kingdom). Bearing obvious close relation to their accent on renewal pneumatology, this second theological emphasis is one that flows from Pentecostals' regarding the Spirit's outpouring as fulfilment of the prophecy of Joel. Given the Spirit's coming in fulfilment of this prophecy, and ushering in the promised eschatological age, Pentecostals are therefore passionate and zealous in carrying out the commission of Christ (Matt 28:18–20), calling people to faith and repentance "for the Kingdom of God has drawn near" (Mark 1:15).[21] Pentecostals regard the narrative of Pentecost—as narrated in Acts chapter 2—as the key interpretative passage for understanding who the eschatological Spirit is and his work of "the last days,"[22] and the Luke-Acts corpus are viewed as the key biblical books (possibly, "canon within the canon") for the work of articulating specifically Pentecostal theology.

19. For the relation of the two—Pentecostal spirituality and Pentecostal theology—see the discussion that follows below as well as the further exposition in chapter 6 of this book.

20. Cf. Faupel, *Everlasting Gospel*; Cartledge, "Text-Community-Spirit," 140; Yong with Anderson, *Renewing Christian Theology*, 15.

21. Land, *Pentecostal Spirituality*, 58–61.

22. Whilst early Pentecostals often viewed "the last days" as a reference to the few remaining days before Christ returns, over the last century of Pentecostalism, Pentecostals have come to recognize that "the last days"—as it is used in Acts 2—is more a reference to the New Testament age, that is, the age between the resurrection of Christ and his return as coming king. That said, whilst the eschatology has shifted a little because of this growing recognition, because (as is stated above) the Spirit is the eschatological Spirit, who empowers and equips his people for godly living and service in the inaugurated eschatological kingdom of God, Pentecostals still retain the eschatological outlook, desiring on-going fillings of the Spirit to participate well in the "now" of the eschatological kingdom of God, whilst awaiting the "not yet" of that eschatological kingdom. See further Land, *Pentecostal Spirituality*.

It becomes evident, therefore, that these two Pentecostal emphases—the renewal pneumatological emphasis and the eschatological (kingdom) emphasis—are intricately interrelated and are arguably the *lead* defining features of the movement. However, these are joined by two further emphases that are also characteristic of Pentecostalism.

Along with the emphases above, Pentecostals emphasize the holistic, embodied nature of a believer as one who encounters the Spirit, and responds bodily (for example in dancing, singing, falling prostrate in worship, receiving healing [bodily and psychologically], laying on of hands), as well as "spiritually," to the Spirit. This is interestingly balanced with a further emphasis on the "supernatural" realm, i.e., the world of angels, demons, and ancestor spirits—or what might be termed the "spirit" realm—giving Pentecostalism a certain dualistic emphasis.[23] These two

---

23. The word "dualism" (with its adjective "dualistic") needs here to be clarified as it is often misunderstood or used as a polemical term in the academic literature (somewhat akin to the way the term "fundamentalism" is used in everyday language). Although there is a vast range of uses for this term in philosophy and theology (see for instance, N. T. Wright's list of 10 uses he finds in just the theological arena [Wright, *New Testament*, 253–54]), as used in this book, it is to be clarified that the term is *not* used to mean the opposing of the physical world to that of the spiritual/immaterial world—as if the spirit realm were good and the material/physical were bad (like on a Platonist worldview). As a healthy doctrine of creation, incarnation, and eschaton emphasize, the material realm is to be as valued as much as the immaterial realm. It is *not* used here, either, in the sense of depicting God and his forces of good in battle against Satan and the forces of evil—that understanding is countered by a healthy doctrine of God and his sovereignty (though this sense of dualism is particularly evident, for instance, in Peter Wagner's Pentecostal work, and to an extent that of the early John Wimber. [e.g., Wagner, *Territorial Spirits* and Wimber and Springer, *Power Evangelism*.]). In this book, the term "dualism" is used in an *ontological* sense, making a distinction between the two realms, the material and the immaterial—both on a macro (whole of reality) level (physical world/spirit beings) and an anthropological level (physical/material bodies, spiritual/immaterial souls). But as stated above, the book recognizes the value of both realms, the downplaying of one or the other being inappropriate.

In terms of grammar, the adjectival use of "dualism" differs across the literature—some preferring "dualistic," others "dualist"—likewise with the terms "monism" and "holism." Generally, this book uses "dualistic" as the adjective, however when joined with another (or even two) of the above adjectives, to avoid regular cumbersome phrasing (e.g., "a 'holistic dualistic' view"), the ultimate adjective becomes the alternative form (e.g., "a 'holistic dualist' position"). This usage of the double adjective form phrases of a technical variety, and so further double adjectival termini technici of an anthropological variety also follow the rule; hence the book speaks of "an 'emergent monist' understanding," "a 'substance dualist' model,'" or "a 'Cartesian dualist' position." In further consistency with the above, this is applied to "monism" and "holism," so whereas being used ordinarily as a singular adjective in which instance "monism," for example, becomes "monistic" (e.g., "a 'monistic' understanding of the human"), when functioning as the ultimate adjective of two (or more), it becomes "monist" (e.g., "a 'holistic monist' position" or 'an 'emergent monist' view").

features bring a natural balance between the spirit world and the physical world in Pentecostal thinking, giving additional emphases to the lead distinctives of eschatology and pneumatology.

Pentecostal Theology of Human Constitution and Its Significance

The doctrine of anthropology, and specifically of human constitution within that, is significant for Pentecostal theology (and indeed for beliefs of all worldviews), both in its illumining the issue of what humans are essentially comprised/"made-up" of, but also in the implications it carries for many important associated matters of theology and philosophy.

By way of some of these implications, one's understanding of life after death, for example, is affected by this doctrine of what constitutes a human being. Relatedly, one's answer to the question of what a person is—plus the extensive ethical issues connected—are affected by the view one holds as regards constitution. The associated metaphysical question of whether an essentialist or relational view is preferable—and the subsequent impact that has on one's understanding of the Trinity—is additionally implicated by the topic. And the nature and reality of spirits—such as ancestral, ghostly, and angelic—are all impacted by one's philosophical-theological doctrine of human constitution. Whilst this list is not exhaustive, (and whilst Pentecostals around the world, depending on their location, will sense the importance of certain of these topics more than they will certain others,) it contributes to highlighting the significance of the topic of human constitution. But furthermore, the doctrine of constitution has significant implications for the Divine-human encounter at the core of Pentecostal spirituality globally—the encounter spirituality that is central and distinctive to Pentecostal theology.

Given the significance of the doctrine of human constitution, it is somewhat surprising that the doctrine has received a lot less attention from Pentecostals than more favored doctrines—such as Pneumatology, Christology, and the Trinity. It should be acknowledged that there has been a thin stream of Pentecostals who have considered this issue over the last hundred years, displaying something of a "trajectory of thinking" on the topic; but only very recently, in the (relatively new) scholarly era of the movement's history, has it received a degree of thorough consideration, particularly by Amos Yong and then Veli-Matti Kärkkäinen.

Introduction

The work of Yong and Kärkkäinen (and scholars who follow in their footsteps[24]) is welcome in the sense that it might encourage other Pentecostals to examine the subject, going some way to filling the dearth. But whilst affirming their contribution in this respect, their work on human constitution is also in need of response, due to debatable contentions they make.

In their work, Yong and Kärkkäinen make two particularly significant contentions regarding human constitution:

1. They reject dualism (of any kind)—with the entailed understanding of the "spiritual" soul (that is, a soul that is immaterial,[25] and ontologically distinct from the body)—viewing such a position as theologically and philosophically flawed.

and

2. They propose *emergent monism* as an alternative view of constitution (espousing that humans are essentially physical beings with a mind that has *emerged out of* and *supervenes on* the brain)—a view they regard as a more laudable constitutional model.[26]

Such is bold theological innovation, but when examined carefully, both contentions show to be problematic. Although recognizing that Yong and Kärkkäinen have good reasons for rejecting *Platonist and Classic Cartesian* dualisms, their arguments do not stand against better, stronger forms of dualism. And when assessed more thoroughly, it is seen that their emergent monist view, in its relation to Pentecostal theology, is not particularly concordant with the four Pentecostal theological emphases expounded; moreover, their view is not philosophically persuasive in the wider field of enquiry. Recognizing the serious implications that their emergent monism would have, then, for other areas of Pentecostal thought, (for example Yong's revisionist belief of emergent angels that arises from his

---

24. See, for instance, Vondey, who follows (albeit from a distance) in the footsteps predominantly of Yong when touching on human constitution in his chapter entitled "Humanity" (in Vondey, *Pentecostal Theology*, cf. 179, 181, 183, 193–97.)

25. That is, an entity that is not material—not made of physical matter (being a non-physical entity, an entity of a spirit nature).

26. To give variation of language, the adjective "constitutional" will be employed through the course of this book in a narrow sense, to refer to work done on the theology of human constitution. It is not used in the grander and more popular sense of meaning "lawful" or "statutory."

emergent position,[27] or his likewise-affected understanding of personal eschatology,[28]) the prospect of Pentecostals following such thinking is not a particularly positive forecast. Further, given the historical Pentecostal trajectory of thought on this issue, and where it stands in the present, the possibility of Yong and Kärkkäinen's work encouraging other Pentecostals also in the monistic direction, and so likewise shaping the future direction of the trajectory, is one that is very real. So, given the problems of these two contentions, the implications these issues would have for other areas of thought, and the current status of the Pentecostal trajectory, response to Yong and Kärkkäinen's work is requisite at this time.

This book seeks to respond and does so in both a critical and constructive manner. After giving an original historical overview of western Pentecostal thought concerning the doctrine of human constitution over the last hundred years,[29] and so ascertaining the trajectory that such Pentecostal theology is on concerning this doctrine, the book identifies scholars Amos Yong and Veli-Matti Kärkkäinen as significant voices toward the end and present of the trajectory—with the potential to influence its future direction. It then reviews and critiques their work on human constitution, on the lines identified above, suggesting that Pentecostals avoid their monistic lead. Having carried out this critique, it then further responds by arguing for and constructing an enhanced Pentecostal philosophical-theological model of human constitution—one termed an "Enspiritable Holistic Dualism"—to redirect the future path of the trajectory.

The model constructed in the book is initially "enhanced" (by the start of the final chapter) in the sense of being more concordant with the Pentecostal emphases and being stronger philosophically than Yong and Kärkkäinen's view (the degree of philosophy entailed in this project underlining the appropriateness of a philosophical-theological approach for

---

27. Yong's revisionist view suggests that angels are entities that supervene on a physical substrate. See further Yong, *Spirit of Creation*, 204–25. For critique of such a view, see Churchouse, "Angels," 97–113.

28. Such as removing the grounds for identity persistence in and through the intermediate state. See discussion in chapter 3 of this book.

29. The limiting of the scope to the western tradition of Pentecostalism is due to emergent monism (as espoused by Yong and Kärkkäinen) having arisen out of that western tradition and so being an issue most prevalently faced by western Pentecostals. Whilst the constructive proposal of the book is certainly applicable to Pentecostals on a global scale, the critical part of the book dialogues and engages specifically with the western tradition—out of which Yong and Kärkkäinen's emergent monism has arisen.

constructing such a doctrine[30]). It is then additionally enhanced through the further constructive work carried out in the final chapter by drawing on the sources of biblical studies, philosophy of mind, and the pneumatology of Pentecostal spirituality [/"Pentecostal pneumatology"][31]—recruited in the earlier constructive chapters. As such, a model is constructed with a better understanding of the spiritual soul (than that rejected/redefined by Yong and Kärkkäinen). Through giving this spiritual soul the requisite attention and indeed prominence in the construction, and by establishing the centrality of the spirit (and Spirit) in the new model constructed, a renewed, enhanced doctrine of human constitution is proposed, so having the effect, in addition, of redirecting the future of the Pentecostal trajectory.

The Meaning and Terminology of the "Spiritual" Soul

As implied in the foregoing section (and as will become evident in the overview of the book to follow), the sense of the soul's adjective "spiritual"—when used specifically in reference to the soul—is precise and distinct in its meaning, but that meaning is one that expands as the book nears its point of conclusion. It is used from the opening chapters in a specifically *philosophical* sense to denote the soul's *immaterial, non-physical* nature (the soul's being of a spirit [/"spiritual"] nature). This *philosophical* sense is the exclusive meaning of the term up until the point of the ultimate

---

30. Philosophical theology as a discipline is ultimately theological, but theology well informed by the insights of philosophy—in this case, the philosophy of mind. Cf. the definition of Moore who defines it more fully, arguing the approach of Philosophical theology "(1) uses philosophy to clarify and confirm the truth of dogmatic affirmations, and (2), is prepared, where consistency with revelation requires it, to modify, suspend, or discipline philosophical positions by reference to the unique subject matter of theology." (Moore, "Philosophy of Religion or Philosophical Theology?" 310). Plantinga likewise confirms, "Philosophical theology is a matter of thinking about the . . . doctrines of the Christian faith from a philosophical perspective." (Plantinga, "Augustinian Christian Philosophy," 291) (Cf. Crisp "[Philosophical theology is] the consideration of philosophical issues in particular theological traditions." [O. Crisp, "Analytic Theology," 471] or Wood, "Philosophical Theology uses the tools of philosophy to investigate the theological claims made by a specific religious tradition" [Wood, "Analytic Theology as a Way of Life," 45]).

31. As indicated earlier in the introduction (and will be further expounded in chapter 4), Pentecostals' distinctive pneumatology arises out of their spirituality, hence the fuller locutions "the pneumatology of Pentecostal spirituality" or "the pneumatology that flows from Pentecostal spirituality" being accurate. But for succinctness and smoothness of phrasing, these fuller locutions will be shortened, from this point on in the book, to "Pentecostal pneumatology" (as per the language in the [square] brackets above).

chapter. However, as the overview below will expound, at that point of the final chapter the term is injected with an additional, *theological* meaning—the term "spiritual" being augmented to mean *pertaining to the Spirit of God* (its being responsible for relating to the Spirit). The primary *philosophical* meaning is what is used throughout the whole of the work, the additional theological layer being added in the final chapter of the book; so, the book concludes by employing the adjective in a deliberately-dual sense of the term—a *philosophical-theological* dual meaning of the soul's adjective "spiritual."[32]

Overview of the Book

In pursuing the goal of proposing an enhanced Pentecostal philosophical-theological doctrine of human constitution—with particular focus on the spiritual soul—Part I of the book sets the scene for this direction by giving the theological historical backdrop to the discussion. Chapter 1 (in this part of the book) gives a fresh historical review of western Pentecostal theological thought as regards human constitution over the last century. In so doing, Pentecostals' consistent emphasis on the authority of Scripture—as the foundation on which they want to ground their doctrine of human constitution—is identified, as is their interest in the concept of the *human* spirit.[33] The underlying theological and philosophical influences contributing to the shaping of their thinking as regards constitution are further identified, leading to a trajectory being highlighted; this trajectory discerns the journey of Pentecostals' evolution of thought on the doctrine—from the early twentieth century up to the early stages of the twenty-first—giving hints as to where Pentecostal thought on the matter might potentially be going in the future.

In part II, the work of the most influential Pentecostal authors to have written on the subject is considered—that of Amos Yong and Veli-Matti Kärkkäinen. As particularly renowned scholars in Pentecostal

---

32. In further delineation of the book's terminology (but regarding a term not so prominent to the book's central thesis/title), it would be helpful, at this point, to clarify the book's use of another term—that of the word "person." The term "person" will generally be used in the book as a word synonymous with human/human being. As the book proceeds towards its close, however, the term "person" will receive a more technical definition, being philosophically and precisely defined in the book's conclusion.

33. As will be seen, the human "spirit" Pentecostals are referring to (displayed in the review of chapter 1) they see as being, in some sense, distinct from the "soul." This will be borne in mind for latter chapters of the book.

studies with substantial influence in the discipline, and indeed as those standing at the (current) present of the constitutional trajectory and so being potential shapers of the trajectory's future, these two specific thinkers are engaged withat this point in the book. In chapter 2, their two important contentions are articulated. Their theological and philosophical reasons for rejecting dualism are identified, and having illumined this variety of issues, their preferred emergent monist view(s) are then subsequently expounded.[34] Following this exposition, their two key contentions are assessed and critiqued in chapter 3 of the book. It is seen that their theological and philosophical reasons for rejecting dualism are only accurate when aimed at Platonist and Classic Cartesian dualisms but do not extend as justification for rejecting dualism per se; their inadvertently rejecting *every* type of dualism through their critique of two particular varieties is fallacious. Further, their emergent monist proposal(s) disclose themselves as unpersuasive in light of the four Pentecostal theological emphases and when exposed to philosophical critique.

Having admonished the emergent monist model as containing philosophical problems and being not particularly concordant with certain Pentecostal emphases (in the [critical] part [II] of the book), Part III begins the constructive project of building an *enhanced* Pentecostal philosophical-theological model of human constitution.

Following a carefully located excursus which expounds and critiques the position of the problematic Platonist and Classic Cartesian dualisms (which follows the end of part II of the book),[35] chapter 4 begins the constructive project by returning to the fount of Pentecostal pneumatology[36]—the source from which the other Pentecostal theological empha-

---

34. Although Yong and Kärkkäinen title their position(s) in different ways—with minor nuances of differentiation—their views are recognized as being very similar, sharing a common emergent monist core. So, identifying this, at the end of chapter 2 and into the beginning of chapter 3, the "proposals" / "models" (plural) give way to viewing their work as an emergent monist "proposal" (singular), only drawing attention to the slight differences when they arise.

35. This excursus is deliberately placed at this point between parts II and III—fitting with the critical-constructive shape of the book. With the Classic Cartesian position being often what is assumed when the phrase "dualism" is heard (see the book's critique of Yong and Kärkkäinen), this view is exposed and critiqued in the purposely located excursus to then clear the path for any dualistic construction to follow. Doing the work of critique at this point makes clear that any dualism to follow is not of the Platonist or Classic Cartesian varieties.

36. Remembering that the phrase "Pentecostal pneumatology" is being employed as a shortened form of the fuller phrasing "the pneumatology of / that flows from Pentecostal spirituality" (see earlier footnote).

ses flow—by engaging with the Pentecostal ontology and philosophical theology of J. K. A. Smith. Expounding and filling out his ontology, Pentecostals' emphasis on the *spirit* realm is illumined—along with its correlated stress on the physical realm—for the chapter to then further proceed to highlight the *intimacy* of both realms—within the Enspirited ontology Pentecostals affirm. Having highlighted these realms and their intimate relation through beginning with Pentecostal pneumatology, the chapter then proceeds to draw on the biblical studies of John Cooper to continue the construction of an enhanced doctrine of constitution. As a philosophical-theological exegete whose work is in much accord with these Pentecostal emphases expounded, Cooper's biblical model is then articulated to provide a solid *scriptural* basis for the development of the constructive project. Whilst maintaining the scriptural value accorded to the physical body—as well as likewise affirming the value accorded to the spiritual soul (and indeed seeking to carefully handle the scriptural meaning[s] of the term "soul"), his biblical holistic dualism—a holistic *soul-body* dualism—is commended at this point in the chapter, to continue the advancement of an enhanced constitutional model.[37]

Having exposited, by this point in the project, Cooper's general biblical holistic dualism, chapter 5 advances within and beyond this work to define the soul and its nature more conceptually. Whilst recognizing and actively signposting a variety of philosophical soul-body dualisms, to which Pentecostal theology might be beneficially drawn, the chapter identifies the model of philosopher Richard Swinburne—namely his (contemporary) substance dualist position—as one of particular attraction for advancing an enhanced Pentecostal constitutional model. Having critiqued Classic Cartesian dualism already by this point in the work—so Swinburne's model is delineated from this view—chapter 5 expounds Swinburne's model, followed by analytical critique of his viewpoint, to

---

37. Following the thinking of Cooper, the phrases "holistic dualism" and "dualistic holism" (and its associates "holistic dualist" and "dualistic holist") could be used interchangeably—the former emphasizing the *ontology* of the human, the latter emphasizing the *functioning* of the human. Cooper, in his key work *Body, Soul and Life Everlasting*, opted for the former, hence following such terminology in this book. However, Cooper more recently reversed his preference to "dualistic holism" (working specifically from the biblical texts) clarifying at the Biola conference "Neuroscience and the Soul" (2013) that, with Scripture's emphasis being more on the *function* of humanity, he wanted to do likewise—hence opting instead for "dualistic holism." The book appreciates this insight and affirms it. Yet being a book emphasizing the spiritual soul, it maintains the former language, drawing attention to the ontology (whilst still affirming the holistic functioning of that ontology).

highlight its potential for serving as a robust philosophical option for further constructing an enhanced Pentecostal anthropology.

Ensuing part III's advancement of a holistic soul-body model that is strong in philosophy of mind, that is founded on biblical exegesis, and in accord with the Pentecostal emphases, chapter 6 (part IV of the book) then continues the project of proposing an enhanced Pentecostal model. To check the model so far established for its Pentecostal suitability, the model so far proposed is tested for "fit" in dialogue with the (spirit-inducing) anthropology of Steven Land's *Pentecostal Spirituality*. From this engagement with Land's pioneering work, it is seen that the spiritual soul so far proposed fits comfortably within the anthropology of Pentecostal spirituality—showing in fact to have fuller capacity for accommodating the "passions," "beliefs," and "practices" so integral to Pentecostal spirituality. This dialogue with Pentecostal spirituality, therefore, suggests that the (immaterial) spiritual soul would be a better (anthropological) center for conceiving of the anthropology of Pentecostal spirituality. But additional benefit is found from this dialogue in stimulating the possibility of *theologically* enhancing the soul, so far proposed in the book. Through considering the concept of "spirit"—the anthropological, human spirit—the chapter then proceeds a step further in its advancement of an enhanced understanding of constitution by considering a place for this (human) "spirit" *within* the spiritual soul.

Through engagement with the biblical work of John Levison and Gordon Fee, and the philosophical work of J. P. Moreland, the so far commended constitutional model (of a contemporary substance dualist variety) is enhanced, in the second half of chapter 6, through the articulation of a (philosophical-theological) understanding of the human spirit as located within the spiritual soul. By then engaging again with Smith's Pentecostal ontology and considering the possibility of this spirit's renewal—being renewable in an on-going sense by the (Holy) Spirit of Christ—this leads to the chapter's proposing of an "Enspiritable Holistic Dualism" as a renewed and enhanced Pentecostal doctrine of human constitution.

As is palpable in chapter 6 (as well as implied in the chapters preceding), it is through concentration on the *spiritual soul* that the (additionally) enhanced Pentecostal doctrine of human is achieved and so presented.[38] Indeed, it is the spiritual soul that *engenders* the enhanced

---

38. The word "additional" (in regard to the doctrine's enhancement) clarifies that the doctrine was initially enhanced in the sense of its being more concordant with the Pentecostal emphases and stronger philosophically than Yong and Kärkkäinen's;

Pentecostal philosophical-theological doctrine of human constitution that the book constructs and proposes. Such a constructive proposal brings, in turn, renewal/redirection to the Pentecostal trajectory of thought on the doctrine of constitution—redirected from the monistic direction towards an enlivened dualistic direction instead. This enlivened direction flows from the proposed Enspiritable Holistic Dualism—the enhanced Pentecostal doctrine of constitution established in this book—with its particular focus on the spiritual soul.

---

by the end of the book, this doctrine has been *additionally* enhanced (or *renewed* and enhanced) by way of the Pentecostal pneumatology of chapter 6.

Part I

Setting the Scene

1

The Doctrine of Human Constitution in Western Pentecostal Theological History

THE DOCTRINE OF ANTHROPOLOGY has been given relatively sparse attention by western Pentecostals—it being a lacuna of thought in their theological work.[1] Although bearing direct relation to the doctrine of pneumatology—an area of particular focus for Pentecostals throughout their history—the doctrine of anthropology has received rather limited treatment and indeed remains a neglected subject in western Pentecostal thought.

Given the disregard of the doctrine of anthropology more widely, it is therefore unsurprising that the topic of *constitution* (within that wider doctrine) has received even less coverage or focus—it being a topic that has experienced a similar related neglect. But whilst it has suffered this shortfall, there have been a handful of Pentecostal thinkers who *have* engaged with the topic and articulated their views on the doctrine in varying formats and styles (for instance, as part of a wider theological project

---

1. It is likewise a lacuna in the theology of Global Majority Pentecostals, but given that anthropological (emergent) monism has arisen in the western tradition—so being an issue faced more prevalently by western Pentecostals—the present work will limit its scope to that western Pentecostal tradition. (Of the limited articulation of the anthropology of Global Majority Pentecostalism, cf. the dualistic nature of such reflected in Anderson, *Spirit-Filled* World; Anderson, *Introduction to Pentecostalism*; and Cox, *Fire From Heaven*.)

such as an encompassing systematic theology). From the publications of this handful of Pentecostal thinkers, discernible trends become evident in their writings—certain *themes* being manifestly common; but in addition to these shared common themes, a *development* of thought also becomes overt across the hundred-year period during which these writings were authored. Spanning from the early 1900s through to the early 2000s this development of thought becomes apparent as do the influences that have *shaped* this progression of opinion; and through analyzing this evolution of thought, and the influences that have shaped its direction, it is possible, then, to ascertain a sense of western Pentecostalism's *trajectory* of opinion concerning the topic. Moreover, identifying this (extending) trajectory gives a degree of scholarly understanding as to the possible future direction of this evolving trajectory of opinion—giving reason for engaging with the topic in the present, to speak fruitfully into that future. Because of the significance of this (developing) trajectory, this chapter will focus on that hundred-year period of Pentecostals' writings on the constitutional topic—to elucidate this trajectory of thought plus the influences that have shaped its direction.

The first half of the chapter will proceed in a chronological, descriptive manner—articulating Pentecostal views on the doctrine of constitution from the time of the early twentieth century through to those expressed more recently at the beginnings of the twenty-first.[2] This will provide a historical overview of Pentecostals' beliefs concerning the doctrine of constitution during the identified century of thought on the topic.

Having documented the writings of the designated hundred-year period, and the views of constitution contained therein, the second half of the chapter will then bring analysis to this descriptive work by identifying the themes common in Pentecostals' thought on the topic from during that century span. Such analysis will also highlight Pentecostals' *development* of thought on the doctrine, and further identify the influences that have shaped that evolution of opinion during the hundred-year period. Having accomplished this "scene-setting" work, the trajectory of western Pentecostal opinion from during that designated era will have become evident by the end of this chapter, giving both locus and *direction of travel* for modern-day Pentecostal discussion concerning the doctrine of constitution.

---

2. Whilst aware that Pentecostalism pre-dates the twentieth century, this overview begins with the anthropological writings of authors who self-identify as "Pentecostal."

Historical Overview of Western Pentecostal Thought Concerning the Doctrine of Constitution

The Early Twentieth Century Magazines (1900s to 1920s)

In the period of time being considered, the earliest western Pentecostal references to the doctrine of human constitution (which was commonly termed in such writings as the doctrine of the constitution of "man"[3]) are the references in the devotional magazines—in "Confidence" and "Pentecostal Evangel."[4] In the former of these magazines, a series of early-edition devotionals entitled "The New Creation, of a Wonderful Salvation—for Body, Soul and Spirit" imply that trichotomy was the position espoused by the magazine's editor and contributory authors—since the earliest days of its publication.[5] This trichotomous inclination is confirmed in subsequent editions; for example, an article in a following edition entitled "The Indwelling and Abiding Trinity," authored by the magazine's editor Alexander Boddy, made a case for an intimate relationship between the trinitarian Father, Son, and Holy Spirit and the

---

3. In recent times contemporary anthropology has tended to adjust its language to speak of the doctrine of "humanity" rather than using the (traditional) language of speaking of the doctrine of "man" (though both idioms are still used in differing anthropological discussions). Whilst I opt to use the contemporary language through the general course of this book, when narrating the views of writers who wrote before this terminological change, their terminology will be retained for historical and citational accuracy.
  Regarding the usage of pronouns, to bring variety from the trend of this chapter (in its usage of "man," "him," and "his"), I have opted, in the rest of the book, to employ the pronouns "she" or "her" in reference to the terms "human," "human being," and "person" (specifically concerning *human* persons). The pronouns "he" or "his" could also be easily employed in reference to such terms—either set of pronouns being equally valid. In recent years the choice of pronoun has become politically loaded—using "he"/"his" is often regarded as "traditionalist," using "she"/"her" is commonly viewed as "progressivist" or "feminist." Neither of these ideologies are what motivate my using the female pronouns I do in this book. I simply affirm that either "he"/"his" or "she"/"her" could be used legitimately as the appropriate pronouns (both of which—as singular pronouns—are preferable to the popular plural term "their"). Because one set has to be chosen, simply for variety and clarity's sake (outside of chapter 1) I opt to employ the pronouns "she"/"her."

4. "Confidence" ran from 1908–1926 edited by the Pentecostal Anglican minister Alexander Boddy; "Pentecostal Evangel" (originally founded as "The Christian Evangel") originated in 1913 and is still published today—having become the official magazine of the Assemblies of God.

5. These early-edition devotionals were penned by Mary Boddy (the wife of Alexander Boddy [who edited "Confidence" magazine]); they were a series of monthly devotionals that ran from December 1909 to August 1910 (excluding the month of June).

respective (human) spirit, soul, and body[6]—again revealing trichotomy to be the favored anthropological position among the magazine's authors and editors. Indeed, from the publication of this article onwards (to the publication's terminus in 1926), the front page of each edition was emblazoned with the statement: "Confidence advocates . . . an unlimited Salvation for Spirit, Soul and Body . . ."—evincing the magazine's clear support of the trichotomous viewpoint.

At a similar time in the era, a trichotomous belief is evident in the magazine "Pentecostal Evangel"; its commitment to trichotomy is represented by an (anonymous) editorial, published in a 1924 edition, asserting that "man, by nature, is trichotomous in his make-up."[7] Whilst an article of a subsequent edition—entitled "Jesus as Saviour of the Soul and Healer of the Body"—might suggest an alternative dichotomous belief being favored,[8] a reading of that article reveals that it is also, in fact, trichotomous in its view of a human being.[9] In other Pentecostal magazines published in the first half of the twentieth century, very similar belief in trichotomy is displayed;[10] these magazines show thorough trichotomous conviction—that man is constituted of body, soul, and spirit.[11]

Watchman Nee and *The Spiritual Man* (Late 1920s)

As the early twentieth century progressed, an anthropological tome was authored by Watchman Nee entitled *The Spiritual Man*.[12] Written in 1928,

---

6. Boddy, "Indwelling and Abiding Trinity."
7. Editorial, "Spirit of Man," 1 and 5.
8. Orwig, "Jesus as Saviour."
9. The ambiguity between title and content potentially suggests that the title was derived from outside the Pentecostal tradition—either as a catchphrase from popular culture or derived from another Christian tradition. (The fact that the title/phrase occurs in other editions of the magazine too might further point in this direction.)
10. E.g., "Bridegroom's Messenger" (of the International Pentecostal Church of Christ), "Bridal Call" (of the International Church of the Foursquare Gospel), "Foursquare Crusader" (and its latter) "Foursquare Magazine" (also of the International Church of the Foursquare Gospel), "The Pentecost" (Independent), "Pentecostal Testimony" (Independent).
11. Because the chapter is interacting with the language of the writers being surveyed, I will, from this point, use the traditional language of "mankind" and "man" interchangeably with "humanity" and "human." I will then in the following chapters return to the contemporary terminology and employ the anthropological language of "human" and "humanity" from that point on.
12. Nee, *Spiritual Man*. Although I am using the word "spiritual" exclusively in a

the work gives a most extensive exposition of a trichotomous theology of constitution. Though Nee did not profess, himself, to be a Pentecostal, his work is necessarily included at this juncture because of the significant influence it had on subsequent generations of Pentecostals.

As an overview of Nee's constitutional thought, his trichotomous anthropology is based on the biblical teaching of 1 Thess 5:23, Heb 4:12, and Luke 1:46–47, but in particular an exposition of Gen 2:7 (the Darby Translation thereof).[13] From this latter passage he highlights that God breathed his Spirit into Adam, so (whilst maintaining a distinction between the Holy Spirit and the human spirit) he asserts that the (human) spirit, therefore, is the premier part of man's being.[14] For Nee, the human spirit is the part that experiences connection with God, it is the means by which man apprehends and communes with God, and indeed it is the aspect which gives to man his sense of "God-consciousness."[15] On the other/opposite hand, Nee wants to assert that the body—of purely "matter" (cf. Gen 2:7)—is the lowest of the three constituting parts and relates to the things of the material world; the body, therefore, is what gives man his sense of *world-consciousness*.[16] According to Nee, the *soul* was given rise to when the newly created human spirit came into contact with the

---

philosophical sense—in the first five chapters of this book—Nee's use of the word "spiritual" (in the overview of his book to follow) is more of a *theological* usage.

13. In the Darby translation these verses read: (1 Thess 5:23) "Now the God of peace himself sanctify you wholly: and your whole spirit, and soul, and body be preserved blameless at the coming of our Lord Jesus Christ." (Heb 4:12) "For the word of God [is] living and operative, and sharper than any two-edged sword, and penetrating to [the] division of soul and spirit, both of joints and marrow, and a discerner of the thought and intents of [the] heart." (Luke 1:46–47) "And Mary said, 'My soul magnifies the Lord, and my spirit has rejoiced in God my Savior.'" (Gen 2:7) "And Jehovah Elohim formed Man, dust of the ground, and breathed into his nostrils the breath of life; and Man became a living soul."

In a more contemporary translation (particularly notable concerning Gen 2:7) these verses read: (1 Thess 5:23) "May the God of peace himself sanctify you entirely; and may your spirit and soul and body be kept sound and blameless at the coming of our Lord Jesus Christ" (NRSV). (Heb 4:12) "Indeed, the word of God is living and active, sharper than any two-edged sword, piercing until it divides soul from spirit, joints from marrow; it is able to judge the thoughts and intentions of the heart" (NRSV). (Luke 1:46–47) "And Mary said, 'My soul magnifies the Lord, and my spirit rejoices in God my Savior" (NRSV). (Gen 2:7) "Then the LORD God formed man from the dust of the ground and breathed into his nostrils the breath of life; and the man became a living being" (NRSV).

14. Nee, *Spiritual Man*, 27.

15. Nee, *Spiritual Man*, 29 (emphasis his).

16. Nee, *Spiritual Man*, 29.

physical body—forming the soul as this third and separate entity.[17] So, the soul, on Nee's trichotomous view, is that entity which gives individuality to (each) man, and gives him his *self-consciousness*.[18]

Given Nee's understanding of the soul, he argues that it is able to function like a go-between; it operates between the spiritual human spirit and the earthly physical body and it can choose which of these entities to favor (plus its associated pattern of behavior).[19] But, as is implied by the book's title, the encouragement of the tome is for the soul to submit to the spirit and for the person to live as the "Spiritual Man."[20] Summarizing it very succinctly, the goal of *The Spiritual Man* is to encourage its readers, empowered by the Holy Spirit, to live according to the (anthropological) spirit—the highest and premier part of man's fundamental constitution.[21]

Myer Pearlman (1930s)

Progressing to the 1930s, Myer Pearlman wrote a work (in 1937) that can be legitimately labelled a "systematic theology."[22] Though preferring to title the volume *Knowing the Doctrines*, and opting not to cite his theological sources in that work, Pearlman observes the usual order followed by traditional systematic theologies and brings some thought-provoking insights within that volume concerning the doctrine of constitution—particularly in its relation to other associated and relevant doctrines.

Of all the Pentecostal thinkers to have written in the first half of the twentieth century, Pearlman offers the clearest definition of a soul; he defines the ("God-breathed") human soul as:

> The life-giving and intelligent principle animating the human body, using the bodily senses as its agents in the exploration of material things and the bodily organs for its self-expression and communication with the outside world.[23]

---

17. Nee, *Spiritual Man*, 27.
18. Nee, *Spiritual Man*, 28–30.
19. Nee, *Spiritual Man*, 25–65, 89.
20. Nee, *Spiritual Man*.
21. Nee, *Spiritual Man*, 27.
22. This has been put in inverted commas because he does not title it as such and is a smaller and more devotional text.
23. Pearlman, *Knowing the Doctrines*, 103–4.

Pearlman's designation of the soul as being an entity that is "God-breathed" comes from his reading of Gen 2:7. He argues, in distinction from Nee, that the verse implies a *dicho*tomous anthropology (as opposed to the trichotomy that Nee wants to espouse), but he acknowledges that 1 Thess 5:23 and Heb 4:12—verses commonly cited in favor of trichotomy—point more in a trichotomous direction than they do in a *dicho*tomous direction. He argues that, in fact, both positions are accurate to a degree, but nuances these understandings by asserting that the biblical terms "soul" and "spirit" represent two distinct (but related) "modes" of man's non-physical substance.[24]

For Pearlman, the distinct "modes" of "soul" and "spirit" are not separ*able* from one another, rather they interpenetrate and permeate each other. He argues that the terms "soul" and "spirit" are used closely in the teaching of Scripture—even interchangeably (at times)—which is unsurprising given that the "soul" and "spirit" are different aspects but of the same "spiritual" entity.[25] But he further nuances this interpretation by noting that "soul" is particularly used in Scripture in reference to the *earthly* life of a person, whereas "spirit" is the regular description for someone who has (physically) died and is now experiencing life-after-death.[26]

Clarifying the interrelation of the soul and the spirit, he writes:

> The soul survives death because it is energized by the spirit, yet both soul and spirit are inseparable because spirit is woven into the very texture of soul. They are fused and welded into one substance.[27]

So, in summary of Pearlman's understanding, there is an intimate relation between the soul and the spirit in the spiritual (immaterial) substance of a human; the "soul" and "spirit" are the two modes of the one spiritual substance.

---

24. Pearlman, *Knowing the Doctrines*, 104.

25. Pearlman, *Knowing the Doctrines*, 104.

26. Pearlman, *Knowing the Doctrines*, 101–2. On Pearlman's thinking, man's mode of "spirit" is, further, what differentiates the souls of humans from those of animals. Pearlman is of the view that both humans and animals have intricate souls but that an animal's soul is less complex and advanced and, not possessing a "spirit," these souls of animals do not relate to God in the unique way humans do (and they do not survive death) (104).

27. Pearlman, *Knowing the Doctrines*, 102.

The Prosperity Gospel (1940s onwards)

The decade of the 1940s saw the origin of the health and wealth movement(s)—the best-known proponent at the time being the televangelist, Oral Roberts. This movement gathered momentum in the following decades, was active through the rest of the twentieth century, and is currently alive and operative in the twenty-first century today; but its inclusion at this point of the review is due to its constant and consistent anthropology—tracing back to the movement's origin in the 1940s.

The prosperity evangelists developed a dictum, asserting that: "Man is a spirit, has a soul, and lives in a body." Nee's trichotomous understanding is evident in the background of this anthropological dictum; indeed, Nee's influence is further apparent in the theological assumption of the "Word of Faith" movement, an assumption that is keen to affirm that the cosmos is controlled by "spiritual" forces (certain *God-given* "spiritual" forces), which have a priority in the cosmos' functioning over other mere physical/material forces.[28] Whilst Nee's thinking is clearly of influence—in both this anthropological and cosmological thinking—there is differentiation in the *nuance* between his anthropology and that of the Word of Faith movement; they prefer to speak of the *spirit* as the true "I" of the human person (by contrast to the preference of Nee, who sees the *soul* as fulfilling that function).[29]

Summary of the First Half of the Twentieth Century

At this point in the exposition, having considered these earlier decades, it can be legitimately stated that the Pentecostals in the 1900s-50s were almost unanimously trichotomous in their anthropology. The one notable exception to this category might be Pearlman but who would probably accept the designation of holding a "neo-trichotomous" anthropological view (or possibly a "neo-dichotomous" view instead). All the Pentecostal thinkers surveyed believed that humans are body, soul, and spirit (with the unique exception of Pearlman who regarded the spirit and soul as dual aspects of the same non-physical part).

---

28. E.g., Hagin, *In Him*, part 1 or Copeland, *Believer's Voice of Victory*, 3.
29. E.g., Kenyon, *Bible in the Light*, 17–18.

E. S. Williams and the 1950s

Advancing to the middle of the century, to the decade of the 1950s, E. S. Williams was the first Pentecostal to write a "Systematic Theology" and to title it as such.[30] With Evangelicalism's growing influence on Pentecostalism during the middle of the century, Williams's work on the doctrine of anthropology (and indeed his *Systematic Theology* as a whole) shows evident appreciation of what can be gleaned from the Evangelical tradition; indeed, his theological anthropology is particularly reliant on sources drawn from across the Protestant tradition(s). By contrast to the volume of Pearlman, Williams shows gladness in acknowledging these sources but strikes similar tones to Pearlman in his theology of constitution.

Similarly to Pearlman, Williams differentiates individuals on the basis of their souls.[31] Williams also differentiates humans from *animals* on the grounds that the former have been made for relationship with God. Expounding on the difference between humans and animals, Williams draws from the concept of the *imago Dei*[32]—plus later Old Testament passages of Scripture[33]—to deduce that humans have been given a higher place in the order of God's creation.[34]

This theme of the difference between humans and animals, and indeed the developing intellectual rigor with which Pentecostals were desiring to think and write, appears to have also influenced the writers of the devotional magazines of the time. For example, E. J. G. Titterington wrote a very short article for "Pentecostal Evangel" entitled "What Genesis 1–3 Teaches About Man," a piece that characterizes both trends. Regarding anthropology, he writes:

> It is significant that the Hebrew word for "create", "*bārā*", used in Genesis 1:1 and 2:3 of creation as a whole and in 1:21 of animal life, is used three times in one verse (1:27) referring to the creation of man. The word "*bārā*" is used in the Old Testament only in the sense of bringing into being something new, something which was not there before.[35]

---

30. Williams, *Systematic Theology*.

31. Williams, *Systematic Theology* 2:94–95, 110–11.

32. Through the course of *The Spiritual Soul* the phrase "the *imago Dei*" will be used interchangeably with its English equivalent "the image of God."

33. In short, the (Old Testament) passages that teach that animals were given to humans both to eat and for the purpose of offering sacrifices.

34. Williams, *Systematic Theology*, 2:110.

35. Titterington, "What Genesis 1–3 Teaches," 26–27.

Titterington makes an interesting distinction in this quote concerning the difference between animals and humans, based on the Hebrew of Genesis 1 (in particular of v. 27)—advancing the discussion of anthropology to a greater depth. His focus on the image of God (v. 27), the distinguishing of humans from animals, and this deepening of theological engagement with anthropology are characteristic of Pentecostal writings during the 1950s—at both popular and academic level. Such themes are reflected, for example, in a subsequent article written by H. E. Fisher in the mid-late 1950s. Contributed, in this instance, to the devotional "Foursquare Magazine," Fisher develops the anthropological discussion an additional step further, introducing (human) "faculties" into the conversation. In his "Does the Bible Teach Physical Immortality," he argues that, by comparison to the human body—which has its five material faculties (that is, its five empirical "senses")—so the soul has five *spiritual* faculties—those of conscience, memory, reason, affection, and imagination. Moreover, along with those of the body and soul, the human *spirit* also has five faculties—those of faith, hope, reverence, prayer and worship.[36] So, based on this anthropology, Fisher then considers the implications for personal eschatology;[37] his focus on human faculties brings a different advancement of thought to the themes displayed by earlier Pentecostal writers (such as those considered previously in the thinking of Pearlman and Williams).

Duffield and Van Cleave, and J. Rodman Williams (1980s)

In the early 1980s, G. P. Duffield and N. M. Van Cleave showed additional development of constitutional thought in their *Foundations of Pentecostal Theology*.[38] Whilst displaying awareness, in that work, of the arguments for trichotomy, they exhibit a more definite inclination towards a *dichotomous* view.[39] Taking their cue from Gen 2:7, they emphasize that mankind has been created with two "gifts"—that is, man has the gift of a (material) body and the (immaterial) breath of God.[40] Duffield and Van

---

36. Fisher, "Physical Immortality?" 9.

37. Fisher adds the interesting comment in passing that the spirit, as well as the soul, returns to God at death (Fisher, "Physical Immortality?" 8). (Again, see the thinking of Pearlman).

38. Duffield and Van Cleave, *Foundations of Pentecostal Theology*.

39. Duffield and Van Cleave, *Foundations of Pentecostal Theology*, 130–31.

40. Duffield and Van Cleave, *Foundations of Pentecostal Theology*, 125.

Cleave strongly affirm the body,[41] but they likewise affirm man's immaterial "breath," and contend that a plethora of words are used in Scripture to refer to this immaterial aspect of his being (such as life, soul, spirit, mind, heart, strength, self, will and affections).[42] Whilst wanting to affirm all of these terms, and arguing that the (particular) terms "soul" and "spirit" are *generally* used in Scripture in a way that is interchangeable, still they want to maintain a distinction between these two terms, given their *precise* usage in Scripture. They argue that the terms refer to the *inner-self* of man in regard to his *different* types of relationships; for them "the soul is [used of] Man in his earthly relationships; the spirit is [employed of] Man in his spiritual and immortal relationships."[43]

Distinguishing the nature of man from that of animals, Duffield and Van Cleave are slightly more nuanced than previous thinkers surveyed. They argue that it is not the spirit per se that distinguishes humans from animals (recognizing that animals are also referred to in Scripture as beings that have a soul and likewise a spirit [Eccl 3:21; Ps 104:25–30]), but rather it is their faculties of *superior degree* that distinguishes humans from animals. Along with this nuanced distinction, Duffield and Van Cleave draw further attention to the unique status of mankind as having been made in the image of God and again want to affirm (what they see as) humans' (exclusive) position as being those who experience life-after-death.[44]

Showing further nuance in their anthropology, Duffield and Van Cleave also contend that, whilst being dichotomous beings, man has a fundamental *unity* to his being, shown by the scriptural mandate that worship is to be offered with all of his heart, soul, mind strength (Mark 12:30)—the whole of his life and being.[45] So whilst man can experience life-after-death—without the physical body—this state is one of "nakedness" (cf. 2 Cor 5:1–10), and it is only when properly embodied that a man is able to function wholly.[46]

Pentecostals' development of thought on the topic of constitution is traced further, during the 1980s, in the anthropology contained in J. Rodman Williams's systematic theology. Between the time that Fisher wrote

---

41. Duffield and Van Cleave, *Foundations of Pentecostal Theology*, 126–29.
42. Duffield and Van Cleave, *Foundations of Pentecostal Theology*, 129.
43. Duffield and Van Cleave, *Foundations of Pentecostal Theology*, 131.
44. Duffield and Van Cleave, *Foundations of Pentecostal Theology*, 129–30.
45. Duffield and Van Cleave, *Foundations of Pentecostal Theology*, 131–32.
46. Duffield and Van Cleave, *Foundations of Pentecostal Theology*, 132–33.

his piece (in 1957) and when Rodman Williams authored his tome (in 1988), mainline Christian denominations had experienced Pentecostal renewal themselves, and indeed neo-Pentecostal churches (or "neo-Charismatic" churches[47]) were likewise adding to the burgeoning of Pentecostalism across the world. Indeed, expressing the same spirituality as that expressed by Classical Pentecostals, J. R. Williams wrote his systematic theology from a *Reformed* theological angle but opted to title that work specifically a "Renewal Theology"; this was due to the Pentecostal leaning and coloring from and with which he authored that theological work.[48] Some of the anthropological threads of the work bear obvious resemblance to those of the Pentecostals so far considered, yet whilst displaying that continuity, Williams's *Renewal Theology* serves to demonstrate how Pentecostal anthropological thought was continuing to progress.

Continuing the development of Pentecostals' anthropological thinking,[49] J. R. Williams affirmed the relationship of humans to animals—and indeed their relation to plants—considering the implications of the Hebrew word "*bārā*" concerning the constitution of man. He sees physical comparison between plants and animals in the "materiality" they both possess, but views the radically new element of animals (owing to God's creating them "*bārā*") as being the *conscious* life they possess. In then considering the nature of humans as a further step in his argument, whilst recognizing them as additionally material beings—(indeed conscious material beings), he views the additionally distinctive element of humans as their being created uniquely in the image of God (created again, "*bārā*")—their being inbreathed by God himself. Explicating this understanding, he states:

> The specific difference [between man and animals] is that man's conscious life includes the range of his intellectual, emotional, and volitional life. This does not mean that animals, especially the most highly developed ones, have none of this. However, with man there is such a great difference in these areas that quantitative measurement does not suffice: there is a quantitative otherness. With the mind man rises into the realm of concepts, ideas and imagination and can even reflect upon himself in his rational self-transcendence; with the emotions man can

---

47. See Anderson's categorization in the introduction to this book.

48. Williams, *Renewal Theology*.

49. Particularly those ideas that are prevalent in the thought of E. S. Williams, Titterington, Fisher, Duffield and Van Cleave, above.

rise to the supersensible realm and may rejoice in the good, the true, and the beautiful; with the will man can put into practice complex energies of self-determination and move beyond the confines of instinct and environment. Man as living soul, by virtue of being grounded in spirit, is self-transcending in every area of his conscious life.[50]

For (J. R.) Williams, therefore, a being's "soul" is the *kind of conscious life* that is possessed by that being.

Like Pearlman, Duffield, and Van Cleave, Williams sees an intimate relationship between man's spirit and soul; he argues that a de-emphasizing of the spirit results in the relationship of man to God being unhelpfully downplayed, in turn reducing the essence of man merely to his intellect, emotion, and volition.[51] But, rather than being a trichotomist, (though he may be reticent in describing himself as a dualist), Williams divulges his constitutional position following lengthy exegesis of Gen 2:7. In his exegesis of the verse he argues that man is constituted from the dust of the ground (hence having a physical body), but that he possesses a (human) spirit (having received the breath of life[52]); as a result of these two entities meeting, man becomes a living soul/being.[53] Nee's influence is, again, clearly evident in such anthropology, yet Williams's individual nuance is also made clear in his following statement:

> As we . . . reflect on man as a "living being" or "soul", we are not to understand this as a third part of man, but as a resulting expression of spirit functioning through body. It might be said that spirit is the principle of man as soul. Soul (or life) is grounded in spirit and so is inseparable from spirit, but it is not

---

50. Williams, *Renewal Theology*, 214.

51. Williams, *Renewal Theology*, 212, and also n58 on that particular page.

52. Similar to Nee, Williams is keen to differentiate between the "breath of God," in Gen 2:7, and the human "spirit" that results. Drawing on Job 33:4, he states "Man does not have a [literal] deposit of the divine Spirit, else he were partly divine . . . . Man's spirit . . . is *inbreathed* by God . . . and is intimately related to, but *by no means identical with*, the Spirit of God." (Williams, *Renewal Theology*, 211 [emphasis mine].)

53. Williams, *Renewal Theology*, 208–14.

a third part.⁵⁴ It is the *whole of life* through which the spirit of man expresses himself.⁵⁵

So, for Williams, the soul comes into existence through the combination of spirit and body and has a vital role in the life of a human. However, being derivative of the spirit, "it is the *spirit and not the soul* that is said to go immediately 'upward' post-death because of the spirit being the primary in the relation of the two."⁵⁶ Having said this, Williams thinks that Scripture is able to also speak of the soul as being present with the Lord post-death (for instance, in Rev 6:9), because the soul is grounded in, and lives out of, the spirit.⁵⁷

Munyon, Arrington, Grudem, and Hart (1990s)

Following the Pentecostal desire to distinguish the nature of humans from that/those of animals, Tim Munyon also addresses the question of "faculties" arguing that the faculties of human beings are a lot more advanced in their nature than those of animals. He gives the particular example of the houses that humans and animals build; human homes are built with reason and imagination whereas animal homes are built from mere instinct.⁵⁸ He further shows himself content, when seeking to "answer" the dichotomy/trichotomy question, to just state the arguments for both views—not taking a particular view, leaving it open for the reader to decide.⁵⁹ Interestingly, French Arrington takes a similar approach—not committing to either of these positions—but he does underline the unified nature of the human (regardless of which position is chosen).⁶⁰

---

54. His related footnotes on dichotomy and trichotomy are interesting: N58 on page 212 states "one of the basic weaknesses in a dichotomous view of man . . . [is] . . . that [on this view] he is only body and soul; spirit being identified with soul. Since soul has basically to do with the intellectual, emotional, and volitional aspects of man, what spirit points to may be eliminated or radically subordinated." Whereas n64, page 213 states "trichotomy, which views man as constituted of three parts, also has a serious weakness: 'soul' is not a third part of man. However, since it is not identical with body or spirit, trichotomy does point in the right direction."

55. Williams, *Renewal Theology*, 213.
56. Williams, *Renewal Theology*, 214 (emphasis mine).
57. Williams, *Renewal Theology*, 214.
58. Munyon, "Creation of the Universe," 215–53.
59. Munyon, "Creation of the Universe," 81–83.
60. Arrington, *Christian Doctrine*, 191–92.

(Similar to [J. Rodman] Williams) Wayne Grudem fits into the category of being a thinker who is Pentecostal by spirituality but who primarily writes his systematic theology from an Evangelical Reformed point of view (displaying his Pentecostal theological views when the pertinent issues arise).[61] He nudges Pentecostal constitutional thinking an additional step further when he states:

> Although the arguments for trichotomy do have some force, none of them provides conclusive evidence that would overcome the wide testimony of Scripture showing that the terms *soul* and *spirit* are frequently interchangeable and are in many cases synonymous.[62]

The discussion is advanced yet further in the work of (Pentecostal Evangelical) Larry Hart.[63] In his work *Truth Aflame,* when considering man's self-conscious nature, Hart makes the revealing comment that: "The writers of the Scriptures and theologians down through the centuries have called this [self-conscious] aspect [the] 'soul' *or* 'spirit.'"[64] The dichotomous inclination that is expressed in the preceding quote is further implied in Hart's reflection on the constitutional question; he poses himself the following question, and then strongly indicates his answer: "Are there two natures within an individual—the physical body and the soul or spirit? The consensus of the church has been that there are."[65]

Post 2000

From the 1990s into the twenty-first century, Pentecostal academia rapidly developed, yet anthropology and the doctrine of constitution within the discipline remained a somewhat neglected area. (Excluding, for now, Yong and Kärkkäinen[66]—whose work will be examined in the book's two following chapters) Only two other significant works post-2000

---

61. Grudem is helpful to the review because he helpfully highlights the growing influence of outside theological influences on Pentecostalism.

62. Grudem, *Systematic Theology,* 481.

63. Hart describes himself as a "Charismatic Evangelical," but in consistency with the terminology employed in this book (see introduction) I have altered this terminology to "Pentecostal Evangelical."

64. Hart, *Truth Aflame,* 242 (emphasis mine).

65. Hart, *Truth Aflame,* 243.

66. Cf. Yong, *Spirit of Creation;* and Kärkkäinen, *Creation and Humanity.*

contributed to the Pentecostal discussion on constitution.[67] The first is an article by William Atkinson—authored in the year 2006—entitled "Spirit, Soul and Body: The Trichotomy of Kenyon, Hagin and Copeland."[68] Much of Atkinson's article is review and evaluation of the trichotomous position, so, as my own evaluation will follow shortly, his article will, here, be reviewed just by way of a mere outline; however, it is interesting to note in his work that, in response to the trichotomy of the Word Faith proponents, Atkinson appears thoroughly dichotomous in his view of constitution. Drawing on the philosophically-informed exegesis of anthropological dualist John Cooper (Cooper being Evangelical by way of theological tradition), Atkinson holds that Scripture teaches a "moderate dualism" (what Cooper terms a "holistic dualism"[69])—to refute the anthropology of the trichotomous Word of Faith teachers. His position can be summarized by his comment: "moderate dualism holds that the true person is the combination of body and soul, such that neither without the other can be regarded as 'I,' or the full person."[70]

The other significant contribution post-2000 is an article of Paul and Cahleen Shrier entitled "Wesley's Sanctification Narrative: A Tool for Understanding the Holy Spirit's Work in a More Physical Soul."[71] Although recognizing that Wesley's sanctification model fits most naturally with a "holistic dualist" model, Shrier and Shrier also suggest in that article that Pentecostals might be glad to entertain a (nonreductive) monistic position (brought to their attention by the work of Nancey Murphy, Warren Brown, Malcolm Jeeves and Joel Green). In contrast to the Classic Cartesian/"radical" view of the soul (that the Shriers think Christianity

---

67. Beyond this book's focus on constitution, Lisa Stephenson wrote a book on a different branch of anthropology, authoring her *Dismantling the Dualisms*. In that work, she argues that the equality of women is not only justified on the grounds of the *imago Dei* in creation, and in Christology, but also in pneumatology—based on Acts 2. The image of God is a vitalizing area of anthropology, but due to the limited scope of this book, the specific area of the *constitution* of humanity is what is being focussed on here, hence not including Stephenson's book in the above review. (Another article that is likewise of interest anthropologically, but not specifically related to the issue of constitution [so has not been reviewed in the above] is Coulter, "Whole Gospel for the Whole Person." [For further Pentecostal works which address different strands of anthropology to this book's focus on constitution, see the literature cited in the relevant footnote of chapter 2.])

68. Atkinson, "Spirit, Soul, and Body," 98–118.

69. Cooper, *Body, Soul, and Life Everlasting*.

70. Atkinson, "Spirit, Soul and Body," 106–7.

71. Shrier and Shrier, "Wesley's Sanctification Narrative," 225–41.

The Doctrine of Human Constitution

adopts), because they are aware of the neuroscientific findings which reveal that human *brain* activity affects the person's will, beliefs, morals etc.—functions traditionally associated with the soul—they think that Christianity should consider the soul as something more physical in substance. Given that the will and behavior of a person are shaped by her regular habits, routines, and practices, this piques the Shriers's interest in Wesley's physical practices of piety—seeing them as disciplines that physically shape the brain, so aiding in the person's sanctification.

Evaluation

Having surveyed the Pentecostal writings on the doctrine of human constitution—from 1909 to 2009—and now turning to evaluate this corpus, there appear to be two evident constants that remain throughout the whole of the literature reviewed. First, Pentecostals evidently hold to *the authority of Scripture*; it is the (ultimate) authoritative ground upon which they want to build their doctrine of constitution.[72] Second, they show desire to maintain *a place for the human spirit* within their doctrine(s) of human constitution.[73] The former is significant due to the bearing it has for methodology—an appropriate methodology being requisite for constructing a Pentecostal doctrine (of constitution). The latter is likewise significant in the potential resource it offers for the constructive theology itself[74]—resource which will be returned to later in the book's constructive chapters.

To maintain the importance of both the constants above, these significant strands will be separated and will bookend the evaluation. Between these two bookends, the development of Pentecostal thought on the doctrine of constitution will be expounded, and the influence of other

---

72. Pentecostals regarding Scripture as the final authority in matters of faith and practice.

73. Even if this latter point is merely to use the word "spirit" (in favor of any other term) in theological anthropology as opposed to seeing it as a separate ontological entity. See chapter 7 for further exploration.

74. The discipline of "Constructive theology" is sometimes more traditionally termed as "Systematic theology." Whereas the accent of the description "systematic theology" is on systematizing (one's understanding of) the biblical texts (so drawing naturally upon tradition, reason, and experience)—in order to form a doctrine, the accent of the description "Constructive theology" is upon constructing/building a doctrine (but again drawn from one's understanding of the biblical texts, as influenced by tradition, reason and experience).

theological traditions—and indeed of philosophical ideologies—will also be explicated to identify *why* Pentecostal thought has developed in the way that it has from the beginning of the twentieth century to the beginning of the twenty-first. These theological and philosophical categories are naturally bridged by the topic of hermeneutics; so, in a section that will evaluate how Pentecostals' *approach* to the Scriptures has affected their doctrine of constitution, a discussion of the pertinent hermeneutics that Pentecostals have employed will intersect and link the discussion of theological and philosophical influences—within this wider section that lies between the evaluation's bookends. Considering these theological and philosophical influences will illumine what has stimulated Pentecostals' development of thought concerning human constitution; further, the *trajectory* of their thought, that has arisen during that century span, will also be revealed—with indicators being offered as to the trajectory's present status (a topic which will then be further addressed in the chapter that is to follow).

The Authority of Scripture

It is particularly clear from the survey that Pentecostals have consistently sought to construct their view of human constitution on the basis of the authority of Scripture. This desire of Pentecostals is one that has been evident throughout the last century, having remained constant from the writings of the Boddys through to the beginnings of the twenty-first century. Despite valuing the place of experience in their theology, the above clearly reveals that Pentecostals hold to Scripture as their final authority when considering their anthropology (as they do, theological doctrine in general). This means that the appropriate methodology for developing a consistently Pentecostal doctrine of constitution must likewise regard the Scriptures as ultimately authoritative and enter into careful exegesis of the relevant passages.

Theological Influences

Undoubtedly Pentecostals' affirmation of the authority of Scripture is not unique to their theology and is a position they have inherited from other Protestant traditions; indeed, concerning the doctrine of constitution, there are many other theological influences that have also fed into Pentecostal thinking and shaped their thought on this topic of anthropology.

Trichotomy Influence

The tripartite anthropology, evident in many of the Pentecostal writings in the earlier twentieth century, was quite distinctive of Pentecostal thought of the time. This body, soul, and spirit anthropology demarcated these Pentecostals from most other Christian traditions—which, in the main, espoused (varieties of) dualism; but again (as with the instance of the authority of Scripture) this trichotomy is not unique to Pentecostal thought, rather it flowed into Pentecostal theology from other theological traditions, bequeathing to Pentecostals a more marginal constitutional view.

The trichotomous view of humanity was never one which enjoyed a majority status in church history—it being one that suffered from associations with heretical thinkers and ideas. Though being espoused by various church fathers,[75] and being held by a *noteworthy* minority of thinkers throughout church history, the position fell into disfavor after the era of the church fathers. This fall occurred particularly because of Apollinarius's use of the belief in his teaching that the (human) spirit in Christ was replaced by pure divine spirit, but also because of the influence Greek philosophy came to have on the viewpoint. In his *Systematic Theology*, Berkhof helps clarify the view's unpopularity, explaining:

> The tri-partite conception of man originated in Greek philosophy, which conceived of the relation of the body and the spirit of man to each other after the analogy of the mutual relation between the material universe and God. It was thought that, just as the latter could enter into communion with each other only by means of a third substance or an intermediate being, so the former could enter into mutual relationships only by means of a third or intermediate element, namely the soul.[76]

So serious was this combination that by the fourth council of Constantinople (AD 869–70) trichotomy was actually condemned. Since then, it has received something of a resurgence from theologians such as Luther,

---

75. Irenaeus, Melito, Justin Martyr, Clement, Origen, Gregory of Nyssa, and Basil of Caesarea were all trichotomists of a sort—though not in the sense that trichotomy might be understood today.

76. Berkhof, *Systematic Theology*, 191.

the ensuing Evangelical Lutherans, and a handful of nineteenth century thinkers[77]—all of whom came to espouse the view in some form. In fact, some four hundred years prior to A. Boddy (who was writing in the 1900s-20s) Luther had made a connection between human trichotomy and the "trichotomy of the Old Testament temple."[78] However, among those early twentieth century Pentecostals, Boddy was certainly not alone in being influenced by this minority tradition; probably the most obvious other example was Nee, whose exposition of trichotomy belies a swallowing of the viewpoint and its history whole, including the first millennium's non-Christian Greek philosophy (as expounded in the paragraph of Berkhof). Nee in turn bequeathed this misunderstanding to the prosperity Word of Faith movement who in turn adopted much of the non-Christian philosophy entailed.

So, whilst being quite distinctive, the trichotomous anthropology, held by early twentieth century Pentecostals, was at least partly inherited from this marginal theological tradition, a stream that was at odds with the prevalent *dichotomous* tradition.

Dichotomy Influence

The position of dualism/dichotomy, then, has been the favored position through church history, a position Pentecostals inherited through the influence of Evangelicalism. Pentecostalism found itself forming closer and closer relationship(s) with Evangelicalism through the twentieth century—Evangelicalism itself having been influenced by major theological thinkers such as Augustine, Aquinas, and Calvin, and these prominent thinkers' dualistic anthropology, in turn, bearing influence in Evangelicalism's anthropology. Although Pentecostalism's partnership with Evangelicalism was officially formalized in 1943 following the National Association of Evangelicals [NAE] invitation to Pentecostals to be a part of the association, Evangelicalism's influence was already evident in the writings of Myer Pearlman. Pearlman's work was the first to show signs of movement in a dualistic direction (as well as his being the first Pentecostal to write a systematic theology) and shows subtle indications of having been influenced by the theology of (the Reformed Evangelical) Louis Berkhof. But even before Pearlman's writing, Pentecostalism's affinity with

---

77. E.g., Roos, Olshausen, Delitzsch, White, and Heard.
78. Pelikan, *Luther's Works*, 21:304.

Fundamentalism (out of which many in the NAE grew [though many then subsequently distancing themselves from such roots—owing to their developing emphasis upon critical scholarly thought]) gave a natural basis upon which the Evangelical-Pentecostal partnership could arise; indeed, as the century progressed, the mutual influence became prevalent with Pentecostalism being Evangelicalized and Evangelicalism Pentecostalized.[79]

By the end of the twentieth century, the shift of Pentecostal anthropology towards dualism—due to the Evangelical influence described above—is evident in the writings of Duffield and Van Cleave; it is further evident in the work of J. R. Williams, Munyon, Grudem, Hart, and then (at the beginning of the twenty-first century,) Atkinson. All these thinkers would gladly recognize Evangelicalism's influence in their theological thought, and many of them would happily identify as Evangelical as well as Pentecostal (as defined in this book's introduction). By the point of 2006, when refuting the anthropology of the prosperity Word of Faith Movement, Atkinson had fully assumed the exegesis and anthropology of John Cooper—an Evangelical philosophical theologian—so, by this point in the trajectory, the shift towards dichotomy appears to have been "complete;"[80] by the time of the early twenty-first century, the preferred Pentecostal viewpoint (of a more academic persuasion[81]) had become dichotomy/anthropological dualism.

Hermeneutics

In surveying the various theological influences above, the issue of *hermeneutics*—employed by Pentecostals throughout the twentieth century—has been gently illuminated. Through further attention to this topic, additional insight becomes apparent as to the reason for the shift from trichotomy to more dichotomous Pentecostal thinking concerning the doctrine of constitution.

---

79. Cf. McGee, "'More than Evangelical,'" 289–300; and Menzies, *Anointed to Serve*, 186.

80. The word "complete" is put in inverted commas because, as will be seen, it appears that dualism may not be the end point on this developing trajectory.

81. It should be noted, of course, that many Pentecostals today maintain a trichotomous position—being unaware of the Pentecostal development of thought on the issue of constitution. Such maintaining of the trichotomous position is due to influence from some of the earlier and more popular writings of their history, as well as literalist hermeneutics (that will be covered in the following section).

Pentecostals' literalist hermeneutic was significant in their early preference for a trichotomous anthropology. Particularly the (oft-cited) passages of 1 Thess 5:23, Heb 4:12, and Luke 1:46–47 were read with this literalist hermeneutic, resulting in their adoption of the trichotomous position as their favored constitutional viewpoint. As seen in the work of A. Boddy and Nee, such a hermeneutical approach was influenced by the inherited Darby translation and the associated hermeneutics of the (nineteenth century) millennial movements out of which the Darby translation arose. Combined with the growing influence of Fundamentalism, this helped to generate the literalist hermeneutics that were adopted by the Pentecostals of the early twentieth century. As described in the previous section, Pentecostals then found a growing affinity with Evangelicalism in the middle of the twentieth century, an influence which also contributed to the shaping of their biblical hermeneutics (as well as having influence in persuading Pentecostals towards a dualistic position). The hermeneutics of such Evangelicals were themselves inherited from the theology of the Reformers—whose theology did much to shape the hermeneutics of Evangelicals (and so, of Pentecostals) in the historical-grammatical sense.[82] Towards the end of the twentieth century the work of Gordon Fee highlights the application of this hermeneutical method by receptive Pentecostals;[83] indeed many Pentecostals today employ this (historical-grammatical) approach, drawing upon Evangelical works on the topic for practical application of this method to their regular preaching and devotional writing.[84] So the Evangelical hermeneutical approach has also done much to shape Pentecostals' thinking and development surrounding the constitution of humanity.

---

82. This approach sees the words of Scripture as the words of God breathed out through the writings of human authors (2 Tim 3:16) with the goal of such hermeneutics being to interpret the original meaning of the Divine/human author (before then applying the principle of the relevant passage to the contemporary situation today). So, on historical-grammatical hermeneutics, much attention is paid to the historical context of the divinely-inspired human author, as well as the literary genre that that author was using, as well as to how such an interpretation fits with the rest of Scripture.

83. Cf. Fee, "Hermeneutics and Historical Precedent."

84. For example, works by (the Evangelical) John Stott—particularly his *I Believe in Preaching*—have been of value to Pentecostals as they have sought to learn from and employ the historical-grammatical approach (cf. Stott, *I Believe in Preaching*).

Philosophical Influences

The preceding discussion of hermeneutics leads naturally into a consideration of the philosophical influences that have contributed to Pentecostals' thinking on the doctrine of constitution and their development of thought on the topic through the hundred-year period surveyed.

Though very suspicious of philosophy, at least *of that which they were consciously aware*,[85] the review given above demonstrates that Pentecostal thought concerning constitution has been shaped by philosophical influences—of which they were most likely *unaware*. An example of this would be Pentecostals' apparent wrestling with the "science" surrounding their anthropology. (The earlier) Pentecostals' employment of their literalist hermeneutic would have naturally brought about conflict with Darwinian evolution, giving insight as to why many of those surveyed felt the need to focus on the issues of the *faculties* of human beings as well as to defend the unique distinctiveness of humanity regarding other living species. Whilst Pentecostal angst, at the time, arose as a result of the evolutionary "science," Pentecostal scholars have subsequently recognized that it is only when the concept of "evolution" is worldview-and-philosophically-loaded (and when literalist biblical hermeneutics are employed) that "evolution" causes problems for theology and theological anthropology.[86] However, being unaware of the distinction between the science and the philosophy (that is sometimes injected), Pentecostals, of the time, viewed "evolution" as a threat to their anthropology, so felt the

---

85. Pentecostals of the time took very seriously (though mistakenly extracting it from its context) the admonishment of Paul in Col 2:8: "See to it that no one takes you captive through philosophy and empty deceit, according to human tradition, according to the elemental spirits of the universe, and not according to Christ" (NRSV).

86. Christian scholars—Pentecostals included—are usually at ease with the theory of evolutionary so long as the models propounded are clearly defined in a *biological* (not philosophical) sense. For instance, (whilst the following model might, itself, be in a process of evolution [the "modern" evolutionary synthesis potentially being surpassed by the "extended evolutionary thesis"]) many would be at ease with Francisco Ayala's definition of the Neo-Darwinian ("modern") thesis—being content to affirm his understanding that evolution entails 1. Descent with modification, 2. Universal Common Ancestry and 3. Genetic mutation and natural selection (Ayala, *Darwin's Gift to Science*). Sometimes proponents will add the word "random" in front of "genetic mutation" in such a definition, which, again, when defined in a careful *scientific* sense (to mean something like "irrespective of its adaptive benefit to the host organism") is acceptable; however, problems arise when metaphysical/worldview commitments are smuggled in—usually under this word "random"—to mean something to the effect of evolution being "unguided," or "blind,"—having no director behind it. (See further Smith and Yong, *Science and the Spirit*.)

need to major on the distinct human faculties and difference between humans and animals.

Further philosophical influences flowed into the anthropological discussion when Pentecostal theology developed into an *academic/scholarly* endeavor. Particularly the "mind-body" question—from the discipline of the philosophy of mind[87]—shaped the academic thought of Evangelicals concerning the doctrine of constitution, and so derivatively influenced scholarly Pentecostal thought on the topic towards the end of the hundred-year period. One can see these issues in the background when reading Grudem and Hart on constitution (in 1994 and 1999 respectively) and it is then a lot more prevalent in Atkinson and the article of the Shriers that followed (in 2006, then 2009 respectively). How aware Pentecostals were of this influence before the end of the century is difficult to identify precisely, yet the philosophy of mind has clearly been an influence towards the current end of the survey as Pentecostal theology has developed into a scholarly endeavor.

Drawing these strands all together (the theological, hermeneutical, and philosophical), the shift from trichotomy to a dichotomy, by the (very) beginning of the twenty-first century, was very much influenced by outside theological and philosophical traditions. Whilst some of these influences were specific to a particular time in the hundred-year period, many of them were prevalent through long periods of the century considered—with some of them still being widespread, and shaping Pentecostalism today. Their influence in the twenty-first century, in the most recent Pentecostal scholarship on the topic, will be clearly displayed in the following chapters; however, before that work is considered, and prior to completing this survey, the second of the two anthropological constants—again, prevalent

---

87. The discipline of the philosophy of mind is one that focusses on a number of different questions to do with the mind-brain relationship—the pertinent question of consciousness being one of particular intrigue for the discipline in recent times. Poured over in contemporary decades by numerous philosophers of mind, Colin McGinn articulates the intrigue and mystery surrounding the conscious mind, asking:

> How can technicolour phenomenology arise from soggy grey matter? [. . .] It strikes us as miraculous, eerie, even faintly comic. Somehow, we feel, the water of the physical brain is turned into the wine of consciousness, but we draw a total blank on the nature of this conversion. (McGinn, "Can We Solve the Mind-Body Problem?" 349)

Whilst something of McGinn's approach to the question is belied in his asking how such a phenomenon "arises out of" the brain (/"is turned into" consciousness), his articulation captures well this particular facet of the philosophy of mind and highlights the importance of the conscious mind for anthropological understanding.

throughout the period surveyed—will be addressed in this chapter's last section, giving focus to the Pentecostal desire for maintaining a place for the human "spirit" in their doctrine of constitution.

The Concept of (Human) Spirit

Although the trichotomous trend was drifting out of vogue by the middle of the twentieth century, Pentecostals still thought that the concept of the human spirit was scriptural in some sense. As the literature surveyed displays, even from the middle of the century onwards, the general feeling of Pentecostals (with a limited number of exceptions[88]) is that there is some kind of a distinction between "soul" and "spirit"—even if that distinction is slight, and difficult to nuance with precision.[89] This commonly leads back to the question of exegesis (and hermeneutics)—what Pentecostals understood by the scriptural term "spirit" when referring to the spirit of a human. Clearly, for many Pentecostals, the classic passages referred to of 1 Thess 5:23, Heb 4:12 and Luke 1:46–47 were paramount in their seeking to understand the concept—though the understanding of these passages became more nuanced from the scholarly era. Although not the place for full exegeses of these passages, some comment about how scholarly biblical commentators have regarded the exegesis of the latter verses is important, so will be briefly addressed at this point (but to receive further attention in chapter 6 of this book).

Among New Testament commentators, 1 Thessalonians 5:23 is consensually viewed as a passage in which Paul is praying for the sanctification of the Thessalonians in the *whole of their human condition*—linking back to his earlier exhortations of 1 Thess 3:13 and 4:3–8.[90] Likewise, the consensus of scholarly exegetes holds that the main point of Hebrews 4:12

---

88. The only real exceptions being Atkinson, the Shriers, and Hart (and possibly Grudem as well).

89. J. Rodman Williams seems to be very much in this category. His wanting to retain the difference between soul and spirit by suggesting that the (anthropological) spirit is the soul's "principle of life"—with some special relationship to God—appears to be an obvious example of such difficulty in identifying and articulating precisely what this distinction and nuance is (Williams, *Renewal Theology*, 212). Even if not wanting to make such a conceptual distinction, Pentecostals want to retain the *term* "spirit" (as the main text above will make clear).

90. Cf. Best, *Epistles to the Thessalonians*; Bruce, *1 and 2 Thessalonians*; Morris, *Epistles to the Thessalonians*, Malherbe, *Letters to the Thessalonians*; Witherington, *1 and 2 Thessalonians*.

is that the word of God is able to penetrate to the very core of a person's being.[91] Adding to this consensus opinion, there is a strong feeling expressed amongst these commentators that it would be "precarious" to build a trichotomous doctrine of humanity upon these verses.[92] Yet, it is interesting that few of these commentators, whilst recognizing that the terms are closely related, are willing to rule out entirely that the spirit is something *distinct* from the soul, even if they do not think of the spirit as a separate substance to the soul.[93] The reader is often presented with comments such as those of O'Brien: [In Heb 4:12] "Spirit and soul are *virtually* identical."[94] But that there might be room for *some* distinction arises from the exegesis of Marshall, who comments regarding 1 Thess 5:23 that:

> [Probably the best reading of the anthropology would be] . . . taking it in the sense that Paul here distinguishes three aspects of the Christian's personality, his life in relationship with God through the "spiritual" part of his nature, his human personality or "soul," and the human body through which he acts and expresses himself.[95]

Fee's comment on the verse is also worthy of note:

> . . . it is very likely, given the way Paul here expresses himself, that he might think of the human spirit and soul as distinct entities in some way. But how he might think of them as different is not at all clear from the rest of his letters. Since he tends to use such terms both broadly and somewhat interchangeably, one is hard pressed to come to final conclusions.[96]

---

91. Cf. Allen, *Hebrews*; Ellingworth, *Epistle to the Hebrews*; Gundry, *Hebrews*; O'Brien, *Letter to the Hebrews*; Stedman, *Hebrews*.

92. F. F. Bruce's word "precarious" helpfully summarizes the feelings of wider commentators on this issue, see both his *1 and 2 Thessalonians*, 129–30 and his *Epistle to the Hebrews*, 113.

93. Cf. Best, *Epistles to the Thessalonians*, 243–44; Bruce, *1 and 2 Thessalonians*, 129–30; Morris, *Epistles to the Thessalonians*, 181–82; Malherbe, *Letters to the Thessalonians* 338–39; Witherington, *1 and 2 Thessalonians*, 173; Ellingworth, *Epistle to the Hebrews*, 263.

94. See further his related comment in a footnote "There seems to be *little* difference in meaning between one's 'soul' and . . . 'spirit'" (O'Brien, *Letter to the Hebrews*, 117n137 [emphasis mine]).

95. He goes on to say "These distinctions are loose, and do not suggest three 'parts' of man which can be sharply separated, but rather three aspects of his being. Paul lists them together here to emphasize that it is indeed the whole person who is the object of salvation." (Marshall, *1 and 2 Thessalonians*, 163).

96. Fee, *God's Empowering Presence*, 66 cf. Fee, *Letters to the Thessalonians*, 230.

So, on exegetical grounds—particularly in the thinking of Fee—the *possibility* of a distinction between the "soul" and the "spirit" seems valid in a biblical sense, even if it is not immediately clear what that distinction is. Having made this biblical distinction, it is important at this point to make clear that the soul in biblical thought is rarely a spiritual entity. Whilst a case can be made for this meaning in the usage in Matt 10:28, the connotation of the word "soul" is not predominantly a spiritual substance/entity; rather (if pressed to give *a* meaning of a term whose sense differs between biblical authors) it is used more to express the essential being/core of the creature—often translated as the creature's "life"/ "life-force" or the "I" of a human person.[97] Such will receive further comment in the following chapters of the book, as indeed will the pertinent issue of whether one can make an *exegetical* case for a spiritual soul and/or spirit; but the concept of the human "spirit," to which these biblical commentators have drawn helpful attention, gives an interesting avenue to explore in the latter chapters of this book.

Summary

The historical review conducted in this chapter has revealed that Pentecostals' theology of human constitution, in the century of thought examined, exhibits a high view of Scripture and a desire to retain (in some sense) a place for the human spirit. The review has also displayed that the writings of that hundred-year period show a development of Pentecostal opinion on the doctrine of constitution, and indeed, a developing *trajectory* of thought. This development of Pentecostal opinion has been influenced by theological and philosophical ideas from (mainly) outside the Pentecostal tradition, but which have colored and shaped Pentecostals' thinking on the doctrine, and indeed shaped their trajectory of thought.

This survey will be brought up to the present—to the contemporary state of the discussion—in the chapter that is to follow, by turning to leading Pentecostal scholars Amos Yong and Veli-Matti Kärkkäinen on the topic. It will be seen that their thought epitomizes many of the strands highlighted in this chapter; indeed, embodying what has been seen in this chapter and magnifying the themes that have been present in the survey, their work gives a strong indicator, not just of where western Pentecostal thought now is on its trajectory, but its potential future direction.

97. See Churchouse, "Healthier Anthropology."

Part II

The Contemporary Pentecostal Anthropology of Yong and Kärkkäinen

2

Yong and Kärkkäinen's Doctrine of Human Constitution

THE PREVIOUS CHAPTER IDENTIFIED that western Pentecostal theology is on a (developing) trajectory concerning its doctrine of human constitution. At the start of the twentieth century, Pentecostals espoused a belief in trichotomy, namely that humans are constituted of body, soul, and spirit; this view then developed, in the following decades, into a softer version of such—Pentecostals showing progression in their anthropological thinking through the mid-latter years of that century. By the end of the twentieth century, and the turn of the twenty-first, they had proceeded in their thinking to holding a dichotomous/dualistic view—seeing a human as body and soul (or alternatively body and spirit). The signs of this on-going advancement, potentially beyond a dualistic position, were then seen in a following article authored by Shrier and Shrier (in 2009) in which they argued that the entity of the soul should be seen as a substance more "physical" in nature (at least, more physical in nature than most dualistic positions are willing to affirm).

What is evident throughout this history, and through this development in Pentecostal thinking, is that Pentecostals have always desired to operate with a high view of Scripture and to build their doctrine of constitution (and indeed their theological doctrine in general) upon this authoritative foundation. They have also maintained an interest in the concept of the human spirit and sought to retain a place for that spirit in their doctrine of constitution. Further, it is evident from the previous chapter that the course of the trajectory has been influenced by outside theological traditions and philosophical considerations that have contributed to the shaping of the direction of this anthropological trajectory.

As will be seen in this forth-coming chapter, the developing trajectory of thought and the influences that have historically shaped it, plus the theme of biblical authority and likewise a place for the human spirit, all continue and indeed are embodied in the most contemporary Pentecostal writings on the topic—the anthropological works authored by scholars Amos Yong and Veli-Matti Kärkkäinen. The writings of these scholars on the doctrine of constitution will be surveyed and expounded in this chapter, bringing further illumination to the trajectory's status in the present and giving indications of its possible future direction. Indeed, recognizing that the work of these thinkers stands in line with the trajectory's direction—taking it an additional step beyond into a monistic understanding of constitution—will illumine the importance of engagement with the topic in the present to both shape the contemporary discussion and the trajectory's future direction.

Amos Yong

Introducing Yong as a Thinker and His Theological Anthropology

Amos Yong is Professor of Theology and Mission at Fuller Theological Seminary. Having published extensively in a wide range of subjects it is legitimate to say that he is Pentecostalism's most prolific theologian and his work is having influential effects both across the Pentecostal academy as well as in further theological arenas.[1] Specifically with regard to theological anthropology—and within that, the doctrine of human constitution—he is the Pentecostal scholar to have written most comprehensively on the subject, and through his full academic treatises addressing the

---

1. Yong is regularly designated by his colleagues as a/the leading Pentecostal scholar, see for instance the opening sentence of Oliverio's review of Yong's *Theological Hermeneutics*: "There is no more influential Pentecostal theologian in the academic world today than Amos Yong." (Oliverio, "Theological Hermeneutic," 4). Cf. the back page of Stephenson, *Amos Yong Reader*; and the compendium dedicated to engagement with his work: Vondey and Mittelstadt, *Theology of Amos Yong*, (in particular) 1–2. Beyond Pentecostal scholarship, particularly his work on disability is celebrated and cited regularly across the theological academy.

constitutional topic he appears to have already impacted the thinking of fellow-scholars in the Pentecostal academy.² His significant works on the issue are those that he wrote between 2005 and 2011—works in which he lays out his anthropology most fully; in the opening half of this chapter, therefore, his major claims on the doctrine of constitution will be surveyed from these noteworthy works. However, to understand more fully why he approaches anthropology in the way in which he does, and indeed why it is that he is attracted to the models of anthropology to which he is, it would be helpful to precede the following review of his work with an outline of his "theological hermeneutic," that is, his theological method in general.

Yong's Theological Method

Yong's method is most fully articulated in his *Spirit-Word-Community*,³ a work in which he sets out his *theological* hermeneutic.⁴ Distinguishing it from a narrower *biblical* hermeneutic, Yong explains that his theological hermeneutic is one which:

> aims at interpreting [not just the Bible but] the totality of human experience—and that includes God and God's relationship with human selves and the world as a whole—from a perspective that is specifically and explicitly grounded in faith.⁵

Whilst seeking to interpret the entirety of the God-self-world reality (the reality of human experience) from a theological perspective, this theological hermeneutic of Yong aims to do so in a manner which is inclusive—leaving the way specifically open for other disciplines of the academy to contribute to this interpretative quest of gathering and discerning truth. In Yong's theological hermeneutic, all truth is *God's* truth—wherever it may be found.⁶ What follows from this understanding

---

2. See the exposition to follow, suggesting his influence in Kärkkäinen's thinking, and (indeed, as was indicated by the footnote in the introduction) influencing (to a degree) the anthropology of Wolfgang Vondey.

3. Yong, *Spirit-Word-Community*.

4. Yong comments that the way in which he uses the terms "theological method" and "theological hermeneutics" are virtually indistinguishable (Yong, *Spirit-Word-Community*, 2).

5. Yong, *Spirit-Word-Community*, 6.

6. Yong. *Spirit-Word-Community*, 305. Truth being "pragmatic, transformative, and liberative. . . and . . . Theologically, truth is said to be salvific and sanctifying" (276).

is that, whilst beginning with his theological assumption that the world is one unified Spirit-charged reality, Yong understands this reality as that which can be understood and interpreted through the (welcome) insights of many different disciplines (such as science, history, philosophy, politics etc.)—all of these disciplines contribute to this quest for discerning truth. Expounding this methodology, he draws upon the description of the "many tongues" of Pentecost as a metaphor to describe his theological method; for him, the many differing disciplines of the academy serve to build (/"proclaim") together a coherent picture of the Spirit's truth.[7]

Application of Yong's Method to His Theological Anthropology

Drawing upon his distinctive methodology, Yong's theological *anthropology* is informed by the disciplines of (neuro)science, philosophy (of mind), and biblical studies, and articulated in a trio of works. Yong's book *The Spirit of Creation* and his article "Christian and Buddhist Perspectives on Neuropsychology and the Human Person" are the two of this theological trio in which he draws particularly upon the "hard" or "natural" sciences (i.e., physics, chemistry, and biology) to inform his theological anthropology—works further enlightened by his research into the philosophy of mind and biblical studies.[8] His *Theology and Down Syndrome* is more in dialogue with the social sciences[9]—specifically disability studies—which help to inform his theology of disability (as part of his wider theological anthropology). Together, the trio of texts display an overall picture of Yong's Pentecostal theological anthropology.

Yong's Rejection of Dualism

In all three of Yong's trio of works it becomes apparent that he is writing in reaction to dualistic understandings of a human being, and his ensuing anthropology expresses a desire to move away from such positions.

---

7. Cf. Mann who engagingly summarizes this approach by stating "we find [in Yong] a call to and method for fidelity to the triune God whose Holy Spirit speaks in many tongues . . ." (Mann, "Traditionalist or Reformist," 220)

8. Yong, *Spirit of Creation*, and Yong, "Christian and Buddhist Perspectives," 143–65.

9. Yong, *Theology and Down Syndrome*. This book was motivated in part by Amos Yong's personal interest in disability studies having grown up with a disabled brother. But as such, it is very much in accord with Yong's overall method, bringing theology into dialogue with a wide range of differing disciplines.

He gives a number of theological and philosophical reasons for rejecting the dualist position(s), which will be surveyed in the following section before moving onto expound his own preferred anthropology and model of human constitution.

Theological Reasons for Rejecting Dualism

Yong makes particularly transparent that his theological reasons for rejecting dualism are because it downplays the scriptural emphases on anthropological *holism* and because it denigrates human *embodiment*. Regarding the first of these themes, Yong makes clear that he wants to move . . .

> beyond traditional (Platonist and especially, Cartesian) dualist definitions of humans as "disembodied souls" toward ontological wholist [sic] understandings of human beings . . . .[10]

For him, the locating of the human identity primarily in the soul is unacceptable because of the scriptural emphasis on the *holistic* nature of a human—one which underlines the importance of the *body*. On the second and related theme of human embodiment, he states:

> . . . human embodiment cannot be relegated to secondary status in any theological anthropology.[11]

And again:

> Only a theology of embodiment can begin to overcome Cartesian dualism and account holistically for the human experience as including other bodies, the environment and technological enhancements or even substitutes for our bodily parts.[12]

---

10. "Christian and Buddhist Perspectives," 147. Note, that Yong uses the term "wholist" (commonly [and in this book] spelt "holist") in a way interchangeable with the term "monist." More will be said about this later, but here it would be useful to define such terms. [W]Holism affirms "the functional unity of some entity in its totality, the integration and interrelation of all the parts in the existence and proper operation of the whole." (Cooper, *Body, Soul, and Life Everlasting*, 45.) Monism is the understanding that an entity ontologically consists of one "stuff" (to use a popular term, but one commonly employed by philosophers for the sake of definition), e.g., "a human consists of (just) physical matter" (as opposed to a dualistic understanding, "a human consists of physical matter and a spiritual soul").

11. Yong, *Theology and Down Syndrome*, 171.

12. Yong, *Theology and Down Syndrome*, 182.

Yong's emphasis on these dual themes of *holism* and *embodiment* arises due to his anthropological starting point; he begins his anthropology with the doctrine of the image of God, seeing this as the key concept for understanding human identity and nature. Specifically, Yong views the foundational verses on this topic—Genesis 1:26–27—as the basis for theological anthropology, verses he identifies as embedded in the creation narrative(s) of Genesis 1 (and 2[13]) and indeed located within the *Hebraic* Old Testament Scriptures (with their Hebraic affirmation of a holistic and embodied view of humanity).[14] As such, he looks to these verses as the foundation for his understanding of humanity.

In contrast to Platonist and (Classic) Cartesian understandings of humanity, which value the spiritual/immaterial soul to the detriment of the physical body,[15] Yong argues that the passages concerning the *imago Dei* in Genesis[16]—in their (physical world-affirming) context—completely undermine these positions.[17] By contrast to these problematic dualisms, he argues that Genesis' verses concerning the image of God emphasize the *physicality/materiality* of humans and the *wholistic* nature of their being.[18] Elaborating his understanding further, and in contrast to "structural"/"essentialist" views of the image—which interpret the image to mean that humans are made *ontologically* like God (in some way[s][19])—Yong is more persuaded by the "relational" understanding of the image. This "relational" view of the image regards humanity as the "thou" made for relationship with God (the "I") and, in turn, also

---

13. See the discussion to follow.

14. This is not to say that the New Testament does not carry this Hebraic understanding too, rather, that that New Testament understanding is grounded in the Hebraic understanding of the Old Testament.

15. As explained in the introduction, the adjective "spiritual" is used in the first five chapters of the book—in reference to the human soul—in a manner synonymous with "immaterial" (in this philosophical sense). At times, the word "material" occurs in these chapters (as an alternative to the term "physical") and so to allow the obvious contrast between (for instance) the "material" body and the "immaterial" soul, on occasions these chapters employ the word "immaterial" instead of the word "spiritual"—for these reasons of syntax and style.

16. Recalling that the book is using the Latin phrase (the) *imago Dei* interchangeably with the English translation (the) "image of God."

17. See the book's excursus (following the end of Part II of the book) for exposition and critique of Platonist and Classic Cartesian dualisms.

18. Yong, "Christian and Buddhist Perspectives," 146–47.

19. Whether that being, for example, by possessing an immaterial/spiritual nature, having a mind, possessing free will (etc.)

with other human beings.[20] So, added to the emphases of holism and embodiment, these themes of materiality and relationality are likewise particularly important for Yong in the constructing of his theological anthropology. With all four of these emphases being grounded in the biblical *imago Dei*, Yong rejects dualistic views and seeks in their place an anthropology which celebrates these four foundational themes.

As regards the concepts of the human "soul" or "spirit," Yong is happy to retain such language (employing the terms synonymously); but rather than understanding the soul as per Christian theology and philosophy throughout the centuries—as a spiritual (and, after death, separable) entity that is ontologically distinct from the body—he wants to retain a more *biblical* understanding of the term. He elaborates this intention by affirmatively citing Dahl, who states:

> [t]he Hebrew mind never produces anything quite like an abstraction; "soul" and "heart" and "flesh" each mean the totality of man considered from different aspects.[21]

Following from Dahl's remark, Yong then proceeds to comment that:

> Theologically speaking, the Hebrew soul or heart captures the *totality* of the human person as he or she stands in relationship to God.[22]

This understanding of the terms is important and will receive further attention in the following chapters, but it is particularly his theological work on the *imago Dei* which leads Yong to dismiss anthropological dualism and to seek, in its place, an anthropology that affirms the scriptural emphases of (anthropological) holism, embodiment, materiality, and relationality.

Philosophical Reasons for Rejecting Dualism

As well as the theological issues identified, Yong also propounds *philosophical* issues with dualism. Indeed, he highlights a number of these

---

20. Yong, "Christian and Buddhist Perspectives," 146–47. See further, Grenz, *Social God* (cf. Grenz, *Theology for the Community*, 168); and Green, "What Are Human Beings?" 3.

21. Dahl, *Resurrection of the Body*, 71–72, cited in Yong, *Theology and Down Syndrome*, 189. (Cf. Dunn, *Theology of Paul*, 54–78.)

22. Yong, *Theology and Down Syndrome*, 189 (emphasis mine).

issues in the following passage—namely the issue of interaction (between immaterial and material substances) and the issue of the neuroscientific data (or the *interpretation of* such data). In the passage he describes these as "theological" problems with dualism, but they are all more accurately designated as *philosophical* issues.[23]

> From a theological [sic] perspective, substance dualists argue, among other points, that only if human beings are seen as souls with bodies, will it be possible for personal identity to persist in the "between" state prior to the resurrection. Even if we grant this point, the problems here are both the Cartesian one about how the material and immaterial realms relate to each other and the more recent neuroscientific evidence that correlates mental life with cognitive brain states.[24]

The issue of interaction is further elaborated by Yong in another of his anthropological works (in a passage which, this time, locates the issue in the discipline of the *philosophy of mind*):

> The mind-body (or mind-brain, or soul-body) problem has persisted for centuries. Various dualisms and monisms have explored how they are related and interact. *Dualist conceptualizations—whether supernaturalist, interactionist, Aristotelian-Thomist, or Cartesian—are increasingly suspect* but provide some explanation for intentionality, the emotions, and top-down/mental causation more difficult to overcome by otherwise.[25]

The question of how an immaterial substance could interact with a material substance is one that Yong views as uncertain and problematic for a substance dualist position,[26] again giving him reason to look for other answers to the mind/soul-body question and to distance himself from dualistic positions. In articulation of the issue of *neuroscience* for advocates of substance dualism, Yong proceeds to comment:

---

23. In the opening sentence of the paragraph, Yong is referring to the theological concepts of the "soul" awaiting the time of "resurrection," so one can see why he uses the term "theological" at the start of this paragraph. But recognizing that the key issue being addressed in that sentence is that of *personal identity persistence*—between the points of an individual's death and resurrection—even this is more accurately designated as being a topic of *philosophy* (along with the issues of interaction and the interpretation of the neuroscience which he goes on to highlight).

24. Yong, *Theology and Down Syndrome*, 170.

25. Yong, "Christian and Buddhist Perspectives," 144 (emphasis mine).

26. Specifically, the issue of how a spiritual (non-physical) soul could relate to a physical body.

> ... the contemporary neurosciences have certainly shown that mental activities are emergent from and in that sense dependent upon brain and bodily functions. This includes, necessarily, the emotive and affective parts of the body....[27]

Yong affirmatively cites Gregory Peterson who summarizes various studies to show that damage to different parts of the brain inhibit and (in some cases) destroy mental functioning.[28] Then he additionally quotes Philip Clayton in support of his comment above who observes that results from the cognitive sciences:

> present a clear challenge to those who would rend thought and affect from its physical substratum.[29]

So, as regards the neuroscientific data, Yong is of the opinion that any place for a distinct and separable immaterial/spiritual soul has been invalidated by such neuroscientific findings; he thinks these discoveries indicate that it is *brain states* which affect mental functioning (and so, therefore, impact on one's personality and spirituality). For him, all the human functions that were traditionally conceived of as being the work of the spiritual soul are being gradually explained away by the neuroscience, which is showing that these mental states are, in fact, dependent on the functioning(s) of the *brain*.

When added to his theological reasons, these philosophical issues leave Yong feeling dissatisfied with any form of dualism, and lead him, instead, to seek elsewhere for an alternative and better model of human nature and constitution.

Yong's Own Anthropological Proposal

Philosophy of Mind

In his constructive theological anthropology, Yong relies upon dialogue partners from the field of the philosophy of mind to give him both insight and theological leverage from the pertinent mind-body discussion(s).[30]

---

27. Yong, "Christian and Buddhist Perspectives," 148.

28. Peterson, *Minding God*, 77–85 cited in Yong, "Christian and Buddhist Perspectives," 148.

29. Clayton, "Neuroscience, the Person, and God," 184, cited in Yong "Christian and Buddhist Perspectives," 148.

30. The mind-body question seeks to explain the relationship between a person's

As seen in his earlier works, he draws primarily on Peterson and Nancey Murphy as his key interlocutors on the mind-body relation; but he then, latterly, advances his work in dialogue with Philip Clayton and so gradually moves *beyond* the philosophy of Murphy as his anthropological thinking develops. Drawing further upon thinkers within psychology, Yong adds further insight to his model from psychologists Malcolm Jeeves and Warren Brown in augmentation of his anthropological sources. All these thinkers hold to monistic and emergentist theories of mind, however, Murphy, Jeeves, and Brown describe themselves as holding to a "nonreductive physicalist" position, whereas Clayton prefers to describe his view as an "emergent monist" position. In clarification of these understandings, "nonreductive physicalists" advocate a position which views the mental as genuinely real; they have room, therefore, in their models for first-person perspective—including rationality, the appropriation of language, top-down causation, and free will[31] (none of which are reducible to mere physical states of the brain[32]). But nonreductive physicalists do not consider the mind as a metaphysically different entity (to the body). Clayton, by contrast, prefers the description "emergent monist"—allowing for the emergence of mind as a distinct metaphysical entity.[33]

Being heavily influenced by Peterson and then Clayton, Yong makes clear that he considers an emergentist view of the mind to be the best solution to the mind-body problem. He views the mind as a *radically* new (mental) property which arose in evolutionary history at a point when the brain reached a sufficient degree of complexity—so progressing his thinking beyond that of a nonreductive physicalist understanding to

---

mind and her physical body; more specifically, it seeks to explain the relationship between a person's (inner subjective) consciousness and her physical states of the brain (cf. chapter 5).

31. Though if William Hasker's prominent view of emergence is correct, it would appear, for the nonreductive physicalist, that this cannot be *libertarian* free will, but only compatibilist free will. For Hasker, libertarian free will is only possible in the event of a property being given rise to that is genuinely completely independent of its subvenient base and having causal powers which cannot be explained by causal interactions at the level of the particles (Hasker, *Emergent Self,* 188). Put in his own words, he comments "If we are to include libertarian free will as an attribute of persons, it seems we shall need to recognize persons, or minds, or souls, as *unitary subjects,* not analyzable as complexes of parts" (178 [emphasis mine]).

32. As opposed to reductive physicalists who argue that everything in the world ultimately reduces to simple physics.

33. Peterson prefers the title "radical emergentism" to describe his view, which is closer to Clayton than Murphy.

embracing a distinctly emergent monist account. To reiterate his view of emergence, the mind (or "soul" or "spirit" [Yong being content to interchange these terms for the "mind"]) has emerged (historically) from the brain; and whilst being *dependent upon* the brain as its substrate it is *irreducible to* this physical substrate.[34] This radically new property of mind is one that *supervenes* on the brain, having been given rise to by the brain's complexity and physical arrangement. Yong is attracted to this view for several reasons (for now focussing on those he terms "scientific" and philosophical reasons[35]). First, he sees it as a view which offers a cogent explanation for the "hard problem of consciousness" (a specific issue in the philosophy of mind).[36] Second, it espouses a view of the mind which is able to account for mental/top-down causation and hence for morality and (compatibilist) free will.[37] Third, it retains the beauty and

34. Yong, "Christian and Buddhist Perspectives," 63, 143–44; Yong, *Theology and Down Syndrome*, 183. Emergentists commonly use the examples of H2O or a wheel to illustrate emergent properties: an oxygen molecule on its own does not constitute a liquid, but when arranged together with two other hydrogen molecules, the property of liquid emerges, the sum being greater than the parts. Likewise, a single molecule does not have the property of being able to roll, but when combined with other molecules into the complexity of a wheel, the molecules together gain a new kind of property— that of being able to roll. (Cf. Sperry, "A Modified Concept," 532–36 and "Mind-Brain Interaction," 195–206.)

35. The reason for putting the term "science" in inverted commas will begin to become evident in the following paragraph but will be made particularly so by the end of chapter 3.

36. Yong, *Spirit of Creation*, 62. The "hard problem of consciousness" is a phrase coined by David Chalmers, a neuroscientist and philosopher of mind (of a naturalist persuasion), who, having sought every possible reductive solution to the mind-body problem, concluded that though science could solve "the soft problem of consciousness" (that is, the problem studious neuroscientists are going to encounter in studying and mapping the brain and its 10^{11} neurons and 10^{14} neural connections), it could go no way to solving the "hard problem of consciousness." Once all the mapping of the "soft problem" has been achieved, the "hard" problem remains of how to explain the reality of a person's *inner* subjective mental life, for instance the reality of her "qualia" (being a person's first-person experience of what it is like to be her) (Chalmers, *Conscious Mind*, 24–25). (Chalmers, though still a naturalist, has moved to a form of "naturalistic dualism" and subsequently, further to a panpsychist position.) Cf. Nagel, "What Is It Like to Be a Bat?" 433–50 for a different slant on the question.

37. Yong, "Christian and Buddhist Perspectives," 148–50; Yong, *Spirit of Creation*, 58–61. For Yong, these first two points—particularly that of top down causation— also give (philosophical) critique of *reductive* physicalism, in that (rather than being purely the result of an unguided Neo-Darwinian process [which at best gives rise to epiphenomenalism {the view that mental states are merely a by-product of evolutionary theory and as such have no causative influence on the brain}]), an emergent mind means the escaping of biological and social determinism by (instead) giving grounds for (compatibilist?) free will.

elegance of a world which (in its entirety) is a monistic entity[38]—having the associated benefit of meaning that it does not impede science's desire to operate according to methodological naturalism.[39] Fourth (and of particular importance to Yong), it is consistent with the contemporary neurosciences.[40]

This combination of philosophical and scientific factors has attracted Yong to his preferred emergentist theory of mind but it is especially the "scientific" dimension that has been of particular appeal.[41] Though the "scientific" basis that he gives for both a bottom-up yet top-down causation has developed from the time of his "Christian and Buddhist Perspectives" to his later *The Spirit of Creation*,[42] that is doubtless part of the position's attraction for Yong—it allows room for the on-going developments in science to strengthen the position over time. As such, in preference to the thinking of Murphy, he (more) closely identifies with the reasoning of Clayton, so favoring the emergent monist position. Yet, at the same time, he is glad that emergent monism is able to retain the scientific/metaphysical desire of Murphy[43]—that of providing a substantial metaphysical position which allows for on-going development and findings within the scientific empirical domain (even if the scientific domain could never *confirm* such a position).[44] Given that this metaphysical/scientific platform is entailed in Clayton's emergent monist proposal—and carries potential for Yong's own constructive approach—Yong favors the model of Clayton (over all the interlocutors he that draws from) and so adopts his emergent model to serve as the philosophical (anthropological) basis upon which he then builds his own constructive anthropology.

---

38. Yong, "Christian and Buddhist Perspectives, 160 and Yong, *Spirit of Creation*, 60 and 145.

39. Yong, *Spirit of Creation*, 61.

40. Yong, "Christian and Buddhist Perspectives," 148.

41. As has been already indicated in the aforementioned sections, what is sometimes designated as "science" by Yong (concerning the topic of anthropology) can require further analytical probing to disclose whether this is the best categorizing term. (See further the review of chapter 3).

42. Compare the development from "Christian and Buddhist Perspectives" 148–50 to Yong, *Spirit of Creation* 59–60.

43. Note, this scientific/metaphysical desire concerns the emergent model *as a whole* (in distinction from holding that the mind *specifically* is a distinct metaphysical entity).

44. Murphy, "Nonreductive Physicalism," 147. (The view's being non-confirmable by science is due to the discipline of science as being one that is always progressing.)

Resolving, to Yong's preference, the question of the relationship of the mind to the body, Clayton's emergent monist position offers much of benefit to Yong for the construction of his theological anthropology. It offers him a model which emphasizes the human brain and body as essential features of human identity (a model which espouses that, apart from the body and brain, consciousness [and self-consciousness] is impossible). It also gives a holistic understanding of the human—affirming embodiment, social/environmental situatedness, and spiritual relationality. Further, it values Scripture's eschatological emphasis on the resurrection of the body.[45] So, in his desire to propose an anthropology which affirms holism, embodiment, materiality, and relationality, Yong sees much of potential in emergence theory; he finds himself attracted to the position of Clayton as he sets out to construct his own theological anthropology, anthropology that he decides to build upon Clayton's emergent monism.

Clayton's Model

Elaborating Clayton's emergentist model—that of attraction to Yong—Clayton advocates a monistic understanding of the world but one which entails an "ontological pluralism" *within* that (monistic) world.[46] Borrowing from the work of Harold Morowitz—who argues that the world hosts up to twenty-eight levels of emergence[47]—Clayton contends that there are many differing levels of emergence which have arisen through the history of the world. Some of these are examples of what he calls "stronger" levels of emergence (for instance, those which occur at the level of biology), some of which he terms "weaker" levels (i.e., those which occur at the level of physics and chemistry); but whilst differing in degrees of strength, he argues that all of these levels display a "family resemblance," exhibiting shared common traits across the variety of strata of emergence.[48] For Clayton, these shared common traits—exhibited at each of these levels of emergence—consist of the following characteristics:

1. The higher level's emerging at a time later in evolutionary history than its lower (subvenient) base (the lower level being what is supervened on by the emergent higher stratum).

---

45. Yong, *Theology and Down Syndrome*, 171.
46. Clayton, *Mind and Emergence*, 148.
47. Morowitz, *Emergence of Everything*.
48. Clayton, *Mind and Emergence*, 61.

2. The higher level's emerging as a result of a sufficient degree of complexity at that lower (subvenient) level (meaning it could theoretically be possible to *predict* the arising of a higher stratum of emergence—based on knowledge of the lower level[49]).

And

3. (Though emerging from the lower level) The higher stratum being non-reducible (in a causal, metaphysical, and ontologically explanatory sense of the term) to its lower (subvenient) level.[50]

Whilst recognizing these shared common traits in the differing levels of emergence, the *distinctive* feature of Clayton's overall view is the ontological (emergentist) pluralism which he espouses (originally derived from Morowitz), a pluralism entailed within his *monistic* view of the world.

This distinctive acknowledged, Clayton (still) shares much in common with Murphy (and other emergentists) concerning his *highest* level of ontology—the emergence of mind. Like Murphy, Clayton emphasizes downward causation as integral to the model, and he likewise agrees with her standpoint that the emergence solution to the mind-body problem is superior to other contenders (such as dualism). This superiority is due, in his mind, to the position's being able to give an appropriate account for the neuroscientific data (which demonstrate, for him, that mental states are "dependent upon brain states").[51] So his view is in many ways similar to that of other emergentists' thinking, yet he is clear to underline that he believes in a *metaphysically distinct* emergent mind, and that his emergent monistic theory is his own unique version due to the *ontological pluralism* he espouses (grounded in philosophical monism).

Clayton's Influence in Yong's Anthropology

Yong prefers Clayton's particular branch of emergentism because it retains the benefits of Murphy's project but additionally gives Yong extra stimulus for his *theological* project. The "emergent universe" espoused by Clayton—with its many different levels of emergence—chimes with

---

49. Even if it the exact relationship between the two levels would be uncertain, as indeed the precise nature of the higher level.

50. Clayton, *Mind and Emergence*, 61, 66, 80–84.

51. Clayton, *Mind and Emergence*, 120–23. What it means for mental states to be "dependent upon brain states" will need closer examination in the following chapter.

Yong's "many tongues" theological hermeneutic, and, indeed operating within that hermeneutic, Yong suggests that science itself is a "many tongues" discipline, which needs to draw upon all of its sub-branches in order to discover truth. Indeed, offering a "pneumatological assist" to Clayton, Yong proposes that Clayton's work is comfortably theologized by considering the Spirit who is immanently present in the world—the one who authored the world and its laws and so animates the "many tongues" of science (as science studies the world of the Spirit).

When focussing the discussion on anthropology in particular, Yong is appreciative of Clayton's model in that it espouses engagement with the ("many tongues") disciplines of (the) science(s) (in this case, particularly those of physics, chemistry, biology, and psychology) to explicate the nature of a human in full.[52] But given the position's contention that the mind is fully dependent on the body to engender mental activity, he is further appreciative of the model in its (deductive) affirmation of human embodiment, materiality, and holism.[53] Finally, Yong is attracted to Clayton's position in that it allows him to advance an indeterminate quantum view of the sciences—one which has room at the micro level for the interaction of the creaturely mind within creation, but also for God's interaction at the macro level of creation too (so paving the way for his theory of divine action which he advances through his book *The Spirit of Creation*[54]).[55]

Biblical Support for the Emergent Monist Anthropology

As well as seeking to build his anthropology on the preceding philosophy and science, Yong also provides *exegetical* support for his theological

---

52. Whilst certain scientists might question whether psychology should be considered in the domain of the sciences, as Yong has already made a case that the mind is not reducible to the brain (contra the views of certain reductive materialist scientists), his instating psychology as a scientific discipline—indeed, as a means of studying of that mind—is legitimated.

53. Again, the meaning of the mind's being *dependent* on the body will need further examination later.

54. See Yong, *Spirit of Creation*, particularly chapters 3 and 4 (though seen throughout the book as a whole).

55. Being a work of philosophy (of science), aimed especially at those in the sciences, Clayton does not say much about God in his *Mind and Emergence*. Whereas, for Yong, his theologizing of Clayton's project is one in which God permeates this (theologized) model.

model. This exegesis provides the means of adopting—but theologically-advancing—the emergent monism of Clayton and constructing it into a theological anthropology that is distinctive to Yong himself. The way Yong undertakes this exegesis is by theologizing Clayton's model by means of exegesis of Genesis 1 and 2[56]—specifically by what he calls a "canonical-pneumatological" reading of these creation narratives.[57]

What Yong means by a "canonical-pneumatological" reading (of Genesis 1 and 2) is a reading which interprets the(se) chapters of Scripture on their own exegetical terms—respecting their specific context and meaning but allowing the theological teaching of later canonical passages to help *bring out* the implicit pneumatological color (of these Genesis accounts of creation). This "canonical-pneumatological" approach allows Yong to place the insights he has gained from Clayton—concerning the philosophy of mind and of science—into a pneumatological doctrine of creation; this, in turn, has the effect of furthering Yong's Pentecostal method—enabling him to view the "many tongues" of (the) science(s) as those which all flow from the authorship of the one Spirit of creation.[58]

Genesis 1:2 is principally important for Yong in the construction of his theological anthropology in that the verse speaks of the identity and function of the *rūach Elōhīm*. In terms of identity, *rūach Elōhīm* can (here) be aptly translated as "'wind,' 'breath,' or even 'storm' of God," but it is most commonly translated as "'spirit' of God"—Yong identifying this spirit as being specifically the *Holy* Spirit.[59] As regards the Spirit's function, Yong draws attention to the Spirit's "hovering" over the waters of creation, contending that the word that is used here for "hovering" is the same word that is used to refer to a hen as she "broods over" her eggs. In the opinion of Yong, therefore, Gen 1:2 alludes to the Spirit's "brooding over" creation and his/her work of giving life to creation.[60] Developing

56. This is similar to an approach he took in his earlier article; see Yong, "Christian and Buddhist Perspectives," 145–50 (although in this former work, he theologizes a less specific supervenience theory of mind than that which he theologizes in *Spirit of Creation*).

57. The "canonical-pneumatological" hermeneutic is his own description of his approach (Yong, *Spirit of Creation*, 152–63) but acknowledges Warren Gage's work (*Gospel of Genesis*) as part of the inspiration for such an approach.

58. And so, these many disciplines of the sciences are then employed for studying the relevant levels of emergence.

59. In light of Yong's canonical pneumatological hermeneutic—which takes into account the related passages of Job 34:14–15; Eccl 12:7; Ps 104:28–29; Ezek 37:1–14; Luke 23:46; and Rom 8:11,18–23 (Yong, "Christian and Buddhist Perspectives," 146).

60. This image of a hen brooding over her eggs is, in part, what leads Yong to opt to

this line of thought additionally, Yong interprets Gen 1:2 as a "bookend" to the creation narrative—with its opposite bookend being the creation of *hā ādām* in Gen 2:7; he views the *rūach Elōhīm*, as depicted in this narrative, as actively working to animate all aspects of creation. Expounding this understanding still further, through drawing attention to the details of Gen 1, Yong wants to affirm that it is specifically the *Spirit* who divides, defines, and differentiates—between sea, sky, and land—and who gives breath to all the living creatures (cf.1:30); indeed, it is this Spirit who breathes the creative words "let there be . . ." on each day of creation.[61] So by way of understanding creation and the Spirit's role *in* creation, Yong is very affirmative of Jay McDaniel who describes it as a world that is "en-spirited by God."[62]

When relating his exegesis to Clayton's model of the "emergent universe," Yong argues that the Spirit (of Gen 1:2) has providentially guided all of the levels of emergence that have occurred through natural history; he states that hints are given throughout the Gen 1 account of the Spirit's having created a world that, itself, is able to create and facilitate these multiple levels of emergence.[63] Yong is of the view that the world was designed to "co-create" along with its divine creator;[64] from the foundational level of physics (a level created directly by God), the world has been subsequently able to give rise to the ensuing levels of emergence—all of which have occurred under the providential guiding of the Spirit of creation.[65]

Of pertinence to the topic of constitution is what Yong is keen to argue concerning the creation of humanity (in Gen 1:26–28 and 2:7). In

---

employ the pronoun "she" when referring to the Holy Spirit. (Yong, *Spirit of Creation*, 172.)

61. Yong, "Christian and Buddhist Perspectives," 146; Yong, *Theology and Down Syndrome*, 181; Yong, *Spirit of Creation*, 152–56. His canonical approach leads Yong to draw upon Pss 33:6 and 104:29–30 to support such a reading.

62. McDaniel, "Where is the Holy Spirit Anyway?," 162–74 cited in Yong, *Spirit of Creation*, 153.

63. E.g., the "let the earth *put forth* vegetation," "let the waters bring forth living creatures of every kind."

64. The idea of a deistic God (who has left the world to create for itself) is excluded on Yong's model by the *co*-creational role of creation (a creation which co-creates alongside and within God's [macro-]creational work.)

65. Yong, *Spirit of Creation*, 158. It should be noted at this point that Yong's theology is in accord with big bang cosmology and Neo-Darwinian evolutionary theory. He does not read Genesis 1 and 2 as (what he calls) a "literal-historical" account of creation, rather he sees it as an account written to combat ancient Near Eastern cosmogonies (152).

one sense he wants to clarify that *hā ādām* is both a part of, and similar to the rest of creation;[66] *hā ādām*, according to Gen 2:7, is literally of the earth—a being made from its physical dust—so there is a close relationship between humans and animals and, indeed, the rest of creation. However, in a complementary but different sense, Yong regards the pneumatological "breath of life" that was breathed into *hā ādām* (2:7)—and the specific designation of humans as having been made in the image of God (1:26–27)—as distinguishing humankind from the rest of creation. In the creational thinking of Yong, the image/likeness of God confers a *special* status on humans as the *pinnacle* of creation; and as bearers of the image of God, they have been given an extra endowment of relationality for purposes of relating to God, one another, and the rest of the created world.[67] Related to this view of the *imago Dei*, Yong identifies the specific task of humanity as caring for and ruling over the rest of creation as part of their divine vocation—a task to be carried out in relation to God their creator.[68]

In terms of Genesis 2 and the further theologizing of Clayton's model, Yong sees emergence theory as at least consistent with Gen 2:7 and in fact he argues that emergence theory helps to elucidate what is implied in the verse. For both Yong and Clayton, the self-conscious mind (/spirit) is the final level (to date) to have emerged within the universe, and this emergent (self-) conscious mind is what distinguishes humanity from the rest of the animal kingdom. Yong claims that the emergence of this human mind (/spirit) is partially explicated in Gen 2:7 in its narration of the Spirit's breathing life into the dust of *hā ādām*; Yong's philosophizing of this verse suggests its acknowledging the fact that the human mind (/spirit) is dependent upon and interconnected with its material substrate—its physical/earthly matter. Yet, whilst holding this in mind, he suggests that the verse also implies that human consciousness and self-awareness is (partly what is) derived from the Spirit's breath of life that has been breathed into *hā ādām*.[69]

---

66. Yong sees *hā ādām* as a reference to *generic humanity* (as opposed to a male Adam [to be followed later by the creation of female Eve (cf. 2:18–25)]).

67. Yong follows the Barthian view that to be made male and female is a significant part of humans being created in God's image (see Barth, *Church Dogmatics*, III/1 41.2).

68. A relationship and task which humans are able to fulfill or sabotage (Yong, "Christian and Buddhist Perspectives," 146–47).

69. Yong, *Theology and Down Syndrome*, 183; and Yong, *Spirit of Creation*, 159. Again, Yong would want to say that this is not a literal-historical piece of literature that he is exegeting, it is in some ways symbolic, allowing room for his interpretation.

Holding this philosophized sense of the verse, Yong sees the creation of humanity as fitting naturally into his canonical-pneumatological reading—for him, these chapters of Genesis portray humans as "dust-enspirited beings." He thinks that this canonical-pneumatological reading has the further advantage of being more in accord with a holistic, Hebraic understanding of humanity (a view favored in contemporary theology) instead of following the traditional Platonist/Cartesian readings. Indeed, he affirmatively cites Old Testament scholar Claus Westermann in support of this case, stating:

> The person as a living being is to be understood as a whole and any idea that one is made up of body and soul is ruled out.[70]

Yong regards this [w]holistic Hebraic understanding (of a person) as the direction in which contemporary biblical studies is pointing, and he ends his exegetical foray (in "Christian and Buddhist Perspectives") by affirmatively highlighting the work of leading biblical scholar Joel Green to this effect;[71] his reason for citing the latter is that Green is an example of a leading biblical exegete who has developed his theological anthropology from the Hebraic [w]holistic understanding above—a perception that Green has gained from his work in biblical studies.

Summary of Yong's Constructive Proposal

In summary, Yong is very much attracted to emergent monism—viewing it as a commendable understanding of the relation of the mind to the body. Having originally valued the thinking of Murphy (due to her "science-based" view of the mind), he moved subsequently to the viewpoint of Clayton—preferring his model of the emergence of mind as another level that has emerged within the wider emergent universe. Recognizing the theological potential that an emergent universe holds, Yong takes Clayton's model of emergence and adopts the model into his Pentecostal "many tongues" model, theologizing Clayton's emergent monist idea with particular exegetical coloring from Genesis 1 and 2. This gives Yong

---

70. Westermann, *Genesis 1–11*, 207, cited in Yong "Christian and Buddhist Perspectives," 147.

71. "Christian and Buddhist Perspectives," 147. There he cites Green's work "Bodies—That Is, Human Lives," 149–73. In his later (2007) work—*Down Syndrome*, 170 and 322n27—Yong also affirmatively cites Green's further anthropological thinking: Green, "What Does It Mean to Be Human?" 179–98.

an anthropology which he views as consistent with the science(s), with a valid answer to the mind-body problem, and a model he has then theologized to give him his own Pentecostal theological anthropology.

Veli-Matti Kärkkäinen

Introducing Kärkkäinen as a Thinker and His Theological Anthropological Work

The second Pentecostal thinker to be considered—who holds a (very) similar doctrine of constitution to that of Amos Yong—is Veli-Matti Kärkkäinen. Like Yong, Kärkkäinen is also a professor at Fuller Theological Seminary—himself being Professor of Systematic Theology. Though he does not consider the doctrine quite as extensively as Yong,[72] his work on the doctrine is similarly significant; he is the latest Pentecostal thinker to have given thorough attention to the subject of constitution, so being the most recent voice to be added to the Pentecostal trajectory.[73] Identifying Kärkkäinen as "Pentecostal" might be viewed as slightly contentious by some, owing to his re-designation of himself as "Lutheran"—in slight difference to his Classical Pentecostal heritage. Some of the Lutheran-colored influence of Pannenberg certainly comes out in his recent work and approach, and Kärkkäinen has been working with Lutherans in a recent pastoral setting (giving some understanding as to why he might re-designate himself such). But given that Classical Pentecostalism is his

---

72. So reflected in this chapter by a shorter exposition.

73. Despite having authored this work in the year 2015, Kärkkäinen's view still stands as the latest Pentecostal exposition to date on the topic. Whilst Wolfgang Vondey has considered the doctrine of "humanity" more recently in a chapter of his (2017) *Pentecostal Theology* (chapter 8), the focus of that helpful chapter is predominantly on the image of God, with only light consideration given to the topic of constitution. Given the specific focus of that chapter (and that when touching on the topic of constitution, it often follows in the footsteps of Yong [albeit from a distance]), it is not considered in this book as a *further point* along on the Pentecostal trajectory/an advancing beyond Yong and Kärkkäinen's work on the topic of constitution. (Other recent works to have considered Pentecostal anthropology have brought interesting contributions to wider areas of anthropology [such as political anthropology]; for instance, Stone's "Holy Spirit, Holy Bodies," [of 2021] has brought thought-provoking insights on the politics of embodiment [cf. Stephenson, *Dismantling the Dualisms*], and D. Augustine's variety of recent works, such as *The Spirit and the Common Good* [of 2019], followed by *The Politics of the Spirit* [2023], have also brought creative contributions to the wider field of Pentecostal anthropology. But having differing foci to the doctrine of constitution, they do not advance this doctrine of focus beyond the [2015] work of Kärkkäinen.)

home tradition,[74] his devotional experience of the Spirit,[75] the articles that he has authored for Pentecostal scholarly journals,[76] and his editing and contributing to Pentecostal scholarly compendiums,[77] to continue to identify Kärkkäinen as Pentecostal (in the sense defined in this book) appears a legitimate designation.[78]

Kärkkäinen's constructive anthropology is laid out most fully in a chapter entitled "Multidimensional Monism" in his volume *Creation and Humanity* (which serves as volume 3 of his wider project *A Constructive Christian Theology for the Church in the Pluralistic World*). Before turning to this chapter, again his overall theological method and its approach to anthropology will be summarized, which will help illumine why he makes the anthropological claims he does and why he is attracted to the view of constitution he is.

Kärkkäinen's Theological Method

Kärkkäinen's systematic/constructive theology espouses a high view of Scripture, but he does not simply systematize all the biblical texts he can find on a topic to produce a doctrine of 'X'.[79] Rather, Kärkkäinen's approach is nuanced, recognizing the contextual nature of theology, and indeed he highlights his own context as that of the "post" world. He expounds this "post" world context as one that is post-modern,

---

74. He describes his home tradition as Scandinavian Pentecostalism (Kärkkäinen, "Surveying the Land," 10) and as such was formerly a Pentecostal missionary (Kärkkäinen "Toward a Pneumatological Theology," 187).

75. In his "Review of Veli-Matti Kärkkäinen's Pneumatology," (3–8) Pinnock comments "I would say this man is personally a charismatic. Who else would know about and cite our beloved Gordon Fee and Roger Stronstad among many others, and who else would so evidently understand existentially what it means to be filled with the power of God? I would say that he understands these texts from the inside. Perhaps he will tell us in his response." (5). In response, Kärkkäinen replies affirmatively (having identified his home tradition) commenting "Professor Pinnock was right in reading between the lines: I have personal experience of the Spirit" (Kärkkäinen, "Surveying the Land," 10.)

76. Kärkkäinen, "Holy Spirit and Justification," 26–39; Kärkkäinen, "Trinity as Communion in the Spirit," 209–30.

77. See Kärkkäinen et al., *Pentecostal Mission*; Kärkkäinen et al., *Loosing the Spirits*; Kärkkäinen, *Spirit in the World*.

78. Pairing the noun "Lutheran" with the adjective "Pentecostal" would be seemingly accurate, designating Kärkkäinen as a "Pentecostal Lutheran."

79. In distinction from a number of the thinkers considered in the previous chapter.

post-foundational, post-structuralist, post-colonial, post-metaphysical, post-propositional, post-liberal, post-conservative, post-secular, and post-Christian.[80] Though clearly not committing himself to all these philosophical ideologies, he recognizes that, as a theologian working within this academic context, much of his theologizing is affected by this atmosphere, and some of these "post" philosophical ideologies are borne out in in his constructive/systematic theology.[81] He also recognizes that his theology is very much influenced by the Lutheran thinker Wolfhart Pannenberg, an influence which he embraces and gladly wants to affirm.

As a clear admirer of Pannenberg, Kärkkäinen adopts his coherentist theory of truth, viewing truth as like a web that is perpetually developing and continuously being built. Given that truth is historically contingent and so constantly evolving, Pannenberg's theology is oriented to the eschaton when the full web (or network) of knowledge will be realized.[82] In the mind of Kärkkäinen, therefore, constructive theology is one of many different disciplines contributing to the web, so he is keen to draw, not just on all the theological disciplines to inform his constructive theology (such as biblical studies, church history, philosophical theology, missiology, ethics etc.) but on disciplines beyond theology too; he seeks to make use of the natural sciences, sociology, cultural studies—and even other religious faiths—to ensure that his contribution to that web of truth is informed by these disciplines, which are likewise contributing to the web in complimentary senses.

Related to his preference for a coherentist theory of truth, Kärkkäinen takes a post-foundationalist attitude to epistemology, seeing knowledge both as tradition-rooted and as that which is understood from a particular historical, cultural, and ideological context. Whilst considering it genuinely possible to contribute to the (developing) web of truth, he argues that *knowledge* (of the truth) is colored by the location in which it has arisen—meaning that such knowledge is fallible. He thinks, therefore, that knowledge needs to be regarded with humility and with an appreciation for what can be learned from others *outside* of the tradition—beyond the context from which that knowledge has arisen. So, he aims, in his work, for his constructive/systematic theology to be:

80. Kärkkäinen, *Creation and Humanity*, 1.

81. Such will become apparent in the exposition of his anthropology to follow.

82. Systematic Theology, for Pannenberg, being the "Science of God" (cf. Pannenberg, *Toward a Theology*; and Pannenberg, *Systematic Theology*.)

> An integrative discipline that continuously searches for a coherent balanced understanding of Christian truth and faith in light of Christian tradition (biblical and historical), and, in the context of historical and contemporary thought, cultures, and living faiths . . . aims at a coherent, inclusive, dialogical, and hospitable vision.[83]

Application of Kärkkäinen's Method to His Theological Anthropology

The philosophical and theological influences in Kärkkäinen's approach are already prominently obvious but are further revealed when considering specifically his theological anthropology.

In a section of his work entitled "The Constitution of the Self and the Image of God," Kärkkäinen initially considers the "loss of [the human] self" through history up to the postmodern age. In light of his exposition, and seeking to bisect what he sees as the short-fallings of the modern and postmodern accounts of the self, he then proceeds to articulate his goal in theological anthropology; he wants to provide:

> A robustly God-referential holistic and communion-driven account [of the human self] based on Trinitarian resources . . . [in which] rationality, physicality, emotions, and sociality all play key roles particularly when the deepest biblical intuitions are rediscovered and put in conversation with current neurological, behavioral and other scientific fields of study, all done with a willingness to learn from theologies of the Global South and female theologians and other liberationists.[84]

As well as the obvious "post-colonial" influence (of Kärkkäinen's "post" world academic context), such a paragraph also indicates something of the "post-metaphysical" influence in his constructive theological anthropological endeavor—an influence helpful to remember when considering his constitutional anthropology.[85]

---

83. Kärkkäinen, *Creation and Humanity*, 1.
84. Kärkkäinen, *Creation and Humanity*, 274.
85. Like the other "posts," it appears that Kärkkäinen is not "anti" metaphysics, rather, he is not wanting to be *constrained* by traditional models of metaphysics.

Kärkkäinen's Rejection of Dualism

In his chapter entitled "Multidimensional Monism: The Nature of Human Nature,"[86] Kärkkäinen reveals a distrust of traditional "substance metaphysics;" it is therefore unsurprising that (substance) dualism does not appeal. For him, any view of an ontologically distinct or separable soul—distinct and separable from the human body—falls foul of his anthropological goal (as articulated in the citation above). In a quote displaying his view of the historical growth (and demise) of dualism through the ages, he discloses his attitude towards dualism:

> While the [modern-day] shift toward a unified, monist, and holistic view is usually attributed to changes in philosophy and particularly (neuro)sciences, Pannenberg reminds us that the shift is "in line with the intentions of the earliest Christian anthropology." [*ST* 2:182] Too often the investigation into the history of the body-soul relationship ignores the fact that, unlike Platonism (which by the end of the second century had become the dominant philosophy), important early patristic thinkers defended the psychosomatic unity even when they continued distinguishing between body and soul (spirit). However, that attempt to hold on to the idea of body-soul unity soon gave way to dualism for the simple reason that, in keeping with the times, *even those theologians who championed the psychosomatic unity did not thereby reject the idea of soul as an independent entity.*[87]

Kärkkäinen's Theological Reasons for Rejecting Anthropological Dualism

Kärkkäinen gives five theological reasons for rejecting dualistic understandings of human beings. First, he regards substance dualist anthropologies as those which locate human uniqueness specifically in the (self-conscious) soul. In a manner similar to Yong, Kärkkäinen finds this problematic because it downplays the place of the body in human

---

86. Although as a theologian, Kärkkäinen clearly has to have some place for metaphysics in his work, his distaste for traditional substance ontologies and metaphysics is strongly implied in polemical comments such as "... dynamic relationality has replaced the hegemony of a static substance ontology" (290) and "It seems to me the Thomistic view . . . has by and large funded substance ontology" (338).

87. Kärkkäinen, *Creation and Humanity*, 309 (emphasis mine). Note, Kärkkäinen (like Yong) is also content to use the terms "soul" and "spirit" synonymously (as indeed he is the term "mind").

identity. On a related theme to this issue, his second theological reason for rejecting substance dualist views is the emphasis such views puts on the "rational" human being. Whilst not elaborating the point in detail, it seems that he is concerned that such an emphasis might lead to unhelpful societal divisions, with those regarded as "intellectual" being seen as a "superior" class of people and those regarded as less intellectual being viewed as "inferior" human beings.[88] Third, he thinks that dualistic views of a human often revise the actual emphasis of Gen 2:7 through unhelpful eisegesis. Rather than identifying *from* the verse that it is the *rūach* of *God* which does the animating and makes human beings distinct, he thinks dualistic anthropology unhelpfully reads *into* the verse the notion that it is the (human) *soul* which serves these functions instead.[89] His fourth reason for rejecting dualism is very closely related to his first, in that he thinks it downplays the body, emotions, and passions;[90] and his fifth reason is that he thinks dualism runs contrary to contemporary neuroscientific findings.[91]

The issue of contemporary neuroscience, the fifth of Kärkkäinen's objections, is one which he expounds in detail—the objection appearing to carry substantial weight for his rejection of dualism. Highlighting the neurological findings—that reveal the firings of the brain's specific neurons in any given instance of human consciousness and/or behavior—he argues that the functions traditionally associated with the soul are also, themselves, displayed by the neuroscientific data as having neural correlates in the brain. As such, he contends that the activities of the "soul" (or what people *thought* were activities of the soul) have now been shown to be linked with what occurs in the physical brain, so the Classic substance dualist model has been shown to be in error. Being important to his case against varieties of dualism, and indeed with the issue's being essential to Yong's rejection of anthropological dualism, the two (now commonplace) stories that Kärkkäinen employs to illustrate the objection will be recounted below, in Kärkkäinen's particular wording.

> ... in the nineteenth century it took dramatic events such as the oft-referred-to Phineas Gage instance to wake up society to the tight link between the brain and human behavior. In

---

88. Kärkkäinen, *Creation and Humanity*, 315.
89. Kärkkäinen, *Creation and Humanity*, 315.
90. Kärkkäinen, *Creation and Humanity*, 316.
91. Kärkkäinen, *Creation and Humanity*, 316–20.

1948 an explosion caused a tamping iron to pierce the skull, exiting from the top of the head, of this twenty-five-year-old New England railroad worker. This led to a serious change in his personality, making this once stable person emotionally and socially bankrupt—yet without any visible effects at all! The obvious lesson from this poor rail worker's incident is simply that brains and neurons have much to do with emotions, sociality, and thoughts![92]

A recent counterpart to Gage is the widely reported instance of the schoolteacher in the U.S. state of Virginia in 2000. He was caught collecting and using child pornography, facilitating prostitution, and molesting a child. Having had his brain examined before criminal sentencing, he was diagnosed with a tumor in the right orbitofrontal lobe, routinely associated with moral-knowledge acquisition and social integration. Upon removal of the tumor, the teacher's behavior returned to normal—but amazingly, after a couple of years, the immoral traits returned, and the reason was the return of the tumor.[93]

Pressing the point even further, Kärkkäinen reveals:

More recently rapid developments in experimental psychology, comparative neuropsychology, and brain-imaging techniques have yielded an amazing array of results, insights, and information about the deep and wide connections between the brain and human behavior at all levels . . . there is no denying the tight link between the functioning of the brain and human behavior. . . . [C]ertain regions or systems have been shown to be linked with particular mental and physical activities, such as memory functions, or error detection and compensation, . . . [but] [n]ot only behavioral, cognitive, and emotional functioning . . . [and moral decision-making in addition, but also] spiritual and religious activities [such as] charismatic Christians' glossolalia (speaking in tongues), or Tibetan Buddhist meditation, or Franciscan nuns' silent prayer, or Carmelite nuns' mystical experiences with God [have been empirically demonstrated as having particular correlations with activity that occurs in the brain].[94]

---

92. Kärkkäinen, *Creation and Humanity*, 317.

93. Kärkkäinen, *Creation and Humanity*, 318–19.

94. Kärkkäinen, *Creation and Humanity*, 318–19. (Content in the rounded brackets Kärkkäinen's, content in the square brackets, mine.)

In light of such neuroscientific data, and the mind's evident dependence on the brain for any given human behavior, Kärkkäinen (and Yong in particular [and in fact the majority of anthropological monists]) reject dualism per se as being falsified by empirical findings.

Philosophical Reasons for Rejecting Dualism

As has been seen in the section above (and similar to Yong's categorization), Kärkkäinen categorizes the issue of neuroscience as a "theological" objection against dualism. Such categorization is somewhat curious and will receive additional comment later (for now being gently adjusted to its more accurate classification as a *philosophical* objection to dualism); but in further similarity to Yong, Kärkkäinen additionally raises the objection of the problem of interaction—between an immaterial soul and material body—as another reason for rejecting anthropological dualism. He states:

> Cartesian dualism (or any other form of dualism, for that matter) is not saved from the problem of mental causation; its challenge is just different from other theories. Ironically, the mind's capacity to work on matter/the physical had become a major problem with the rise of modern science as hylomorphism was left behind (in which "mind/soul was but one instance of form" and thus could be thought of as having causal effects).[95]

Whilst handling the issue in historical perspective (and so phrasing the issue in the past tense) Kärkkäinen very much retains this as a problem for Cartesian dualism(s) (if not for hylomorphic/Thomistic dualisms as well[96]). How an immaterial substance could interact with a material substance is a problem that is posed to the dualist, and one he perceives as unanswered by dualistic thinkers. As such this gives him additional reason for rejecting the dualist position(s), leading him to seek for an alternative model instead of these dualisms considered.

---

95. Kärkkäinen, *Creation and Humanity*, 313–14. (Kärkkäinen's use of inverted commas are his citing the wording of Murphy [from Murphy, "Human Nature," 7].)

96. See chapter 5 for a brief articulation of the hylomorphic/Thomistic dualisms.

Kärkkäinen's Own Anthropological Proposal

Having rejected anthropological dualism, Kärkkäinen looks to contemporary philosophers of mind for an alternative conception of human nature. His own constitutional anthropology uses the nonreductive physicalist models of Murphy and Brown (cited above) as inspiration and buildings blocks which help him construct his own model—one he entitles "multidimensional monism." He initially draws upon Murphy's model, appreciating its emphasis on the physical, considering her nonreductive physicalism as providing a satisfactory account of the neuroscientific findings. But he is critical of certain aspects of her model concerning the relationship of the mind to the brain. For example, he thinks that the "intentionality" of certain mental states (that is, their "aboutness"/"object-directedness"[97]) is a difficulty for her position, as is the property of "qualia" (that is, the property of "what it is like" [for the subject to be experiencing, for instance, a sensation][98]). He further thinks it problematic for Murphy to build a metaphysical position from a scientific basis.[99] So whilst respecting the science and physicality of the view, he moves from nonreductive physicalism towards his preferred "multidimensional monist" view—a model very much in line with the "emergent holism" of Ted Peters, but Kärkkäinen is also content with the description "emergent monism" (as espoused by Clayton and Yong) as an alternative accurate label for his "multidimensional monist" standpoint.[100]

Emergent monism is attractive to Kärkkäinen because of its emphasis on physicality/materiality but (appreciating the reality of consciousness as that which is so other to the physical realm) it also allows him to affirm that the mind *has* to be something metaphysically different to the brain.[101] Further, the emergent monism of *Clayton* appeals to Kärkkäinen

---

97. For example, a person might think *about* the world, or might think *of* a friend; in contrast to the physical brain state which is not *about* or *of* anything (the brain state simply *is*), certain mental states such as thoughts have intentionality—they are object-directed/have the property of "aboutness."

98. In such an instance, a neuroscientist would be able to discover what is occurring in the person's brain when that person is experiencing the sensation (for example) of (seeing) green (or more specifically, being-appeared-to-greenly); but that scientist could never have the *first-person* knowledge of *what it is like* for that person to be experiencing that sensation of green—certain mental states (in distinction from brain states) having this distinctive property of qualia.

99. Cf. Kärkkäinen, *Creation and Humanity*, 326–31.

100. Kärkkäinen, *Creation and Humanity*, 341.

101. On the model, the mind emerged at some point in human history, and as a

in its providing different ontological levels, so facilitating the different levels of comprehension of the world that are brought about by the many disciplines of the academy. As regards this latter point of attraction, rather than thinking in nonreductive physicalist terms that physics is the only means of giving a natural explanation of the world (with God being drawn upon to give the spiritual explanation), Kärkkäinen is attracted to this emergent monist model in that it allows the genuine employment of other scientific explanations—such as those of biology, chemistry, psychology etc.—to fill out humans' understanding of the universe without the physicalist temptation to simply reduce it all to physics. Recognizing the value of all these disciplines, Kärkkäinen is influenced by Clayton's model, and when added to his integrative approach to theology as well as his desire to honor the neuroscience, this combination of factors makes such a position even more appealing to him. As such, through his ventures into the philosophy of mind and engagement with his dialogue partners in that domain, Kärkkäinen feels he has obtained a strong view of human nature, being particularly drawn to Clayton's model of emergent monism.

As regards the theologizing of his preferred (emergent monist) model, Kärkkäinen draws upon the biblical studies of Joel Green and N. T. Wright for exegetical insight and support in the advancing of his *theological* multidimensional monism. He is attracted to Wright's (Dunn-colored) understanding of Paul's anthropology—one which gleans from Paul's New Testament letters an anthropology that presents the human as a "differentiated unity."[102] Wright argues that Paul's anthropological terms (e.g., "mind," "heart," "body," "soul," and "spirit") emphasize the whole of the human being but from different (and complimenting) angles (e.g., "mind" refers to the entire human as a thinking, comprehending being, "body" refers to that whole human person as a physical being etc.). In this Dunn-tinted understanding, these anthropological terms denote the human's many different dimensions but all referring to that same entire person.[103] When applied to Kärkkäinen's preferred model from

---

mental property, supervenes on the brain. However, the relationship between brain and mental states is not *identity* type, but *token* type, namely different mental states can arise from the same brain states due to different social, environmental, and historical contexts. This he calls "multiple realizability" (322–24).

102. Wright, "Mind, Spirit, Soul and Body," 11–12.

103. Wright, "Mind, Spirit, Soul and Body," 13–15; Cf. Dunn, *Theology of Paul*, 54–78. For further analysis see Churchouse, "Healthier Anthropology," 113–15.

the philosophy of mind (that of emergent monism), this brings forth a theological color to contribute to his overall theological anthropology—namely his "multidimensional monism."

As regards the terminology of the "soul," because the term has such an established history—in both the Christian and non-Christian traditions—Kärkkäinen thinks that the word should be retained (despite his dislike of its *acquired* meaning) because of its wide usage in Scripture and the benefit it has for interfaith consideration.[104] However, he thinks theologians should *redefine* the word and that it should be used to refer to the *whole of the human person* (as per the thinking of Dunn/Wright)—moving away from traditional understandings which view the soul as the "immortal" part of a human.[105] Once having redefined the soul in this manner, he thinks theologians should then employ this more accurate understanding and indeed re-educate the laity as to the term's (now) more biblical and accurate meaning.[106] Kärkkäinen is also drawn by the idea of using the word "spirit" instead of "soul" to emphasize humans' "more-than-physical" nature. Attracted by the idea of Karl Rahner, he suggests referring to human beings *as "spirit"* to underline their "more-than-physical" nature—a human's being deeply embodied (by nature) but also "one who reaches out to the transcendent, even to God."[107]

As such, Kärkkäinen brings certain thought-provoking theological ideas and seeks to build them (similarly to Yong) upon the emergent monist model of Clayton. Given that he does not theologize the favored emergent monist position to the same extent as Yong, the overview of Kärkkäinen's position above is not as extensive as the preceding exposition of Yong's view. However, having explicated the anthropology of both thinkers, one can see that much of what Kärkkäinen proposes is very similar to that of Yong, making further exposition unnecessary given that the essential ideas have already been expounded.

---

104. Kärkkäinen, *Creation and Humanity*, 346. (Though wanting to make clear [following Green and Wright] that the term has a very different meaning to the one it has gained through history.)

105. Kärkkäinen, *Creation and Humanity*, 345–46.

106. Kärkkäinen, *Creation and Humanity*, 346.

107. Kärkkäinen, *Creation and Humanity*, 347, drawn from Rahner, *Theological Investigations*, 21:42.

Summary of Yong and Kärkkäinen's Anthropology and the Current Place of the Trajectory

The above has surveyed Yong's and Kärkkäinen's anthropology with specific focus on their understanding of human constitution. It has highlighted that their own positions arise in reaction to dualism(s) which they see as facing insurmountable theological and philosophical challenges; in response, they both propose models of human constitution that they view as stronger and preferable in light of the relevant theological and philosophical issues. Both thinkers are comfortable with terming their models as "emergent monist" (even if Kärkkäinen finally opts for the title "multidimensional monism").

Having traced the trajectory of Pentecostal thought, in chapter 1, from trichotomy to the more physical "dualism" espoused by the Shriers, the exposition given above makes clear that Yong and Kärkkäinen have subsequently gone the next step to advocating a full monistic position. Being the latest-to-date contributions to the Pentecostal scholarly discussion, this is where academic Pentecostal writing currently stands on the topic of human constitution; as such, it is influencing the scholarly Pentecostal community. However, it would be pertinent to ask, at this point, whether Yong and Kärkkäinen's reasons for rejecting dualism are as strong as they contend; and indeed, is their preferred emergent monist model genuinely a better model? Before allowing the trajectory to continue in the monistic direction these thinkers are advocating, careful analysis and critique of these contentions are in order; so, such will form the focus of the following chapter, which will address these two key contentions.

3

A Critique of Yong and Kärkkäinen's Doctrine of Human Constitution

IN THE PREVIOUS CHAPTER, two key anthropological contentions of scholars Yong and Kärkkäinen were laid out concerning the doctrine of human constitution; first, that anthropological dualism is to be rejected—for a variety of theological and philosophical reasons—and second, that emergent monism is preferable as an alternative constitutional model. In this chapter, both these contentions will receive critical focus, as will important related matters concerning their anthropology surveyed in the previous chapter.

The chapter will initially begin by considering the relationship between thinkers Yong and Kärkkäinen, followed by reflection, from their work, on what can be gleaned concerning the "field" of theological anthropological inquiry and how that impacts what is to follow in the constructive parts of this book. Following these initial considerations, their two key contentions will be addressed; their first will be considered through assessing their theological and philosophical reasons for rejecting dualism (and indeed those of the dialogue partners upon which they rely). Then, their second contention will be considered, assessing the concordance of their (preferred) emergent monist model with the Pentecostal theological emphases, and then reviewing the philosophical rigor of this preferred anthropological model. Having given scrutiny to both these contentions, the chapter will close at a point of having gained substantial conceptual insight as to the strength of both contentions, and to the validity of both contentions for the present discussion of Pentecostal anthropology.

The Relationship of Yong's Work to That of Kärkkäinen

From the survey carried out of their views, in the work of the preceding chapter, the similarity of the positions held by Yong and Kärkkäinen became evident concerning their theological anthropology. This similarity is not surprising given their friendship and collegiality at Fuller Seminary. Indeed, they both draw upon the same dialogue partners, being attracted to them for the same reasons. Influential as these dialogue partners are—two of whom are also based at Fuller—it is plausible that Yong and Kärkkäinen came to their positions independently through discussion with these dialogue-partners. Given the dates of their anthropological writings, and indeed their friendship and collegiality, another plausible explanation is that Yong, himself, was of direct influence in the thinking of Kärkkäinen.[1] Whichever of these is more accurate, the very close similarity of their views makes it straight forward to assess their work because almost all of the major components of their constitutional thinking are the same and so the views of both thinkers can be considered together when considering the aforementioned two key contentions.

Given the very close likeness of the views of Yong and Kärkkäinen, that Kärkkäinen is (likewise) content with the label "emergent monism" for his anthropological model,[2] and that the underlying emergent monism of both scholars is fundamentally the *same* model (drawn from scholars Murphy and particularly Clayton), Yong and Kärkkäinen's

---

1. This suggestion is made all the more plausible when it is recognized that Yong's influence is definitely evident in Kärkkäinen's work in other areas—such as in his thinking on the theology of religions (cf. Kärkkäinen "Pentecostal Pneumatology of Religions," 173–75). Kärkkäinen's affirmative overview of Yong's work in this area and his ending a chapter in the compendium above by encouraging "Pentecostals of all stripes, along with their mainline counterparts, [to] join hands and minds in *Discerning the Spirit(s)*" (180)—the latter being the title of Yong's book *Discerning the Spirit(s)*—suggests Yong's (appreciated) influence in the theology of Kärkkäinen. The fact that they have both written warmly of one another and each other's work (cf. Yong's "Whither Evangelical Theology," 60–85), as well as being friends and colleagues at Fuller would further the contention that Yong has been of influence in Kärkkäinen's theological *anthropological* thinking.

2. Along with his "Multidimensional Monism" label.

constitutional model will be referred to in the singular through the course of this chapter when carrying out the analysis of their anthropological work.³ Once having considered their individual methods (in the immediate section below) the chapter (and then rest of the book) will speak of their model/view in the singular (instead of speaking of their models/views in the plural).⁴

Yong's and Kärkkäinen's Methods, and the Field of Inquiry for Investigating Human Constitution

Much could be said concerning the methods employed by scholars Yong and Kärkkäinen. However, (brief) comment will be limited to assessment of their approach when considering the doctrine of constitution specifically. The theological methods of both thinkers reveal the importance of philosophical engagement for the constructing of systematic theology, with their doctrine of constitution displaying the significance of the philosophy of *mind* for the construction of this doctrine of theological anthropology. As was seen in the previous chapter, both scholars were dependent on dialogue-partners drawn from the discipline of the philosophy of mind to give them a philosophical basis for their doctrine of constitution. As such, the degree of philosophy entailed reveals the doctrine's relevant field as being *philosophical* theology (not just *systematic* theology)—recognizing the philosophical engagement required for the apposite handling of the doctrine. So, when proceeding to parts III and IV—the *constructive* work on the topic—this book will likewise take heed of this insight, and approach the constructive project informed by the insights of philosophy, engaging particularly with specialists in the philosophy of mind. The choosing of these specialist thinkers—to serve as dialogue-partners for the constructive project—will be carried out carefully and fittingly, in light of the critique given in this chapter concerning the anthropology of Yong and Kärkkäinen.

---

3. So, (as just modelled) the chapter will speak about "Yong and Kärkkäinen's work," and likewise use the singular to refer to their emergent monism.

4. And on the (very) limited handful of occasions where any *theological* differentiation occurs (there being little to no philosophical differentiation), such differences will be drawn out in the course of the exposition.

Response to the Critiques of Dualism

Engaging with the Theological Critiques

It was seen in the previous chapter that Yong's theological reasons for rejecting dualism were based on his work on the *imago Dei*. Addressing the verses of Genesis on the topic, in their context of Genesis 1 and 2—and indeed in their wider context of the Hebraic Old Testament Scriptures— he dismissed dualistic anthropology as giving insufficient emphasis to the themes of (w)holism, embodiment, materiality, and relationality, that he finds in these narratives of creation. Kärkkäinen's reason for rejecting dualism was due to its locating biological life and human rationality in the entity of the soul. He thinks the consequence of this understanding is that it downplays the physical body (with its desires, passions, and emotions) raising the possibility of such dualism then leading additionally towards types of societal hierarchical dualism, with oppressions (such as sexism and racism) the possible result of these forms of dualism.[5] These theological reasons for rejecting dualism are distinctive to Yong and Kärkkäinen respectively, however, both of them are united in rejecting anthropological dualism due to the findings of the "neuroscience" and the "theological" problem dualism faces when confronted by this "neuroscientific data."

As has already been noted, to "theologically" reject anthropological dualism because of "the findings of contemporary neuroscience" is actually an error of category; (rather than being an issue of theology [or science], it is actually a *philosophical* issue [so will be considered as such in what follows in that relevant section below]) but the presence of this error of category, in the writings of both Yong and Kärkkäinen, suggests that an outside theological influence has colored the anthropological thinking of both scholars. Indeed, through closely examining both scholars' works, it seems that they have been influenced away from anthropological dualism by biblical scholar Joel Green—whose exegetical and theological thinking (as well as his philosophical assumptions) appear to be what

---

5. In his work, Kärkkäinen acknowledges that (psychosomatic) dualism was the view held by the early church fathers ("Creation and Humanity," 293 cf. 309), and that dualism both has been, and is, the default view of a human—held by people from all over the world, both now and throughout history (citing many works in support of this fact [307–8]). He also recognizes that anthropological dualism has been the traditional and received Christian position through church history up until the present (308), leaving the reader a little surprised at his definitive rejection of dualism—but displaying how convinced he is of his reasons *against* anthropological dualism.

underlies their "theological" objections and their desire to thoroughly reject (all forms of) anthropological dualism.

The Influence of Joel Green

Yong favorably references Green as giving further exegetical support to Yong's own "wholistic," embodied, and monistic anthropology.[6] And indeed, Kärkkäinen similarly shows respect for and exegetical dependence upon Green's exegesis for his monistic proposal[7]—his latter pages being populated with affirmative reference to Green.[8] Because of Green's evident influence upon the thought of both Yong and Kärkkäinen, Green's general (exegetical) theological anthropology will be briefly expounded below, to be followed by a critique of that work. Due to the very close similarity of thought—of Green's work with Yong and Kärkkäinen's—this critique of Green will therefore entail critique of Yong and Kärkkäinen's ideas, which will provide much of the basis for a response to their theological objections against dualism.

As a precursor to the account that is to follow, Green advises that, when speaking of humanity's nature, the biblical passages often handle the question implicitly; they sometimes *assume* a view of a person, other times *counter* alternate views, and at other times *imply* a particular view whilst discussing *renewed* humanity's nature.[9] Given this state of affairs, he warns that exegetes need to proceed with care but identifies a collection of passages that give clues as to Scripture's anthropological view.

GREEN'S ANTHROPOLOGY OF THE OLD TESTAMENT

Green cites four Old Testament [O.T.] texts which indicate something of Scripture's anthropology: Psalm 8, Psalm 144, Job 7:17–18—which all have their basis in Genesis 1:26–27. He argues that all four of these passages afford the following anthropological insights:

6. Yong, "Christian and Buddhist," 147. Cf. chapter 2 of this book.

7. Kärkkäinen also draws upon N. T. Wright's anthropology, specifically his conference paper "Mind, Spirit, Soul and Body: All for One and One for All, Reflections on Paul's Anthropology in his Complex Contexts." Whilst that paper is not considered here, see Churchouse, "Healthier Anthropology" for scrutiny of the anthropology espoused by Wright in that paper.

8. Cf. Kärkkäinen, *Creation and Humanity*, 333–36.

9. Green, *Body, Soul and Human Life*, 46.

1. that a human is to be defined relationally—not in structural/essentialist terms,

2. a human has continuity with, but a higher vocation than animals,

   (because)

3. the person bears the image of God,

   (and)

4. (the person) is viewed within these passages as a bio-psychospiritual unity.[10]

As is evident from outlining these points, Genesis 1:26–27 is the O.T. basis for Green's theological anthropology, so he gives focussed attention to these two foundational verses (in recognizing that the other three passages are related and flow from this key anthropological source).

Much of Green's anthropology and understanding concerning Genesis 1:26–27 appears to be written in reaction to essentialist views of a person—in particular, the Platonist and Classic Cartesian views. In the place of these understandings, he wants to emphasize the *relational* aspect of humans that he finds in these verses of Genesis. A lot of this relational accent appears to have been influenced by Karl Barth's work on the passage, who emphasizes the *covenantal* nature of these verses in their context of Genesis 1. For Barth, and therefore for Green, the emphasis of these covenantal verses is humans being made as relational beings—made for relationship with God (their creator), for relationship with one another, and for relationship with wider creation (the covenantal setting of these particular verses). By contrast to the traditional reading(s)—of Gen 1:26–27—Green thinks it is mistaken to derive from this passage an essentialist view of a person (i.e., one that defines a person essentially as possessing certain indispensable faculties [e.g., faculties of mind and free will]). Instead, he elevates the relational view—seeing a person as a "being-in-relation"[11]—as a view which flows more persuasively from *ex-egesis* of the biblical text. In a concise summary of the *imago Dei*, he states:

> What is this [the *imago Dei*] quality that distinguishes humanity? God's words affirm the creation of the human family in its

---

10. Green, "What Are Human Beings?"

11. The relational view of a person—the "being-in-relation" view—argues that humans are interrelated, interconnected beings who find their true personhood in relation with others.

relation to himself, as his counterpart, so that the nature of humanity derives from the human family relatedness to God. The concept of the *imago Dei*, then, is fundamentally relational, or covenantal, and takes as its ground and focus the graciousness of God's own covenantal relations with humanity and the rest of creation.[12]

With regard to Gen 2:7 (and its relation to 1:26–27), Green wants to emphasize that the "nephesh" of this particular verse—the "nephesh" that God breathed into the "man"/*hā ādām*—is not some unique immaterial soul;[13] he views such a reading as *eisegesis*, associating this view with (the Greek-colored reading of) Philo, and claims that such eisegetical readings have aided the growth and propagation of essentialist views—views that have been subsequently bequeathed to and, indeed, through the church, being prominent throughout the two millennia of church history. Rather, he argues, this *nephesh* (of Gen 2:7) is the same *nephesh* of Gen 1:30—the *life-giving* breath of God which he breathed into *all* of his creatures—a gift of life and endowment bestowed on *all* the creatures of Genesis 1.[14] Indeed, in a manner that stresses the *interconnection* of humanity with creation as a whole, Green comments:

> Genesis 1–2 does not locate the singularity of humanity in the human possession of a "soul," but rather in the human capacity to relate to Yahweh as covenant partner, and to join in companionship within the human family and in relation to the whole cosmos in ways that reflect the covenant love of God.[15]

Having expounded the Genesis verses, with their emphasis on bountiful life that flows from covenantal relation with God, Green then advances, by contrast, the O.T.'s teaching on death—portraying it as the very opposite, as the end of relational life. He argues that the O.T. shows very little interest in the location of humans who have died;[16] he wants to emphasize, instead, that the O.T. portrays death in very stark and absolute terms—that even relationship with God is lost at the end of physical

---

12. Green, *Body, Soul, and Human Life*, 63.

13. The idea that God breathed into the first human an immaterial soul—taken as the teaching of Gen 2:7—is commonly recognized as an *eisegetical* reading of the text—associated with (the Jewish Hellenistic philosopher) Philo.

14. Green, *Body, Soul, and Human Life*, 64.

15. Green, *Body, Soul, and Human Life*, 64.

16. Green, *Body, Soul, and Human Life*, 146.

A Critique of Yong and Kärkkäinen's Doctrine

life.[17] Indeed, as a means of affirming his point that the O.T. defines a human person in relational not essentialist terms, he defines death very starkly as "the cessation of life in all of its aspects, and especially the severance of all relationships—relationships with God and with every person and with everything in the cosmos."[18]

Green's Anthropology of the New Testament

In regard to New Testament [N.T.] anthropology, it becomes evident from Green's exegesis that he has regularly had to refute a commonly held misconception. The oft-heard misconception (held widely in popular thinking) is that the O.T. is monistic in its anthropology, due to its Hebraic horizon and worldview, but the N.T., by contrast, is dualistic, due to the N.T. writers being influenced by Hellenistic thought of the time.[19] Green redresses this misconception, initially, by highlighting its incorrect underlying assumption, namely, that most Hellenistic philosophy, at the time of the N.T. writings, was classically Platonist in form. He then corrects this assumption by highlighting that the N.T. documents were written in the context of the first century Roman world—a world in which most Greek philosophical thought was *monistic* in its view of a human being. He then further corrects the misconception by showing that the primary influence on the N.T. writers was the *Hebraic O.T. writings*, not Hellenistic thought as supposed. So, disposing of the misconception, he comments that, at the time of the N.T. writings, "In short, support for body-soul Dualism is minimal."[20] However, by contrast to the misconception, he then wants to argue that, like the O.T.'s teaching, the N.T. is actually *monistic* in its view of a human being.[21]

Drawing from his area of prominent expertise, Green highlights this holistic understanding of humanity and salvation from the pages of the gospel of Luke, giving particular focus to the transformation of those who encountered Jesus. A dramatic example of such an encounter, highlighted in Green's anthropology, is the story of the Gerasene demoniac (Luke 8:26–39) who, before encountering Jesus, was: naked, demonized,

17. Green, *Body, Soul, and Human Life*, 147.
18. Green, *Body, Soul, and Human Life*, 147.
19. Green, *Body, Soul, and Human Life*, 51–52.
20. Green, "Response," 194. See also the extended discussion in Green, *Body, Soul, and Human Life*, 51–53.
21. E.g., Green, *Body, Soul, and Human Life*, 54–180.

homeless, he was uncontrollable and engaged in self-harm, he was religiously unclean, lacking in human identity, and (both literally and spiritually) was living among the dead. As a result of his encounter with Jesus, the man left: liberated from demon oppression, fully clothed and now in control, sent back to his home and community, restored to mental health, and portrayed as a disciple with a vocation to tell others what God had done for him.[22] Green argues that the holistic nature of humanity—and hence salvation—is evident throughout the gospel of Luke (and also the other gospels too); for him, a N.T. anthropology should take account of this view of humanity, recognizing human beings in their entirety as fully-orbed holistic beings.

Critique of Green's Anthropology

Having surveyed Green's anthropology, the similarity of ideas should be evident between his thoughts on the topic and those of Yong and Kärkkäinen. Again, given the dates that they authored their works, and their collegiality at Fuller seminary, it is very plausible that the anthropology of Yong and Kärkkäinen—and specifically, their objections against dualism—derive from their colleague Joel Green. Whilst helpful in certain areas, this influence is problematic in others, and with his thought being key to the anthropology of his colleagues—Yong and Kärkkäinen, critique of their thought on the topic will be naturally entailed as the chapter ensues to assess Green's theological anthropology.

The holistic emphasis is very clear in Green's theological anthropology. As a specialist in gospel studies, and understanding the holistic nature of salvation described in the gospels, it appears that he has been glad, then, from this start-point to accept the relational view of the *imago Dei*. Drawn to Barth's relational view of the image, and seeing that worked out in Psalms 8, 144 and Job 7:17–18, from there he has extrapolated this relational-holistic understanding to human personhood generally. As a result of this extrapolation, he is naturally drawn to the Hebraic themes of community, relationality, embodiment—which shape human identity and character—giving a helpful holistic color to his theological anthropology. Because of these biblical themes,[23] he views anything other than

---

22. Green, "What Are Human Beings?" 3.

23. And in addition (and support) of these themes, Green's postgraduate studies in *neuroscience* have added to his thoughts on anthropology. He draws attention to the phenomena of neuroplasticity to provide further insights to the topic highlighting

monism as conflicting with biblical thought and he is outspoken in his rejection of Platonist dualism and/or the essentialist view of a person.

Whilst he helpfully draws out these biblical themes of community, relationality, embodiment, and holism—exegetical work that is of great value for what it contributes to anthropological understanding—there are certain philosophical assumptions implicit in Green's theological anthropology which have the effect of skewing his thinking regarding the monism/dualism debate. These philosophical assumptions are initially difficult to identify because they are embedded among insights that are valuable, but they need to be uncovered due to the influence they have on his anthropology. A prevalent example of such is how Green helpfully draws attention to the *implicit* nature of Scripture's anthropology meaning that anthropology has to be *inferred* rather than exegeted directly; from this correct and helpful assertion, Green proceeds to derive his four anthropological principles (drawn collectively from Gen 1:26–27; Pss 8 and 144; Job 7:17–18), which (to remind) assert the following:

1. that a human is to be defined relationally—not in structural/essentialist terms,
2. a human has continuity with, but a higher vocation than animals (because)
3. the person bears the image of God (and)
4. (the person) is viewed within these passages as a bio-psychospiritual unity.[24]

Under careful examination, it can be agreed that principles 2, 3 and 4 are helpful; but as regards the first of Green's four anthropological principles, his deriving the conclusion that humans are relational *as opposed to* essentialist beings appears, on a first reading, to be a false dichotomy (given that one could both hold to an essentialist view and understand the person's theological vocation and purpose as relationship with God). But actually, on closer scrutiny, it appears that Green is assuming a *philosophical* understanding of these terms, and has committed himself to the (ontological-)relational view of a person—seeing this philosophical view

---

that certain behaviors of a person are based on her *context* and regular *practices*. When added to his biblical studies, all of this provides helpful material for considering areas such as Christian epistemology and ethics. (See Green, "Sacred and Neural"; and Green, *Body, Soul, and Human Life*, 115–22.)

24. Green, "What Are Human Beings?"

of a person as prevalent in Scripture's understanding of a human.²⁵ To arrive at this understanding, he proceeds from the holistic soteriology of Luke, to that of the N.T. gospels generally, to the holistic worldview of the O.T., to the passages concerning the *imago Dei*; this then brings him to his conclusion and first principle that the Bible is "relational not essentialist (/structuralist)" in its view of a human person. Yet whilst most theologians might agree upon the *theological* nature of humans as those having been made for relationship with God, (and, indeed, with other humans, and creation), Green takes a philosophical step further to extrapolate from this theological point that the Bible infers an ontological-relational view of a person—as opposed to an (ontological-)essentialist view of a person; for him, he infers from scriptural *theology* a *philosophical* position that persons are ultimately "beings-in-relation" as opposed to beings with certain fundamental metaphysical faculties.

One might actually agree with the steps/method Green uses to draw towards this philosophical standpoint yet disagree with his conclusion; that is, one could appreciate his elucidation of Luke's holistic soteriology, agree that this brings light to that same emphasis throughout all the N.T. gospels, and endorse his Barthian understanding of the *imago Dei*, while yet disagreeing with the conclusion that the relational *ontological* view of a person follows from these steps in his argument/method. Moreover, what Green fails to see is that some kind of "essentialist" understanding of a person is necessary *for* advocating a relational view, in that the being that is said to be in relation can only be a *personal* being-in-relation if that being possesses some sort of (essentialist) properties that are specific to

---

25. The ontological essentialist view of a person, in contrast to the (ontological) relational view of a person, might be helpfully explicated at this point by (briefly) giving the history and content of the *substance* view of a person (given that that commonly underpins essentialist view[s])—as well as those of the relational view of a person. In terms of the former, Boethius's substance definition of a person is seen as the classic view of antiquity; he defined a person as "an individual substance of a rational nature" (Boethius, *Liber de Persona et Duabus Naturis*, c.3) (Boethius in turn drawing upon Aristotle for his definition of a substance [and the essentialist aspect of Boethius's view being the *rational nature* of the substance]). This view of a person was then developed through Richard of St. Victor, Aquinas, and Scotus and, until recent times, this has been received as the standard traditional view and known as the "substance" view of a person. However, due to a discontent with substance metaphysics, a number of recent thinkers have turned to a more "relational" metaphysics—and associated views of a person—defining a person instead as a "being/creature-in-relation." The relational view has particularly been developed by Zizioulas (*Being as Communion*) and, as seen in the work of Green, Yong, and Kärkkäinen, is favored among some theologians (and philosophers) in the present.

and distinctive of personhood (such as the metaphysical faculties of self-conscious mind and free will).[26] Indeed, though Green (/Barth) might be correct that theological covenantal relation is what is being referred to in Gen 1:26–27,[27] such a view cannot be sustained without a stronger philosophical view of a person to underpin that relational view.

The issue of personhood will be returned to and further expounded later in the book, however, some of the issue's significance is pertinently highlighted at this juncture by considering the effect Green's ontological-relational view has on his view of personal eschatology. Whilst affirming the resurrection of the body, his views on the nature of personhood give him no grounds for affirming (personal) identity persistence over time—from the time of a person's physical death to the time of her final resurrection; having gone out of existence at death (and with no room in his view for the intermediate state), the person that receives a resurrection body can, at best, be only a *replica* of the person she was before her physical death. Considering John Locke's helpful dictum that "one [identical] thing cannot have two beginnings," it could not be the case, on the view Green espouses, that the person at the resurrection is (philosophically) *identically* the same person as she was prior to death[28]—it could only be a mere *replica* of that person.[29] The ramifications this has for Yong and Kärkkäinen's eschatology will be returned to later in this chapter but it should be evident from this discussion that the ontological-relational view holds theological and philosophical problems, and effects other important topic such as the issue of personal eschatology.

Having considered Green's anthropology, enough has been seen by this point to recognize that there are considerable problems therein. Being integral to the anthropology of Pentecostals Yong and Kärkkäinen, it would be helpful to succinctly expound these problems by way of the following two summaries.

---

26. This position will be elucidated, and the topic of personhood expanded, in the relevant discussion in the book's conclusion.

27. Though current exegesis of the texts emphasizes the *vocational* nature of the *imago Dei*—an idea explored more fully in the book's conclusion (cf. Churchouse, "Distinguishing the imago Dei.")

28. To clarify, this is a *philosophical* difficulty with Green's view. It is conceivable that an attempted counter-response would be to say that no-one will be "identical" at the resurrection to who she was prior to death, due to being in possession of a (re)new(ed) resurrection body, but that would be to blur the precise issue of philosophical *identity* with a general theological sense of the person's having been *transformed* in nature.

29. Cf. Churchouse, "Healthier Anthropology," 119–20.

First, in following the work of Green, Yong and Kärkkäinen inherit his opinion that all dualistic forms of constitution have to be dismissed in light of Genesis' (affirmative) teaching concerning the embodiment, relationality, and holism of human persons. This indeed would rule out Platonist or Classic Cartesian dualism as they are inconsistent with these biblical themes,[30] but there are better and contemporary forms of dualism that also gladly affirm all these themes yet receive little to no consideration from Green, Yong or Kärkkäinen—being those merely rejected under the generic banner of "dualism."

Second, although Gen 1:26–27 and 2:7 are a natural place to begin consideration of theological anthropology—i.e., beginning with the *imago Dei*—in following the thinking of Green, scholars Yong and Kärkkäinen make the same mistake as he does in confusing the Hebraic *theological* emphases (of Genesis 1 and 2) with the more *philosophical* and relevant question of the nature of human constitution. Whilst these opening chapters of Genesis address the issues of the "who" and "why" of humanity (or humanity's "identity" and "vocation"),[31] these chapters say little about the "what" of humanity (or indeed "how" it was they were created). Indeed Genesis 1 and 2 seem uninterested in the question of constitution.[32] But in recognizing the absence of comment on the constitutional nature of a human in these opening chapters of Genesis, it does not therefore follow that Scripture assumes a monist understanding of a human being. What is here being further confused is functional holism with ontological monism.[33] Whilst teaching anthropological holism, no ontological anthropology can be deduced from Genesis 1 and 2 alone. In trying to assert anthropological monism from Genesis 1 and 2, Green,

---

30. Platonist and Classic Cartesian dualisms will be fully expounded and critiqued in the excursus that follows the end of this chapter, but in short, a Platonist view regards the immaterial/spiritual soul as metaphysically good but the physical body as bad—positing an *unhelpful* (metaphysical) dualism between the body and soul (in which the body becomes akin to a prison from which the spiritual soul wants to escape); a Classic Cartesian view regards the soul and body as two interacting substances but both of which having differing functions—the soul being responsible for thinking, spiritual experiences, desiring etc., the body being responsible for breathing, digesting, excreting etc.

31. Cf. Walton, *Lost World*; and Wenham, *Genesis 1–15*.

32. Meaning that dualists would be unwise to read constitutional thinking into Gen 2:7 (for instance) (it also being unwise, therefore, for Amos Yong to read emergent monism into the verse).

33. As the following chapter will further reveal, this misunderstanding is one that J. W. Cooper's work identifies—seeing it as commonly inherent in the minds of biblical exegetes.

A Critique of Yong and Kärkkäinen's Doctrine

Yong, and Kärkkäinen are making the category error of confusing identity and vocation with that of constitution.

So, with these key critiques underlined, (Green,) Yong and Kärkkäinen's theological challenges to dualism are undermined. None of their theological objections are problematic for a good holistic or psychosomatic dualism, they simply rule out the strawmen.

Engaging with the Philosophical Critiques

The Neuroscience Objection

Yong and Kärkkäinen show a common tendency to view neuroscience as a *theological* issue, or more specifically as a "scientific" objection against anthropological dualism. As suggested, the source for such categorization is plausibly Green, given that such an assertion appears regularly in his theological anthropology. Although Green's work has been commendably bolstered by his graduate studies in neuroscience, to categorize this objection against dualism as a "theological" or "scientific" objection is a further category mistake. Rather, it is only when the neuroscientific findings are interpreted—from a particular *philosophical* slant—that any objection might be raised.

Whilst the incorrect *categorization* is apparent in Green's biblical work, and so likewise appears in the anthropology of Yong and Kärkkäinen, the actual source of the objection appears to be the philosopher Nancey Murphy—who worked in collaboration with Green on the compendium *Whatever Happened to the Soul* (and whose work Yong and Kärkkäinen drew upon [likewise] for insights in the philosophy of mind). In the opening chapter to that work, Murphy summarized her position and that of her fellow collaborators; she admits that, historically, some form of dualism has been the predominant anthropological view as regards the mind-body question, but in observing the tide of philosophers who have left dualistic positions in favor of varieties of (mind-body) physicalism—combined with the rapid *advances in neuroscience*, which she regards as eroding away any place for a soul in the discussion—she notes that these advances have led both herself and her compendium's colleagues to reject the dualistic position.[34] She comments:

---

34. Murphy, "Human Nature," 1–29.

> Science has provided a massive amount of evidence suggesting we need not postulate the existence of an entity such as a soul or mind in order to explain life and consciousness.[35]

And in a second and pertinent article, she re-affirms her position above, stating:

> It is becoming increasingly obvious that the functions once attributed to the soul or mind are better understood as functions of the brain. These developments in neuroscience, along with the judgment that no account can be given of mind-body interaction, have resulted in a near total rejection of dualism in philosophy of mind.[36]

Murphy's comments and statements above bely a *mistaken* understanding of the implications of the neuroscience, but an understanding that has been absorbed into the thinking of Yong and Kärkkäinen, causing them to reject all dualist positions due to what the neuroscience has supposedly revealed. In a quote that illustrates the case (and one that suggests Murphy's influence, further, in Yong's thinking concerning interaction [of the immaterial soul with the material/physical body]), Yong articulates the following comment when considering substance dualism:

> . . . the problems here are both the Cartesian one about how the material and immaterial realms relate to each other and the more recent neuroscientific evidence that correlates mental life with cognitive brain states.[37]

What has been confused in this quote, here, of Yong—and indeed what has been confused in the thinking of Murphy—is the objective neuroscientific data with the *philosophical interpretation* of such. Neuroscience has clearly shown that, under ordinary embodied conditions, human consciousness and mental activity is *functionally dependent* upon the brain; one can see the relevant neurons firing when, for example, a person thinks, or acts, or experiences. Whilst this causes problems for Classic

---

35. Murphy, "Human Nature," 18.

36. Murphy, "Immortality versus resurrection," 77. See also Kärkkäinen who contends "While in the past, body-soul dualism was assumed to be the default position, in light of the current scientific knowledge, theology has also come to a new appreciation of the fact that "we know conscious and self-conscious life only as bodily life, . . . bodily functions condition all psychological experience." (Kärkkäinen, *Creation and Humanity*, 309 [citing Pannenberg, *Systematic Theology* 2:181–82 in his sections using inverted commas]).

37. Yong, *Theology and Down Syndrome*, 170.

Cartesian dualism, it causes no such problems for other views espousing a spiritual soul; indeed, whether one holds to a contemporary substance dualist interpretation, a reductive physicalist understanding, a position entailing emergence—all these mind-body views are *philosophical interpretations* that take full account of contemporary neuroscientific data (as well as seek to address the many *philosophical* questions to be considered regarding the mind-body relation).

Given how commonly this "objection" is raised, it is worth emphasizing the following response; the issue of the findings of neuroscience is problematic for *Classic Cartesian dualism,* but not for stronger varieties of dualism. Whilst Classic Cartesian dualism will be covered in much fuller detail subsequently (due to its negative and distorting impact on discussions of anthropology) in short, this problematic dualist model advocates that the body has one set of functions, and the soul has another set—and the two substances interact but have separate and individual functions—which is why it suffers problems with the findings of contemporary neuroscience (as highlighted by Murphy). But no current-day philosopher of mind holds to that Classic Cartesian position; rather all contemporary dualistic positions take full account of the neuroscientific data—indeed welcoming its current findings and anticipating its further discoveries.[38] Such philosophers of mind are more philosophically nuanced, recognizing the evident *correlation* between mental states and the relevant associated brain states, and are content to recognize that a human is ordinarily dependent on the functioning of her brain for the functioning of her mental activity.[39] All contemporary mind-body views—including dualist views—recognize this *functional* dependence of

---

38. Due to the overly hasty advancing of the neuroscience as an objection to the soul, it may be helpful to draw attention to the well-known neurologist Wilder Penfield—arguably the father of modern neuroscience—whose neuroscientific work actually helped him arrive at a dualistic position. Penfield discovered that, though he was able to stimulate the brains of numerous patients in order to make them raise an arm (for example), the patient would always say that it was Penfield who was *making* her do this action—it was not an action chosen by the patient herself. After an exhaustive study of the cerebral cortex, this led Penfield to conclude that "there is no place in the cerebral cortex where electrode stimulation will cause a patient . . . to decide" (Penfield, *Mystery of the Mind,* 77).

39. The word "ordinarily" is part of this description to clarify that *in a normal, embodied* condition, the human soul is functionally reliant on its brain, but in disembodied conditions (seen for instance in the accounts of Near-Death Experiences [cf. Habermas, "Evidential Near-Death Experiences," 227–46]), mental activity is still possible (whilst not being the norm)—this understanding allowing for continued mental functioning in a (temporarily) disembodied afterlife.

mental activity upon the mechanism of the brain, but this does not make the mind and the brain the same thing, or suggest that the mind emerged from the brain. Indeed as was pointed out by John Eccles—Nobel laureate for his work on brain science—a pianist is functionally dependent on a piano in order to make music, but that does not mean that the pianist and the piano are identical (or that the pianist emerged from the piano); it just highlights that there is a close relationship between the (conscious) pianist and the mechanism of the piano.[40] Yong is, therefore, inaccurate to comment that,

> . . . the contemporary neurosciences have certainly shown that mental activities are *emergent from* and in that sense dependent upon brain and bodily functions.[41]

In counter to Yong's emergentist assertion, a (contemporary) substance dualist interpretation of the mind-body question would make the alternate philosophical contention that there are two *distinct* substances (the spiritual soul and physical brain) and that these substances interact—the mind/soul's mental states being correlated with (physical) states in the brain.[42] To clarify and emphasize the point, on this philosophical interpretation of the mind, the soul is indeed *functionally* dependent upon the brain in ordinary circumstances—indeed, a person's *soul* experiences pain (for instance) due to the C-fibres in her body relaying that sensation of pain through the brain to the spiritual soul—but the soul is actually the agent; it is the *soul* that thinks, decides, desires (being examples of its mental states) by *using* the brain and the associated C-fibres for carrying out its operations. In short, the brain is the instrument, the soul is the conscious agent.

Both emergentism and dualistic interactionism are *philosophical* interpretations of the neurological findings and are both thoroughly consistent with, and take account of, all the relevant science. Again, the only dualistic position that would suffer from Murphy, Yong, and Kärkkäinen's objection would be a straw man variety of dualism—the Classic Cartesian view. However, for research into human constitution seeking to engage with positions in their *strongest* forms, such an objection does not

---

40. See for example his dialogue with Karl Popper in Popper and Eccles, *Self and Its Brain*, 495.

41. Yong, "Christian and Buddhist Perspectives," 148 (emphasis mine).

42. In the philosophy of mind, the words "mind" and "soul" are interchangeable on a substance dualist position.

apply. In fact, the issue is put quite starkly by scientist and philosopher Daniel Robinson:[43]

> Truth be told . . . it is fair to say that, whatever it was about the mind-body problem that made it a philosophical problem in the first instance, developments in the brain sciences have done nothing to solve, settle, or eliminate it. . . . [Regardless of the neurological findings] . . . the vexing fact [is] that the available and even foreseeable findings can be applied with equal evidentiary force to such radically different solutions to the mind-body problem as interactionism, parallelism, epiphenomenalism, eliminativism, supervenience etc. It would seem that there is no *experimentum cruces* that will tell so thoroughly for one solution and against all the rest as to establish *the solution*. To the extent that a problem is a bona fide *scientific* problem if and only if there is some imaginable experiment that will settle it, the mind-body problem would have to be judged as falling outside the boundaries of scientific modes of verification. For this reason, if for no other, little is gained by today's philosophical advocates who reach for one another "finding" to support a pet conjecture.[44]

The Problem of Interaction

Yong and Kärkkäinen's other philosophical objection to dualism is the issue of interaction. This classic objection, raised ever since the time of Descartes, focusses attention on the problem of how an immaterial substance could interact with a material substance and is the most commonly advanced difficulty against dualistic views. Indeed, dualistic views are often dismissed out of hand because of this traditional but trending objection. However, despite having been used so commonly in rejection of dualist views, when the objection is examined more closely, it shows to be comparatively weak when considered against the better dualistic models. The stronger form of the objection attempts to reject dualism on *epistemological* grounds,[45] namely no mechanism has been put forward

---

43. Robinson, in his career, has been a consultant to the American National Science Foundation, as well as to the National Institutes of Health, and the government's Department of Health and Human Services.

44. Robinson, "Minds, Brains, and Brains in a Vat," 55–56 (emphasis his).

45. By contrast, less precise versions of the "problem of interaction" seek to argue that it is not possible for an immaterial substance to interact with a material substance

for explaining *how* the different substances interact—leaving a gap in human knowledge. But if two entities exist, and it is apparent that they *do* interact, to not (yet?) know *how* that interaction occurs is no grounds for rejecting the view.[46] The interaction of *God* (a spiritual entity) with the *universe* (a physical entity) is one accepted by Yong and Kärkkäinen (as likewise by Murphy and Green), despite not knowing the exact mechanics of that interaction.[47] So, if one contentedly allows the latter, it should also be the case for the former. In a similar but more forthright critique (one that refutes the wider/looser versions of the argument as well as the tighter epistemological version), leading emergentist philosopher William Hasker has condemned the objection, commenting:

> There is . . . the ancient, and by now extremely boring, objection that causal interaction between diverse substances such as mind and body . . . is impossible. . . . Once we have recognized that, as Hume long ago taught us, *all* causal relations are at bottom conceptually opaque, this hoary objection should be relegated to its appropriate place in the dustbin of history.[48]

With advocates in recent times appearing to sense some of the weakness of the classic objection, contemporary advocates have offered substantiating augmentations of it by appealing to the "conservation of energy" issue. This augmentation of the objection argues that an action occurring in the brain, that is stimulated by a mental state (originating in the soul), would need to have been brought about by at least some form of energy-momentum exchange in order to cause the physical brain state; but this would violate the conservation of energy principle by introducing extra energy into the world—a world which has a precise and limited amount of energy. However, as (the philosopher of physics) Robin Collins has responded, this augmentation of the objection relies on models of physics that were prevalent at the time of Descartes, which have since been

---

on apparently metaphysical grounds. But these looser constructions of the argument are inadequate in that they assume the hidden (but unjustified) premise that X cannot causally influence or interact with Y unless X *is like* Y.

46. Cf, Swinburne, *Mind, Brain, and Free Will*, chapter 5. Interestingly, the philosopher of mind Colin McGinn suggests that a mechanism of interaction may well exist but be beyond the intelligence capabilities of humans to *ever* comprehend. See McGinn, *The Problem of Consciousness*.

47. In his *Spirit of Creation* chapters 3 and 4, Yong gives a creative exposition of what a Pentecostal theology of *Divine action* might look like. However, Divine action, and the *mechanics of* that (inter)action are different categories, and not to be confused.

48. Hasker, "Emergent Dualism," 104 (emphasis his).

exposed as inadequate and outdated by contemporary physics. Expounding on this issue, he writes:

> [this augmentation] fails when one considers that energy conservation is not a universally applicable principle in physics and that quantum mechanics *sets a precedent* for interaction (or at least law-like correlation) without any sort of energy-momentum exchange, or even any intermediate carrier.[49]

Further:

> ... The fact that so many leading philosophers have trumpeted the energy conservation objection as a fatal blow to dualism, without carefully examining the relevant physics, should make us suspicious that the widespread rejection of dualism within academia is based more on the fashion of the day than on sound argument.[50]

Given this assessment, and the inadequacies of the classic formulation, this popular and long-held objection—the "problem of interaction"—now appears rather dated and worn. Rather than providing grounds for a philosophical rejection of dualism, by contrast it has been seen to be deficient in its attempt to critique dualist positions.

Summary of Yong and Kärkkäinen's Challenges to Dualism

In sum, the reasons Yong and Kärkkäinen put forward for rejecting *Platonist* and *Classic Cartesian* dualisms are strong, and they join a long line of thinkers in their (valid) critique of these positions. But whilst they seem aware of *other* varieties of dualism, they apparently reject these dualisms likewise—for the same reasons that they reject the strawmen. Such rejection is conceptually mistaken, and in fact none of Yong or Kärkkäinen's objections—either theological or philosophical—are problematic for a good, contemporary, psychosomatic (or holistic) dualism. To reject all forms of dualism due to problems with two (notorious) varieties is a classic erroneous case of "throwing the baby out with the bathwater."

---

49. Collins, "Energy of the Soul," 133 (emphasis mine). Collins's chapter in *The Soul Hypothesis* is a condensed version of his "Modern Physics and the Energy Conservation Objection to Mind-Body Dualism," *The American Philosophical Quarterly* 45 (2008) 31–42.

50. Collins, "Energy of the Soul," 133.

Both scholars seem to assume that dualism espouses a soul that is ontologically distinct from the body, but that is *separate* in its functioning to the physical functions of the body. But better forms of dualism advocate a soul which is ontologically distinct and spiritual, and indeed might be separ*able* following death, but that in ordinary circumstances functions *in intimate relation with* the body. Such better forms of dualism will be considered in the second half of this book, advancing beyond the limited viewpoints considered by Yong and Kärkkäinen. But having mistakenly rejected dualism per se, might it be that, regardless of the mis-critiques of dualism, Yong and Kärkkäinen's preferred anthropological model—their *emergent monist* position—is a strong and healthy alternative itself to serve as the basis for a flourishing anthropology? Does their emergent monist position stand as a model that is philosophically and theologically robust, so giving an alternative commendable model upon which to build a theological anthropology?

In assessing their emergent monist viewpoint, again, the philosophical strength of the position will be considered. But considering their anthropology as that carried out within the corpus of *Pentecostal* theology, their work will, first, be assessed as regards its concordance with the *Pentecostal* theological emphases as articulated in the book's introduction.

Pentecostal Theological Assessment of Yong and Kärkkäinen's Emergent Monist Proposal

It might be recalled from this book's introduction that there are certain theological emphases that are commonly more pronounced in the Pentecostal theological tradition. In very succinct summary (of what is, there, more fully articulated) Pentecostal theology characteristically displays the following theological emphases:

1. A renewal pneumatological emphasis
2. An eschatological (kingdom) emphasis
3. A holistic anthropological emphasis
4. A "supernatural" dualistic emphasis (stressing the spirit realm not just the physical[51])

---

51. Although the term "supernatural" is regularly employed by Pentecostals, the term is rather unhelpful as it tends to create a *divide* between the physical and non-physical (or material and immaterial) realms. This will be seen more clearly as the book

A Critique of Yong and Kärkkäinen's Doctrine

Whilst the predominant emphasis of the four is Pentecostals' renewal pneumatological emphasis—from which the other three flow—the three following theological accents are also additionally prominent in Pentecostal theology. Together these emphases form a quadrant of theological emphases that are commonly more pronounced in the Pentecostal tradition (than tends to be the case in other Christian theological traditions). As such, it is instructive to assess the concordance of Yong and Kärkkäinen's emergent monism with these four theological emphases and so to ask, in that sense, how harmonious their model is with the Pentecostal theological tradition.

From the expositions of chapter 2, it becomes quickly apparent that Yong and Kärkkäinen's emergent monist model is very much in accord, *theologically*, with the first (and primary) emphasis—Pentecostals' renewal pneumatology. Particularly in Yong's theological anthropological model, he consistently allows such pneumatology to inform, "assist," and enhance the theology he is proposing; indeed, the pneumatology is his means of developing Murphy's and Clayton's model into his own theological model—a model that might, in effect, be titled a "Spirit-energized" or "Pentecostal" emergent monism. Whilst some of Yong's exegesis of Genesis 1 and 2 is questionable—for instance, his idea that Gen 2:7 forms a pneumatological "bookend" with Gen 1:1,[52] and it being possible to read 2:7 in a philosophized sense to support his emergent monist proposal—his theological "pneumatological-canonical" reading (of Genesis 1 in particular) is interesting and engaging, and brings a vivid renewal pneumatological emphasis and coloring to his proposal. Whilst the model of Kärkkäinen is less explicit in a pneumatological sense, because of its similarity to Yong's anthropological proposal, his could likewise be affirmed as being concordant with this Pentecostal emphasis (even though that renewal pneumatological concordance is not the focus of his anthropological project).

Their emergent monist proposal is also in accord with the third of the theological emphases—the holistic anthropological emphasis and understanding of a human being. Both scholars repeatedly emphasize,

---

develops—particularly through dialogue with J. K. A. Smith—however, recognizing that it is common parlance amongst Pentecostals, here the word is retained, yet placing it in inverted commas to draw attention to the author's unease with the term.

52. Gen 2:4a is usually taken exegetically as the booked to Gen 1:1, before the second creation account begins in 2:4b (cf. Churchouse "Distinguishing the imago Dei," 273–75 and the list of Genesis commentators [end note 14] that have been drawn on in affirmation of this exegesis).

throughout their anthropological works, the theme of embodiment as the natural state of a human being. Whilst recognizing that true spirituality is had in relation with the life-giving relational Spirit, they strongly maintain that such relationship is most fully displayed and experienced in holistic, embodied form. As such, it is very clear that their emergent monist proposal gladly comports with this third Pentecostal emphasis—their view being happily concordant with both the first and third emphases as articulated above.

As regards the eschatological orientation inherent in Pentecostal Theology—emphasis two as denoted above—this requires further theological probing. This eschatological emphasis is characteristic of Pentecostal theology in its emphasizing the eschatological kingdom of God (and the pouring out of the eschatological Spirit)–resulting in Pentecostal desire to be (continually) Spirit-empowered for missional living in the period of "the last days"—living in the "now" of the eschatological kingdom whilst awaiting its promised "not yet." On this macro eschatological level, Yong and Kärkkäinen's proposal would appear to be concordant with this general eschatological emphasis.[53] Indeed, their model very much affirms the physical, holistic nature of the eschatological resurrection body—a theme that has received greater prominence, in more recent years of the tradition, within Pentecostals' over-arching eschatological outlook and emphasis. But with the theology of final resurrection developing in Pentecostal prominence, that has also naturally meant that the theme of Pentecostals' *personal* eschatology has also required consideration—as was implied by some of the work carried out in the survey of chapter 1 of this book. (Putting some theological flesh on the philosophical bones of identity persistence,) Pentecostals have traditionally held, and standardly hold in the present, to belief in the *intermediate state* from the time of a person's death to the time of her final judgment/resurrection.[54] This belief is prevalent through the literature of the Pentecostal tradition.[55] But Yong and Kärkkäinen's emergent monism rules out any

---

53. Given all the more indication when considering Yong's thought concerning anthropology in relation to his thinking on Divine Action (Yong's thinking concerning Divine Action puts a "dunamis/teleological" stress on the working of the [eschatological] Holy Spirit). (See Yong, *Spirit of Creation*.)

54. Daniel 12:1–2 implying that all will be raised on the day of judgment, some to everlasting life, some to everlasting destruction.

55. Cf. Pearlman, *Knowing the Doctrines*, 370–71 (Pearlman specifically disavowing the soul sleep hypothesis on the basis of Isa 14:9–11; Ps 16:10; Luke 16:23; 23:42; 2 Cor 5:8; Phil 1:23; Rev 6:9); Williams, *Systematic Theology*, 178; Arrington, *Christian*

A Critique of Yong and Kärkkäinen's Doctrine 103

place for this intermediate state. When physical death occurs, (on their view) the mind's biological substrate, the brain, also dies at that point as well, and so the person/mind goes out of existence—going extinct until final "re-creation" (note "re-creation" not "resurrection"). Being aware of this theological implication, Yong muses on the topic:

> I am unsure what to think about the traditional doctrine of the "intermediate state" given my commitments to an emergentist anthropology. If human beings are constituted by (even if irreducible to) their bodies, then there can be no proper human "existence" after death and prior to the resurrection of those bodies. However, the biblical data can be read in a way that does not necessarily demand a dualistic construal of the relationship between the human soul and body. Even the appearance of Samuel to the medium of Endor can be understood as made possible by a resurrection theory. Clearly, while much more work needs to be done in this area, at the very least it can be said that an emergentist anthropology takes the resurrection of the body as constitutive of human personhood and identity in the afterlife much more seriously than any dualistic view can.[56]

The last sentence of the paragraph seems uncharacteristically polemical for Yong (and the explanation of Samuel's appearance unlikely), but leaving such polemics aside, there are two further issues disclosed in this quote which add to the related philosophical problem of identity persistence over time. First, Yong recognizes that the doctrine of the intermediate state is traditionally what Pentecostals have wanted to espouse;[57] but he is content to jettison the doctrine due to his commitment to emergentist theory. Second, remembering his previous comment that Paul does not believe in re-creation (following a period of nothingness/extinction at the physical death of a person), Yong's discarding the intermediate state means that he is forced to adopt exactly that position—the re-creation view he recognizes as being one that is contra Paul. As for Kärkkäinen, he clearly feels these difficulties shown by his citing the view of Polkinghorne and, to a similar effect, John Zizioulas,[58] but giving no

---

Doctrine, 238; Horton, "Last Things," 606–13 (who argues on the basis that Moses and Elijah appeared with Jesus at the transfiguration that there has to be some kind of existence between death and final resurrection) and Grudem, *Systematic Theology*, 816–24.

56. Yong, *Theology and Down Syndrome*, 287n21 (printed as an end note on page 337).

57. Cf. n55 above.

58. Zizioulas states "[w]hat gives us an identity that does not die is not our nature,

grounds in his writing for espousing belief in an intermediate state, or anything but replica re-creation. So, related to the philosophical issue of identity persistence over time, their emergent monist view has a problem with personal eschatology, making their view less concordant with the Pentecostal eschatological emphasis.

Whilst the issue regarding the second Pentecostal emphasis is concerning a *component within* the emphasis, the problem as regards the fourth of the quadrant of emphases—the Pentecostal accent on the *dualistic* nature of the world (accentuating the "supernatural"/spirit world as well as the physical world)—concerns the emphasis as a whole. The emergent monist conception of a human, though not necessarily *excluding* the spirit world, sits less concordantly within this dualistic world that Pentecostals stress in their theological thought. As Yong himself has commented:

> belief in a spirit-filled cosmos is *endemic* to Pentecostal spirituality.... [This spirit-filled cosmos is a world] that includes not just the Holy Spirit but also angels, demons, and other spiritual beings and powers.[59]

Within this dualistic reality, God and angel (spirits) exist without a physical substratum. So, to argue that the spirits/souls/minds of *humans* need a subvenient physical base for their (ontological [not functional]) existence seems surprising and unconvincing. It should be acknowledged that Yong has admittedly offered a revisionist emergent view of angels, in consistency with his theory of the emergent world, contending that they *do* in fact have a subvenient physical base.[60] Whilst having addressed this revisionist view elsewhere, it is idiosyncratic of Yong and an implausible understanding of angels,[61] but underlines the point that he recognizes that the emergent monist view is not particularly in accord with the Pentecostal emphasis of the dualistic world—a world that is richly populated with spirit(ual) beings that do not have a physical substrate (to be further explored in the following chapter).

---

but a personal relationship with God." Zizioulas. "Holy Trinity," 58 cited in Kärkkäinen, "Creation and Humanity," 348.

59. Yong, *Spirit of Creation*, 174–75 (emphasis mine). Yong has elaborated this point much more fully in his *Discerning the Spirit(s)*, 127–32, 234–55 and 294–308. However, it is only in his more recent book that he has sought to give a full interpretation of these phenomena.

60. Yong, *Spirit of Creation*, 175–207, 213–21.

61. See Churchouse, "Angels," 104–8.

In light of the above assessment, whilst it would be unfair to assert that Yong and Kärkkäinen's emergent monism is *discordant* with the four Pentecostal theological emphases, because it carries specific problems in regard to the issues of personal eschatology as well as a credible doctrine of angels, it is not particularly *concordant* with the eschatological and "supernatural" dualistic emphases; therefore, it does not especially commend itself as a preferable *Pentecostal* model. But, having identified these issues, those of a (more) theological nature, their model requires further review, this time of a *philosophical* nature. So, in returning to their model again, and their preferred philosophical dialogue-partners, their emergent monist view will once again be assessed, now from the philosophical angle of scrutiny.

Philosophical Assessment of the Emergent Monist Proposal of Yong and Kärkkäinen

Strengths and Weaknesses of the Murphy and Clayton Project

In terms of its philosophical basis, Yong and Kärkkäinen's anthropology is dependent on the philosophical theory of emergence. Consistent with the "many tongues" methodology of Yong, and Kärkkäinen's coherentist approach (methods in which both expect to find truth discovered through many different disciplines of the academy), both thinkers have drawn from this emergentist model—particularly from the philosophy of mind—as the basis for their constructive theology and filled out those findings with their own theological insights. This philosophical-theological nature of their approach is one that is apropos, but similar to their reliance upon Green (to provide the biblical studies for their theological model) their emergentist philosophy is reliant on the philosophy of Murphy and Clayton; so again, critique of both of these thinkers' emergent monist projects will naturally entail critique of Yong and Kärkkäinen's emergentist model.

In considering the mind-body problem, to arrive at their own distinctive models, some of the thinking of Murphy and Clayton is strong, being philosophically clear and robust. Particularly their refutation of the reductive physicalist position (as giving inadequate explanation for the hard problem of consciousness) shows rigorous philosophical thought, and so Yong and Kärkkäinen are on solid ground in following in their footsteps in this regard. But there are considerable philosophical problems with the models of Murphy and Clayton which are then also assumed into the projects of both Yong and Kärkkäinen. The issue of the "science"—that is integral to Murphy's model—has already been addressed above, so repetition of that critique will be avoided here. Indeed, once Murphy's "scientific basis" had been assumed, by both Yong and Kärkkäinen, they moved beyond her model—preferring that of Clayton. As such, the philosophy of Clayton will be the focus of particular assessment, given that he is the lead influence and dialogue-partner in the anthropology of Yong and Kärkkäinen.

A Closer Examination of Clayton's Emergentist Project

As was identified in chapter 2, Clayton recognizes that unless there are more than just two kinds of properties in the world (just mental and physical properties), his position collapses into a mental-physical dualism.[62] So, to avoid this latter position, he follows Morowitz in arguing that there could be as many as twenty-eight differing types of properties in the world—but all being derived from the one same monistic stuff. Such a view seems to escape dualism by inserting a gradient between the pure physical property $[P_p]$—the base level of the gradient—and pure mental property $[M_p]$—the top level of the gradient. Between these bottom and top levels, Clayton argues that more and more (unique/sui generis) emergent properties have arisen through the course of natural history, and so, far from there just being a simple ontological dualism (M_p having emerged from P_p), there are *multiple* examples of emergence that have occurred during this evolutionary natural history—each new property having arisen as a new sui generis property from the subvenient level below. The reader, on this proposal, is prepared *psychologically* for the (otherwise) arresting distinction between the conscious mind and the physical brain through being given this "gradient" hypothesis; if history is *full* of comparable and regular instances of such *sui generis* emergence, then the difference between the brain and mind—and indeed the emergence of the latter from the former—seems one that is less stark, with the reader being psychologically prepared for this additional level of emergence. Yet this plurality-of-emergence model is only "successful" through

---

62. Clayton, *Mind and Emergence*, 156.

blurring the difference between *structural* and *sui generis* emergence (or as David Chalmers has coined, between *weak* and *strong* emergence[63]).

As J. P. Moreland has carefully delineated, a structural (/weak) emergent property is one that is "constituted by the parts, properties, relations, and events at the subvenient level."[64] Concerning this structural kind of emergence, all scientists and philosophers are ready to acknowledge examples of such in the natural world. However, by contrast to these structural examples, the emergence of a conscious *mind* would be an example of a radically new kind of emergence—a *sui generis* (/*strong*) kind of emergence—Moreland delineating this type of emergent property as "a completely new kind of property different from those that characterize its subvenient base."[65] When this careful distinction is made, it is acknowledged (in the philosophy of mind) that mind is the *only* example of such *sui generis* (/strong) emergence. So, to try and explain away this real issue of *sui generis* (/*strong*) emergence by appeal to multiple examples of *structural* (/weak) emergence is fallacious reasoning. When the illegitimate extrapolation is highlighted, Clayton's gradient model is exposed, showing it a problematic emergent monism for Yong and Kärkkäinen's theological construction.

Indeed, pertinently related to this issue with the theory of emergence, there is a growing suspicion amongst scientists and philosophers that "emergence" is actually just a *description* not an *explanation* of a phenomenon.[66] Rather than addressing the question as to how mind came into existence (and possibly motivating Clayton's alternative proposal), the growing scholarly concern is that "emergence" is just a *re-phrasing* of the issue rather than actually a plausible *solution*—giving additional philosophical predicament to Clayton's emergent monist proposal.

On this theme of emergence theory more widely, it is worth highlighting, in brief, certain issues that have been raised in the philosophy of mind which have led philosophers away from preferring emergentist theories of mind. First, David Barnett has critiqued its central thesis that

63. The terms "weak" and "strong" emergence were first coined by neurologist and philosopher of mind David Chalmers. See Chalmers, *Conscious Mind*.

64. Moreland, "Mental vs Top-Down Causation," 135.

65. Moreland, "Mental vs Top-Down Causation," 135.

66. Clayton himself admits "Much of the suspicion about emergence within the scientific community stems from the sense that emergence is sometimes used as a 'magic pill.' That is, scientists complain that, in certain treatments, emergence seems to represent a strange mystical power within evolution that constantly works to lift the universe to new levels of reality." (Clayton, *Mind and Emergence*, 47).

complexity plus arrangement of parts gives rise to a conscious mind. Using a variety of thought experiments, he counters that in no parallel or *more* complex arrangements does a (philosophically) simple conscious mind come into existence through the complexity and arrangement of parts, so there is no reason to think that this should happen in the instance of the mind-brain relation.[67]

Second, there are further thought experiments that imply that the mind/soul is ontologically distinct, and a separable entity from the brain. For instance, the oft-used duplication arguments that are proffered to demonstrate that the essential "I" is distinct from one's physical brain and body.[68] Relatedly, certain arguments from "conceivability" (when joined with Leibniz' law of non-identity) are put forward to make the case that if it is *possible* to conceive of something that could be true of yourself (Y) but not true of your brain and body (B)—such as waking up to find yourself with the body of a different human or animal[69]—then there is something conceivably true of Y that is not true of B, therefore Y is *not* B and so you are not the same entity as (or inseparable from) your physical brain.

Third, research done into near-death/out of body experiences suggests the ontological distinctness (and unusual separability) of consciousness from the brain/body. Instances of near-death experiences, with

---

67. Barnett (drawing upon Ned Block's analogy of arranging the required number of people in the space of an appropriately large country, e.g., China) proffers the thought experiment of the correct number of people standing in the right relation to one another, with the right nature, and in the correct structural formation—all with the appropriately advanced radios—to emulate the configuration and interaction of the parts of a brain. Even with exactly the number, structure, nature, and relations—and so exact configuration to emulate the brain—one would not expect those billions of people to then give rise to some overall conscious Subject, so there is no reason to expect it with the normal human brain. Even more complex than the human brain is the configuration of the universe, yet it does not give rise to consciousness, so why think that something less complex, namely the human brain, would give rise to such a phenomenon? (Barnett, "You Are Simple," 161–74 [cf. Block, "Troubles with Functionalism," 268–305]). (Even if one were to seek to counter Barnett and Block's critique taking the route of panpsychism [the idea that the whole of the universe is proto-conscious, so given the right conditions, conscious minds of certain animals and humans are given rise to by this proto-conscious universe], this would not solve the issue for the emergentist of why *one* conscious mind arises through the configuration of the brain as opposed to many conscious minds (as per the universe [on the panpsychist view]) (and the panpsychist view suffers the fundamental issue in the first place as to how to explain this supposed "fifth" dimension of the universe—that of "proto-consciousness" (to add this supposed fifth dimension to the accepted four dimensions of physics).

68. See Swinburne's use of such an argument, expounded in chapter 5 of this book.

69. For instance, Kafka's *Metamorphosis*.

medical evidence provided (that which demonstrates that the patient's brain was "flat-lined" [according to the EEG] during the time she was having a *conscious* experience), indicate that the brain is not the bearer of consciousness or the "experiencer"/"Subject" of consciousness; these experiences suggest that some other—distinct and separable—entity must be the bearer of consciousness instead.[70]

Fourth, people yielding just one layer of cortex—such as people born with Dandy Walker syndrome—clearly display self-conscious minds.[71] Contra the emergentist theory (that consciousness is given rise to by an intricate and complex arrangement of the layer upon layer of carefully interwoven cortex), this suggests that the mind exists *regardless* of this complex configuration of the brain.

All of these critiques from the philosophy of mind bring difficulty for emergence theories of mind in general, adding to the difficulties for Clayton's *specifically*. As such they add to a cumulative case that is mounting *against* the viability of Yong and Kärkkäinen's attempting to build upon Clayton's emergent monist model. But further to these significant

---

70. The topic of near-death experiences [NDEs] is an area of research that is gladly affirmed (in its validity) in the writings of Amos Yong (cf. *Spirit of Creation*, 196–207). The findings of NDEs—experiences that have occurred throughout history and across the world—display a large quantity of stories that share a core of similar details. (Examples of the core common details include: the Subject speaking of experiencing a "light" during her NDE, travelling up some kind of tunnel, speaking with heavenly persons, feeling at deep peace in the experience, feeling reluctance to return to her body—such details being both core and common, regardless of the culture in which the Subject lived or at what time in history the NDE occurred). Of particular philosophical interest are the (recent) near-death accounts (indicated in the main text above) in which the Subject is able to recount events that occurred whilst she was in a comatose state—particularly the very recent accounts in which intense medical monitoring has been active throughout the whole of the episode, able to verify that the patient's cortex was entirely shut down during the entire of the (conscious) episode. Accounts in which patients describe rising up out of and looking down on their comatose bodies—in the context of the hospital ward—and are further able to recount verifiable details during the experience (such as where certain surgical instruments were placed in the ward, discussions doctors/relatives had *outside* the ward, or even events occurring further afield during that time) give empirically testable claims. Where validated, such accounts then give further argument for thinking that an essential person/bearer of consciousness is ontologically distinct and separable from her brain.

71. These findings suggest that, contrary to the emergence view (that would say that consciousness is given rise to by an intricate and complex arrangement of the neurons—in the layer upon layer of carefully interwoven cortex in the brain), that the existence of mind appears regardless of the complexity and arrangement of the brain, and indeed its existence is not dependent upon intricate and complex configuration of the brain.

problems, the issue of identity persistence—from the time of a person's (physical) death through to the time of her resurrection—is also problematic for Yong and Kärkkäinen in their seeking to build their models on the viewpoint of emergent monism.

Personal Identity Persistence between an Individual's Death and Resurrection

Both Yong and Kärkkäinen are attracted to emergentism because it emphasizes the embodied nature of a person—affirming the scriptural teaching concerning the resurrection body at the eschaton.[72] Yet, their emergent monist idea—like emergent monism in general—suffers the same difficulty as was seen in the critique of the thinking of Green: it provides no philosophical grounds for maintaining personal identity persistence from the point of a person's physical death through until the time of her resurrection. Both Yong and Kärkkäinen are aware of this issue and seek to escape the philosophical problem by appeal to a suggestion made by scientist-theologian John Polkinghorne; Polkinghorne suggests that each person has a complex information-bearing pattern—or blueprint given by God—which God then uses to re-exemplify the person at the time of the resurrection.[73] But as indicated in the discussion above (when considering Green's thought on the issue), this is not a sufficient response because what God would be doing in such an instance would be a work of *re-creation/replication* (as opposed to resurrection). As Yong himself acknowledges (in his citation of Gordon Fee):

> . . . for Paul, resurrection is neither resuscitation (which preserves continuity) *nor re-creation (which severs identity)*; rather, since "flesh and blood cannot inherit the kingdom of God" (1Cor 15:50), Paul teaches a resurrection of the body that preserves but also transforms *personal identity*.[74]

---

72. Yong, *Theology and Down Syndrome*, 171. Of course, giving an eschatological emphasis to his view.

73. Cf. Yong, *Theology and Down Syndrome*, 279 and Kärkkäinen "Creation and Humanity," 348–49 citing Polkinghorne, *Sciences and the Trinity*, 161.

74. Yong, *Theology and Down Syndrome*, 273 citing Fee, *Corinthians*, 776–77 (emphasis mine). Although this is moving into theological territory (having been assessed in an earlier section), it is particularly the aspect of *identity persistence over time* that is being considered here, so remaining in the area of philosophical assessment.

In fact, unless a person has/*is* a spiritual soul—a soul that survives her death and persists until her resurrection—there are no grounds for affirming that that person at the resurrection is identically the same person as herself prior to death.[75] As was seen in the critique of Green, views that do not espouse a spiritual entity—some kernel of the person's being—have no grounds for saying that the person alive at the eschaton is *identical* to the person prior to death, because nothing ontologically survives the death of the person. To repeat what was argued above, this means that the person at the resurrection can only be a *replica* of herself, a replica of the "I" that she was prior to death.[76] So (being an unfortunate philosophical complement to their difficulty with the intermediate state) Yong and Kärkkäinen's model is deficient in the philosophical issue of identity persistence over time, adding a further philosophical problem to their emergent monist proposal.[77]

In sum, there are a number of philosophical problems with Yong and Kärkkäinen's preferred emergent monism. The model they are drawn to from Clayton has idiosyncratic problems, the emergence theories of minds more widely (but of which Clayton's is an example) have been critiqued on a number of grounds, and the issue of identity persistence (from a person's death to the resurrection) brings further philosophical issue. As such, their emergent monism appears unpersuasive philosophically.

Summary

The purpose of this chapter has been to consider the two contentions of Yong and Kärkkäinen that were expounded in the previous chapter, namely, that dualism (of any kind) needs to be rejected due to the

---

75. Polkinghorne's suggestion that God remembers the blueprint/pattern of the human appears an ad hoc attempt to maintain belief in an individual's identity persistence through to the time of resurrection.

76. Remembering that "One thing cannot have two beginnings" (Locke, *Essay II*, xxvii, 1).

77. Yong shows a level of awareness of some of these problems but rather than describing these issues as "problems," he prefers to describe them as "questions for further inquiry" or areas where "much more work needs to be done" (cf. "Christian and Buddhist Perspectives," 160; and *Theology and Down Syndrome*, 287n21 respectively). Yong's sympathetic categorization might be granted were there just one or two issues to be accounted for but given the range of difficulties with his emergent monist position, to categorize them in the way that he does appears (unusually for Yong) to be an instance of special pleading as opposed to a legitimate categorization of these problems for his position.

theological and philosophical challenges it faces, and second, that emergent monism is preferable as an alternative constitutional model.

As regards their theological and philosophical challenges to dualistic views of constitution, the challenges Yong and Kärkkäinen offer are certainly valid refutations of Platonist and Classic Cartesian dualisms; however, they bring little by way of challenge to a holistic, psychosomatic variety of dualism. Platonist and Classic Cartesian dualisms are so predominant in the minds of Yong and Kärkkäinen that it appears they equate the idea of "dualism" with essentially these two types of dualism—seeing "dualism" as synonymous with these two (problematic) kinds. Given that these two dubious views are so defining in Yong and Kärkkäinen's anthropology (and indeed in the anthropology of Green, Murphy, Clayton, and others[78]), these dualisms require particular attention before the book can progress to its subsequent constructive chapters. As such, the Platonist and Classic Cartesian dualist viewpoints will be in receipt of their own required excursus, following the close of this chapter, to elucidate these views more fully and highlight why it is that they are problematic; it will also make clear that what follows, in the constructive parts of this book, is *not* a model endorsing of either of these strawmen dualistic positions.

As regards their second contention, Yong and Kärkkäinen's emergent monist proposal is one that is not especially concordant with the quadrant of Pentecostal theological emphases; whilst being agreeable with emphases 1 and 3, it shows inconsistency with emphases 2 and 4, meaning that the model sits less concordantly with the Pentecostal quadrant as a whole. Moreover, when investigated philosophically, and examined for conceptual rigor, Yong and Kärkkäinen's emergent monism shows to have considerable philosophical problems. These include the difficulties it encounters when scrutinized by the philosophy of mind, and its difficulties with the issue of identity persistence over time, problems which render their preferred emergent monism as philosophically unpersuasive.

For this variety of reasons, it has been seen that neither of their two key contentions, concerning human constitution, are intellectually persuasive. The three dialogue-partners that lie behind Yong and Kärkkäinen's work on human constitution appear to have done much to lead them both in a less helpful anthropological direction, with the corollary

---

78. Cf. the theological anthropology of N. T. Wright and M. B. Thompson, responded to in Churchouse, "Healthier Anthropology."

of this being that both Yong and Kärkkäinen themselves have articulated an anthropology that itself has the potential to lead other Pentecostals (and non-Pentecostals) down a similar monistic path. As such, having focussed—in this part of the book—on critically assessing the anthropology of Yong and Kärkkäinen, the book will proceed more constructively to developing an enhanced Pentecostal model of constitution, one that is theologically and philosophically preferable to that put forward by Yong and Kärkkäinen, and one bringing renewed direction for the Pentecostal trajectory of thought on the topic. But before proceeding to this constructive work on the topic, the book will give the requisite excursus to delineate the problematic Platonist and Classic Cartesian dualisms that have been so influential in the discussion (so far). It will become explicit, in so doing, that the constructive work to follow espouses neither of these problematic dualistic views.

Excursus

Excursus

Platonist and Classic Cartesian Dualisms

HAVING ASSESSED THE WRITINGS of Yong and Kärkkäinen, it has been seen that they disavow dualistic anthropology because they equate anthropological "dualism" with Platonist or Classic Cartesian dualism.[1] So it would be helpful to pause at this point to articulate these two problematic dualisms in order to identify the difficulties contained therein and reveal why it is that these dualistic positions bring forth the evident displeasure of Yong and Kärkkäinen (and indeed of their wider colleagues). Moreover, in identifying and critiquing these viewpoints and exposing their drawbacks and pitfalls, this will help the project to advance *beyond* these problematic positions, clearing the way for the constructive work to follow—that of proposing a more nuanced, *enhanced* model of constitution—in parts III and IV of the book.

It will become evident, in delineating these views, that the earlier *Platonist* dualism—whilst still holding a level of influence in certain theological arenas—does not carry as much potential for affecting the present discussion as Classic Cartesian dualism. As the exposition below will reveal, and once explicated for what it espouses, Platonist dualism shows itself to be evidently incompatible with Christian theology. So, whilst

---

1. This disavowal is similarly prominent in the literature of biblical studies where both Platonist and Classic Cartesian dualisms are regularly and continually critiqued. Because of the disdain for these two dualistic viewpoints within that discipline too, it is easy for biblical scholars to fall into the same mistaken equation as articulated in the main text above. Cf. Churchouse, "Healthier Anthropology."

succinctly summarizing this dualism to draw out this incompatibility, it is not given so much space in this excursus as Classic Cartesian dualism. Indeed, a lengthier overview of Classic Cartesian dualism is requisite in light of what is to come in the following chapters to distinguish this second problematic dualism from those forthcoming anthropological models (those contemporary models of dualism that are more nuanced in nature). So, this excursus will briefly outline and critique Platonist dualism, then more fully articulate and critique Classic Cartesian dualism, to identify these two problematic dualisms; this will allow the moving beyond both these positions—in the constructive chapters to follow—to advance an enhanced view of dualism through a preferable view of the spiritual soul.[2]

Platonist Dualism

In Plato's anthropology, a human is a material being with an immaterial soul, but the soul (in his understanding) denotes the person's *principle of life* (having no theological connotations). In distinction from the souls of other living beings, a human soul, for Plato, has rational capacity—able to understand the realm of the immaterial "Forms."[3] In fact, Plato thinks that a human already knows these Forms even before having been taught them (a teacher's role being simply to guide the student to *understand* these already known Forms); he deduces from this that these Forms must have been previously known to that person before she was born.[4] As a result of this deduction, he concludes that a human soul itself must have pre-existed and therefore, in fact, *be one of* the eternal Forms.[5]

---

2. Because both Plato and Descartes employed the terms "immaterial" and "material" as an opposite pairing, in articulation of their viewpoints, their language will be retained in this excursus until the closing paragraph when the term "spiritual" (in the philosophical sense) will be returned to (with the preferred correlative term being "physical").

3. In Plato's metaphysics, this realm of the immaterial "Forms" is a non-material abstract world of universals—a realm of eternal, bodiless, and changeless objects that cannot be known empirically but only known through intellect/reason (this being in contrast to the *material* realm—the world of "particulars"—which, with its entities made up of [destructible] parts, is a realm that can be understood by the use of the empirical senses). Plato, *Phaedo*, 78b–80b.

4. Plato, *Meno*, 82b–86b.

5. Plato, *Phaedo*, 81c–d.

Articulating his view of the soul more fully, Plato viewed the human soul as tripartite; he termed the top part of the soul the *logistikon* (referring to the reasoning part of the soul), the bottom part the *epithumetikon* (the part that is responsible for the person's bodily desires), and the middle part the *thumoedies* (referring to the "spirit" part of the person).[6] In Plato's tripartite view of the soul, the *logistikon* is always trying to control the *thumoedies* and *epithumetikon*.[7] For Plato, a human requires all three, but the reasoning part must dominate in order for well-being to result. Although all three are parts of the soul,[8] really the "soul" of this soul is the *logistikon*—the "rational" core of the soul; and whilst embodied in a material body, this *logistikon* is being held back from its pursuit of attaining truth—Plato's view being famous for describing the soul as imprisoned in the body.[9] So, the reasonable soul, on this view, is seeking freedom from the confines of the body, so that it might return to the realm of the Forms. But being an *eternal* Form, it will be subsequently re-incarnated in another earthly body, being continually re-incarnated until it has led a suitably philosophic life, at which point it is able to fully jettison *thumoeides* and *epithumentikon* and never return to earth—remaining with the Forms forever.[10]

Although the mature Plato moved beyond this position, what has been detailed above is the view entailed in the legacy of Platonism. From this exposition it should be clear that such a view is acutely inconsistent with Christian theology and doctrine, suffering from the following variety of problems.

First, the Platonist dualist view is very stark in its denigrating of the body—viewing the body as an obstruction for the (eternal) soul, a confining and depraved material body that restrains/has imprisoned the soul. But as such this puts forward an unhelpful dualism between the

---

6. But for Plato, this "spirit" part of the soul represents the *passions* (such as anger, shame, ambition)—the term having no theological referent.

7. Plato using the example that when a man sees a beautiful woman, the reasoning part of his soul is filled with wonder at the woman's beauty, whilst the bodily aspect wants to move forward to suggest the pleasures of sex to that woman, whilst, at the same time, the spirit part recognizes the shame that that act would entail (highlighting that, whilst not as dignified as the reasoning part of the soul, the spirit helps [the *logistikon*] keep the bodily desires in check (Plato, *Phaedrus*, 253d–257b).

8. The "soul," to this point in the excursus, having been used in a contemporary sense of the word to refer to the bearer's inner mental life.

9. Plato, *Phaedo*, 82a–e.

10. Plato, *Phaedo*, 80d–82c.

immaterial human soul (an entity which is regarded as good) and the material human body (an entity that is regarded as bad)—a view incompatible with Scripture's affirmation of the physical/material world. In contrast to the Platonist worldview, the Christian doctrines of creation, incarnation, and (re)new(ed) creation very much affirm the physical/material world as a reality that is (also) good, so this bifurcation of the ("good") immaterial realm and the ("bad") material realm is an unhelpful dualistic outlook and in discord with Christian theology.

Second, the Platonist model discloses as problematic in its regarding the soul as *eternal*—that is, uncreated in nature, and continuing to exist forever—when the only eternal being (according to the teaching of Scripture) is the uncreated Creator; only *God* himself is eternal.

Third, the Platonist dualistic model is deficient in that it regards the soul as an entity that will be re-incarnated again and again until reaching its final "eschaton"—that of remaining forever with the eternal Forms. This is contrary to the Christian eschatological hope which espouses the soul's being re-united with a *resurrection* body, living eternally in (re-)embodied form.

Given this range of problems with the Platonist dualist view, it should be very clear that this position is inconsistent with Christian theology and anthropology, and it is obvious why Christian scholars are keen to reject this dualism and view of the soul.

The Classic Cartesian Substance Dualism of René Descartes

As with the instance of the (more mature) Plato, it is questionable as to whether the position that bears the name "Cartesian" is *actually* the position that Descartes, himself, espoused. But like with the exposition of Plato, the below will expound the view that has been traditionally associated with Descartes—what I have decided to term "Classic" Cartesian dualism.[11]

Similarly to Plato, Descartes was a rationalist and his epistemology was primarily based upon the knowledge that the intellect can acquire

---

11. The word "Classic" is used in recognition, not just of its association with Descartes through history but, that there are a variety of *contemporary* Cartesian dualisms espoused and defended today in the philosophy of mind; to group all these together under "Cartesian dualism" would be inadequate and not account for the differences between the Classic and the contemporary views.

without the use of the body.¹² His renowned "I think therefore I am" dictum was a natural outworking of this rationality and from which his key argument arose for his (comparably) renowned substance dualism.¹³ In that argument for substance dualism, Descartes contended that he could undoubtedly conceive of his existence (given that he is the mind who is doing the thinking[14]), however, he could not undoubtedly conceive of the existence of his material body; therefore, he (as the thinking thing) must be a distinct and separate substance to his material body.[15] This argument formed the lynch-pin for his substance dualist view but he later added a second argument for his viewpoint—that of the indivisibility of the mind.[16] In this second argument, he argued that, whilst able to conceive of the body as being divisible into parts,[17] he could not conceive of the mind as being likewise divisible into parts, therefore, the mind has to be a different substance from that of the material body.[18]

---

12. This giving rise to his "First Principles." (By contrast to these rationalist foundational principles, he viewed empirical understanding as a less certain basis of knowledge due to the possibility of the senses being deceived [so regarding empirical knowledge as a *secondary* type of knowledge].)

13. Descartes thought of a substance as a "thing capable of existing independently" (Descartes, Meditation III, *Philosophical Writings*, 1:30).

14. Under the term "thinking," Descartes appears to have included doubting, understanding, affirming, denying, willing, imagining and sensing. See his *Philosophical Writings*, 2:19.

15. And indeed, Descartes thought that he could exist without his body.
Descartes's full quote is: "my essence consists solely in the fact that I am a thinking thing. It is true that I may (or, to anticipate, I certainly have) a body that is very closely joined to me. But nevertheless, on the one hand I have a clear and distinct idea of myself, in so far as I am simply a thinking, non-extended thing; and on the other hand I have a distinct idea of body, in so far as this is simply an extended, non-thinking thing. And accordingly, it is certain that I am really distinct from my body and can exist without it." (Descartes, Meditation VI, *Philosophical Writings*, 2:54).

16. As will be seen, the term "mind" for Descartes became synonymous with the term "soul."

17. For example, if a foot or arm became separated from the rest of the parts of the body.

18. Descartes's full argument is laid out in the following quotation: "there is a great difference between mind and body, inasmuch as body is by nature always divisible, and the mind is entirely indivisible. For, as a matter of fact, when I consider the mind, that is to say, myself inasmuch as I am only a thinking thing, I cannot distinguish in myself any parts, but apprehend myself to be clearly one and entire; and although the whole mind seems to be united to the whole body, yet if a foot, or an arm, or some other part, is separated from my body, I am aware that nothing has been taken away from my mind. And the faculties of willing, feeling, conceiving, etc., cannot be properly speaking said to be its parts, for it is one and the same mind which employs itself in willing and in

By contrast to the Aristotelian-Thomistic tradition, Descartes rejected the idea that a person is a (rational) soul-body entity—in which the *whole* of that soul-body entity is the being that is doing the thinking. Instead, he developed a contrary position; he espoused that thought occurs *specifically* in the thinking substance—namely, in the mind[19]—a substance that is immaterial by nature (by contrast to the body which is material).[20] Although Descartes was of the view that interaction occurs between the immaterial soul and the material body, and that the soul uses the body for memory, sense-perception, and imagination, for Descartes, the latter were *secondary* modes of thought, providing a less pure form of knowledge (as per his rationalist principles).[21] As such, he equated the soul *with the mind*, and in so doing he narrowed the soul from the Aristotelian-Thomistic view (which regards an organism's soul as its principle of life[22]) to simply viewing the soul as a thinking thing.[23]

---

feeling, and understanding. But it is quite otherwise with corporeal or extended objects, for there is not one of these imaginable by me which consequently I do not recognise as being divisible; this would be sufficient to teach me that the mind or soul of man is entirely different from the body, if I had not already learned it from other sources" (Descartes, *Meditations on First Philosophy*, 97).

19. In differentiation to Aristotle and Aquinas who contended that the ensouled body is the substance, Descartes thought that the immaterial mind (the thinking thing) is the substance—distinct from the body. Descartes's thinking was a major influence in changing the metaphysical landscape—contributing significantly to the intellectual shift from the preference for hylomorphic metaphysics to the favoring of a corpuscularian metaphysics in the modern-day period.

20. Descartes understood "immaterial" substances to be those that are non-spatial and unextended; whereas "material" substances he understood as those that *are* spatially extended (extended in length, breadth, and depth). Note, for Descartes, matter and space are not separable—there is no space that is not filled with matter, which means that for him "spatial" extension = constituted by extended matter.

21. As earlier indicated, for Descartes, imagination, memory, and sensation were secondary modes of the mind but with a special dependence on the body. But subsequent (early) moderns did not maintain Descartes's distinction of pure and secondary mental states (Rozemond, "Descartes' Dualism," 388).

22. So giving its organism functions of growth, nutrition, motion etc.

23. His fuller thinking in this area is encapsulated in Descartes, *Philosophical Writings*, 2:246 where he comments "the first men did not perhaps distinguish between, on one hand, that principle in us by which we are nourished, grow, and perform without any thought all the other functions we have in common with the brutes and on the other hand, that principle by which we think. They applied to both the single term "soul." Then, noticing that thought is different from nutrition, they called that which thinks "mind," and believed that it is the principal part of the soul. I, however, noticing that the principle by which we are nourished is entirely different from the principle by which we think, have said that the term "soul" is ambiguous when it is used for both.

Although Descartes broadened the views of his predecessors to regard this "thinking thing" as an entity that doubts, understands, affirms, denies, wills, imagines, and senses,[24] he discarded the previous opinions (drawn from the Aristotelian-Thomistic tradition) with their emphasis on teleology and function,[25] and the soul became specifically the mind—the "thinking" thing (/the "Subject"[26]).

Descartes thought that the point of *interaction* between the immaterial soul and material body was the human *pineal gland*—a tiny organ in the center of the brain.[27] He thought that this gland played an important role in the causation of bodily movement and was involved in imagination, memory, and sense perception (the secondary "modes" of the mind). In elaboration of this idea, he suggested that, leading up to the pineal gland there were arteries full of "animal spirits"—(something akin to) a "fine wind" or "air"—that brought physical sensations to this central gland; these "animal spirits" informed the soul/mind, and were reciprocally the means of the soul's carrying out its will in the body.[28]

Whilst evaluation of this view will follow, it is worth mentioning, at this point, a particularly noteworthy facet of this distinctive position of Descartes—concerning the nature of humans and animals (after which evaluation will proceed). Regarding the soul as a thinking substance (of a rational [first-person] nature), Descartes concluded that the soul must be unique to human beings. Further departing from the views of his intellectual forebears, he concluded that animals do not have souls, viewing them merely and simply as automata (espousing that [whilst reacting to external stimuli] animals do not have sensations or thoughts). He further advanced his distinction, of the uniqueness of humans from animals, through reflection on the human capacity to develop and communicate

---

And in order to understand it as the first act or principal form of man, it must only be understood as the principle by which we think. To this I have as much as possible applied the term "mind," in order to avoid ambiguity. For I do not regard the mind as a part of the soul. But as the whole soul which thinks."

24. See earlier footnote and Descartes, *Philosophical Writings*, 2:19.

25. One of Descartes's "fatherly insights" he bequeathed to modern philosophical thought that followed him was the jettisoning entirely of teleological cause.

26. Subject being capitalized to denote its referring to a being with first-person experience.

27. Descartes reasoned that, having two eyes and ears, but only seeing/hearing one thing, this central gland must be the place where the soul and body interact.

28. Note, for Descartes, the mind is "an intellectual substance" (Descartes, Meditation VI, *Philosophical Writings*, 2:54) so although it *has* a will, the intellect is more basic to the mind because the will depends on it.

in *language*; he contended that the capacity for humans to communicate in language, flowing from their distinctive rational capacity, further differentiated them from (non-linguistic) animals.[29] For Descartes, therefore, the human realm was markedly distinct from the animal realm—the former being unique in their possession of an immaterial mind/soul.

In short, Descartes's substance dualist position was distinctive and has had vast effects on the subsequent centuries of philosophy and theology. More widely, his method has had the effect of contributing to the elimination of human teleology within philosophy and academia as a whole. More specifically, he has re-framed the previously debated *soul*-body question and bequeathed it to subsequent generations of thinkers as the *mind*-body question; and within that re-framed *mind*-body debate, he has handed down the "substance dualist" paradigm, his idiosyncratic version being the most renowned view of that particular title and what has commonly been inherited (/"heard") by generations of thinkers who have followed.

Not surprisingly, this Classic Cartesian dualism has received substantial attention and critique. Most of that has focussed on his key argument for substance dualism, and on the issue of interaction between soul and body.[30]

Regarding the former matter, concerning his key argument for substance dualism, it has regularly been pointed out that this argument is an argument from ignorance. Whilst Descartes could undoubtedly conceive of him*self* as existing, whereas he could not undoubtedly conceive of his body existing—hence bringing about his conclusion that (as the thing that is doing the thinking) he is a distinct and separate entity to that of his material body—it is important to hear the objection of Antoine Arnauld in response. Arnauld (a contemporary of Descartes) countered that it is possible that the rational mind and the material body are actually one

---

29. This pre-empting the (more fully-fledged) Chomskian language argument which states that a machine could be programmed to utter words, but only a soul could form concepts and put them into meaningful language. See Chomsky, *Language and Mind*.

30. Whilst these two strands are commonly how Descartes's position is attacked, an interesting (though not commonly cited) *theological* critique was additionally posed by Louis de la Forge—a contemporary of Descartes—who contended that if the soul is pure intellect and not able by itself to sense or imagine, then in the intermediate state, it would be without any particularity; its knowledge derived from sensations would fade, and the soul would just be left with merely abstract ideas—such as those of maths—to contemplate (cited in Cottingham, "Cartesian Dualism," 241).

and *the same* entity, and that the thinker is just simply ignorant of that fact.³¹ If this is the case, then, (as helpfully drawn out by Hatfield):

> [the thinking/rational Subject] could doubt the existence of body (including his own body) while affirming his existence as mind alone, simply through ignorance of his real identity.³²

This critique was one that Descartes came to recognize—apparently feeling the force of the objection. Due to his recognition of the strength of the counter, whilst still retaining his argument's conclusion, he gradually backed away from this argument—which had been key for his view of the mind and his substance dualist position.

The question of interaction was another significant thorn for Descartes's substance dualism. In letters from Princess Elizabeth (dated the May 16, June 20, and July 1) in the year 1643 (and with replies, from Descartes, in between, that she considered as not very cogent responses), she re-posed the question to Descartes as to how an *immaterial* substance (i.e., a soul) could interact with a *material* substance (i.e., a body). This question has been posed to (substance) dualists ever since Princess Elizabeth originally penned the objection.³³ But in addition to this pertinent issue (and as an objection that has grown very prominent), the greatest objection to Descartes's view was arguably the *scientific* issues entailed in his mechanism of interaction. Once the function of the pineal gland had been empirically demonstrated,³⁴ Descartes's idea of "animal spirits" was exposed as scientifically inept. Cottingham helpfully captures the landslide that followed this scientific critique:

> Once Descartes had taken the vital step of assigning so many of the traditional functions of the "soul" to the minute physical mechanisms of the nervous system, it was only a matter of time before Western science would go all the way and make even the residual *ame raisonable* redundant.³⁵

---

31. See Hatfield, *Descartes and the Meditations*, 246.
32. Hatfield, *Descartes and the Meditations*, 246.
33. So being addressed in the relevant section of chapter 3 of this book.
34. It has been shown to be an endocrine organ which secretes (the hormone) melatonin (an organ supplied by *veins* not arteries [contra Descartes's theory]).
35. Cottingham, "Cartesian Dualism," 252. Feeling the implications of these problems, even those sympathetic to Descartes's work sought to follow his substance dualist position but from a distance; for instance Malebranche rejected Descartes's idea that there was causal interaction between mind and body and opted instead for parallelism (parallelism contending that the mental world and physical world do not interact, they

So, whilst the substance dualism of Descartes has had major impact on the history of western academia, these two identified problems undermine the credibility of Descartes's position, meaning his distinctive dualistic model has never been hugely in favor (either at its origin or in subsequent years). Yet, as has previously been highlighted, his view is frequently "heard" when the position of "substance dualism" is considered by modern-day scholars—or indeed, the viewpoint that scholars envisage when they conceive of a soul that is ontologically distinct from the body.[36]

Whilst substance dualism cannot be merely reduced to the Classic Cartesian variety, these critiques of Descartes's position reveal that he unhelpfully divides the functions of the human body and soul instead of viewing them as functional unity. Contra the *biblical* viewpoint, which (as was highlighted by Yong and Kärkkäinen) entails an anthropological functional holism, Descartes *separates* many of the functions of the soul from those of the body, so, as the Classic Cartesian view stands, it would be an inadequate dualistic model for articulating a biblical and Pentecostal anthropology.

Having made these critiques above, it should be acknowledged that the *foundations* of Descartes's position have facilitated a number of fresh dualistic models—models that have learned from his substance dualism but been refined in the contemporary period in light of the findings of modern-day science and the nuances of philosophy of mind. By contrast to the model of Descartes, these models affirm and value the unity of body and soul, giving potential for then bringing forth a better conception of the human soul, in turn, providing the means of constructing an enhanced anthropological doctrine. Therefore, as the book advances its project, it will do so by shedding the problematic dualisms, and their views of the spiritual soul—the Platonist and Classic Cartesian understandings being relinquished from this point in the book. But it will discard these problematic dualisms in a way more nuanced in manner (to that which was previously observed in the writings of Yong and Kärkkäinen). That is, whilst jettisoning Platonist dualism entirely, and whilst recognizing the problems of the *Classic* Cartesian model, the relevant *contemporary*

---

have just been designed to run parallel to one another, so when a mind thinks and acts, in the material world the "effect" occurs, though there is no interaction between the two.) Leibniz and Berkeley, on the other hand, rejected Descartes's basic mind assumptions even though they retained his view of substance dualism.

36. See Churchouse, "Healthier Anthropology," 26–27.

substance dualisms—those that have drawn from their previous forebear but honed and improved their models, in light of modern-day science and philosophy—will be heeded in following chapters as the book progresses, now, to construct an enhanced Pentecostal doctrine of human constitution.

Part III

Towards an Enhanced Pentecostal Philosophical-Theological Model of Human Constitution

4

Biblical Holistic Dualism in Light of a Pentecostal Spirit-Filled World

IN PARTS I AND II of the book, Pentecostal understanding(s) of human constitution in western Pentecostal theological history were considered, and the Pentecostal trajectory of thought on the issue illumined. After considering Pentecostal thought on this doctrine from the beginnings of the twentieth century through to the beginnings of the twenty-first, the constitutional anthropology of Yong and Kärkkäinen was examined—standing at the present and current-day "end" of the trajectory with potential for shaping its future. Certain areas of these two thinkers' work were seen to be helpful concerning the doctrine of constitution—namely their desire (in accord with the tradition) to ground their theology in the final authority of Scripture and indeed having a place for the (human) spirit in their understanding of constitution. Likewise, their affirmation of the human body and the *holistic* nature of the human was seen to be beneficial—being helpful reminders of the themes that are of importance to Pentecostals. But in addressing their two key contentions—that dualism (of any variety) is theologically and philosophically flawed, and their proposing of emergent monism as a better model instead—it was seen that these two contentions were problematic and, in fact, fallacious. The first contention is only helpful in regard to *problematic* dualistic models (i.e., Platonist or Classic Cartesian dualisms) but not applicable to stronger dualistic models, and their emergent monist proposal is not particularly concordant with two of the four Pentecostal theological emphases, nor is it a model that is philosophically persuasive.

In wanting to proceed, then, to construct an enhanced Pentecostal philosophical-theological model of human constitution, these insights and critiques will be heeded and indeed learned from in the following constructive parts of the work. But in wanting to shape this project further in a Pentecostal-theological manner, this chapter will begin with the Pentecostal pneumatology of J. K. A. Smith—specifically his Pentecostal pneumatological ontology—to provide a Pentecostal start-point and worldview from and within which to develop this enhanced Pentecostal doctrine.[1]

Smith is a well-suited dialogue-partner for stimulating this Pentecostal start-point and (spirit-filled) worldview due to the considerable attention he has devoted to Pentecostal spirituality and pneumatology. Within his philosophical work on these topics (especially in his book *Thinking in Tongues*), he has helpfully articulated an ontology that is particularly clear and expositive of the physical-spiritual world that Pentecostals inhabit and believe in.[2] This "spirit-enchanted" ontology arises out of the second of the elements he has identified which comprise the *Pentecostal* "social imaginary" (or Pentecostal "worldview")—the social imaginary that is inherent within Pentecostal spirituality. Given that this social imaginary is so integral to Pentecostal spirituality (and

---

1. As was seen in the introduction, and will be further seen in Smith's exposition, Pentecostals' distinctive pneumatology—and indeed pneumatological ontology within that—arises out of their spirituality. As such, "the pneumatology of Pentecostal spirituality" would be an accurate fuller locution for what is more concisely phrased, above, as "Pentecostal pneumatology," but for succinctness and smoothness of phrasing, the diction "Pentecostal pneumatology" is employed—both here and in the following chapters—as a shorthand for the fuller description.

2. Smith is a continental philosopher teaching in a Reformed theological university (Calvin University). But having wide interests, Smith has also contributed to the *Journal of Pentecostal Theology*, as well as written other significant theological texts demonstrating his ability to straddle not just theology and philosophy but also the Reformed and Pentecostal traditions. The text of preference to be drawn on for this chapter is his Pentecostal Manifesto *Thinking in Tongues*. He and Yong are the thinkers to have gone furthest in attempting to articulate Pentecostal spirituality from a philosophical as well as theological perspective. Whilst both employ their own individual terminology, there is much in common in their work, and Smith, like Yong, is regarded as a lead philosopher and theologian by the Pentecostal academy. In this instance, Smith has been chosen as the preferable of the two thinkers due to his (arguably) clearer salvation-historical theology worked out in his Spirit ontology—the ontology and theology to be exposited in the main text (to follow).

hence to Pentecostal theology), it will briefly be outlined as a whole to provide illumination for the following project (of building an enhanced Pentecostal doctrine of constitution)—the constructive work that will develop throughout parts III and IV of this book. Having overviewed Smith's social imaginary, the rest of this (first) half of the chapter will then turn specifically to the second of the elements—namely the "spirit-enchantment of the world"—to focus on the engaging ontology derived by Smith from this second of the imaginary's elements. Once this ontology is made explicit it will provide a clear and definite steer—to be aided by the insights established from parts I and II of the book—as to which exegetical thinker(s) would be appropriate for the project as it continues in developing an enhanced Pentecostal model of human constitution.

J. K. A. Smith's Pentecostal Social Imaginary

Explicating how the Pentecostal social imaginary/worldview arises, Smith begins with the assumption—shared by the consensus of Pentecostal scholars—that Pentecostalism is a renewal *spirituality* (as opposed to a set of doctrines).[3] As was highlighted in this book's introduction, this Pentecostal spirituality emphasizes participants' on-going (transformative) encounter(s) with God through the Holy Spirit of Christ, being open to experiencing God's Spirit in (more) unexpected, spontaneous, and dynamic ways, as well as those (more) formal, expected, and calm.[4] However, in further elaboration, Smith identifies Pentecostal spirituality more fully as a set of worship practices which "carry" the Pentecostal worldview or "social imaginary" within them. He argues that through participating in Pentecostal worship practices, a believer imbibes this "imaginary"/worldview[5]—it becoming her presuppositions or pre-theoretical set of assumptions through which she then sees and experiences the world. Smith argues that this worldview has five elements to it:

---

3. Smith, *Thinking in Tongues*, 26–27.

4. See further the sections "Defining Pentecostalism" and "Scholarly Pentecostal theology" in the book's introduction.

5. Whilst acknowledging Smith's terminology of the "Pentecostal social imaginary," as personal preference the language of the "Pentecostal worldview" seems slightly clearer, so that terminology will be employed from this point on. (Others, such as Yong, prefer to speak of the "pneumatological imagination" to convey the same idea) (cf. Yong, *Spirit-Word-Community*.)

1. "A radical openness to God,"[6] (from which all the other elements follow)
2. An "enchanted" theology of creation and culture,
3. An affective narrative epistemology,
4. A non (Platonist) dualistic affirmation of embodiment and materiality,[7]
5. An eschatological orientation towards mission and justice.

These are all aspects of the worldview that Pentecostals imbibe from participating in Pentecostal worship practices;[8] but it is specifically the second element—an "enchanted" theology of creation and culture—that is key to this chapter, so will be specifically expounded and engaged with in this opening half of the chapter.

Expounding this element more fully, Smith is of the view that Pentecostals assume:

> An **"enchanted" theology of creation and culture** that perceives the material creation as "charged" with the presence of the Spirit, but also with other spirits (including demons and "principalities and powers"), with entailed expectations regarding miracles and spiritual warfare.[9]

From such a definition, Smith elaborates an insightful Pentecostal ontology—an "Enspirited Creation" ontology—within which he gives particular attention to the person of the *Holy Spirit* and his relation to the created world.[10] This will be further expounded in the exposition that is to follow, however, it is worthy of note in *Smith's* elucidation, that there is little to no attention given to the "other spirits" Smith mentions in his statement above. Such an account would have been helpful given

---

6. Having had a renewing encounter with the Holy Spirit, further encounters are expected.

7. That is, a dualism (unlike that of Plato) which does not oppose the spiritual and physical worlds (as if the spiritual world were good, the physical world, bad).
In a footnote on page 42 Smith clarifies where he stands regarding (anthropological) "dualism," stating: "Pentecostal spirituality remains dualistic . . . insofar as it maintains an ontological distinction between spirit and matter and affirms the existence of immaterial entities." (Smith, *Thinking in Tongues*, 42n69).

8. Smith, *Thinking in Tongues*, 31–47.

9. Smith, *Thinking in Tongues*, 12 (emphasis his).

10. Further contained in this ontology, he gives a helpful articulation of science and miracles also.

the implications it has for anthropology but, being unfortunately absent from his exposition, it requires some additional thought on the issue and further "filling out" of his second element. So, after articulating Smith's (*Holy*) Spirit-ontology, the chapter will further fill out this element of Smith's Pentecostal worldview with an exposition of angels, given that the physical world (on Smith's thinking) is one enspirited by spirit*s* (plural) not just by the (singular) Holy Spirit.

Smith's Pentecostal Ontology

Using his original language of "enchantment" (which he contentedly uses synonymously with the term "enspirited") Smith asserts that an enchanted creation—and hence enspirited ontology—is central to Pentecostal spirituality. He states:

> Endemic to a Pentecostal worldview is the implicit affirmation of the dynamic, active presence of the Spirit not only in the church, but also in creation. And not only the Spirit, but also other spirits. Thus, central to a Pentecostal construal of the world is a sense of "enchantment."[11]

Smith rejects the standard bifurcation of the natural and supernatural world—viewing this unhelpful division as an overhang from the Enlightenment. The idea of an independent universe, which follows its own autonomous laws and regularity—into which God sometimes intervenes "supernaturally" (to do works such as miracles and giving of revelation)—Smith regards as, at best, a *deistic* view of the cosmos. Dismissing this bifurcation, Smith advocates a differing view of the world and its relation to God. His view of the God-world relation emphasizes the Holy Spirit's *immanence* to and within the created order,[12] describing the world (and culture within it) as:

---

11. Smith, *Thinking in Tongues,* 39. Or see also his comment "This sense that all of creation—nature and culture—is charged with the presence of the Spirit is implicit in the prayers and practices of Pentecostal spirituality." (40–41).

12. This use of "to" and "within" might draw attention—raising the question of Pentecostals' doctrine of God (in relation to creation). I address this question, and whether Pentecostal theology is panentheistic in Churchouse, "How Could (Some) Pentecostal Theology Be Analytic Theology?"

> . . . suspended in and inhabited by the Spirit such that it is always already *primed* for the Spirit's manifestations [such as miracles].[13]

Smith's progression towards such an ontology shows influence from Radical Orthodoxy—a theology with which he identifies (and has adapted into his own Reformed mould).[14] Smith's (Reformed) version of this theology likewise espouses a *participatory* ontology, one that is affirming of the world's *materiality* but in a clear and nonreductive sense, Smith clarifying that the world has its existence "only insofar as it participates in, or is suspended from the transcendent Creator."[15] Affirming, along with this emphasis, the "significant sense in which the transcendent inheres in immanence,"[16] the concept of incarnation is a particular theme of importance within his distinctive participatory ontology. As such, Smith wants to thoroughly reject the Enlightenment's perspective concerning the autonomy of nature, recognizing that nature exists in being *only through participating in God*.[17]

Giving *Pentecostal* color to this participatory ontology (and being content to use the terms "world" and "creation" as synonymous with the term "nature") Smith advances an additional step further to argue that nature exists and has its being *only through participating in the realm of the Spirit*[18]—allowing him to advocate that creation is a world that is "enchanted," namely, a world that is full of the presence of the Spirit (and spirits).[19] This Pentecostal additional coloring (to his Reformed-tinted participatory ontology) is one which has developed through the reception of a "pneumatological assist" that was offered to Smith by Yong. Yong's

---

13. Smith, *Thinking in Tongues*, 101 (emphasis his).

14. See Smith, *Introducing Radical Orthodoxy*.

15. Smith, *Thinking in Tongues*, 100.

16. Smith, *Thinking in Tongues*, 100. Note, "immanence" in this sentence refers to the ontological status of the material world as opposed to the sense of God's being immanent.

17. See Smith, *Introducing Radical Orthodoxy*.

18. Smith, *Thinking in Tongues*, 101–2.

19. Three other Pentecostal writers to have explored the Spirit's relation to the world are Cartledge, Vondey, and Chris Green. Although preferring the concept of "sacramentality," Vondey and Chris Green's projects happily dovetail with Smith's project (and sometimes draw upon Smith's ideas). Likewise, though preferring the concept of "Mediation," Cartledge's project also has close affiliation to that of Smith (cf. Vondey, "Between This and That"; Green, *Towards a Pentecostal Theology*; Cartledge, *Mediation of the Spirit*; Vondey, "Theology of the Altar").

suggested assist was that Smith could enhance his participatory ontology by viewing creation as "suspended" in the realm of *the Holy Spirit specifically* (as opposed to suspended in God in general).[20] In accepting and employing this assist, a more pneumatological and Pentecostal color is brought to Smith's participatory ontology, demonstrated by the following quote from his book *Thinking in Tongues*:

> ... we might say that nature is always already suspended in and inhabited by the Spirit such that it is always already *primed* for the Spirit's manifestations. Pentecostal spirituality and practice don't merely expect that God could "interrupt" the so-called "order" of nature; rather, they assume that the Spirit is always already at work in creation, animating (and reanimating) bodies, grabbing hold of vocal cords, taking up aspects of creation to manifest the glory of God.[21]

Such a passage is indicative of Smith's enspirited creation ontology—a Pentecostal ontology that has evidently benefited from Yong's pneumatological assist; but the assist is also of value in its having drawn forth Smith's operative theological framework for appropriating this refined Pentecostal participatory ontology. This theological framework was helpfully articulated by Smith in his immediate and grateful rejoinder to Yong in an article of receptive response—an article in which he gives a creation-fall-redemption context from and within which he applies his enspirited creation ontology.[22]

Smith makes the case in that article (entitled "The Spirit, Religions, and the World") that, indeed, the world participates in the realm of the Holy Spirit, but the church participates in the Spirit in a special, distinct manner. Taking Yong's assist in a personal direction of his own, Smith makes a distinction between the world's participation in the Spirit—being dependent on the Spirit for existence even though in broken relation with God—and *the church's* participation in the Spirit (being dependent on the Spirit in glad harmony/relationship with God). In that article of grateful rejoinder, Smith elaborates this distinction by speaking of "structural" participation and "directional" participation in the Spirit. "Structural" participation is had by something (specifically, someone) that does not participate fully/properly in God—it has merely a structural *existence*

---

20. See Yong, "Radically Orthodox."
21. Smith, *Thinking in Tongues*, 101 (emphasis his).
22. See Smith, "Spirit, Religions, World."

which (though not acknowledging of him) it owes to the life-giving Spirit of God. "Directional" participation is had by someone that *does* fully/properly participate in God and is properly ordered or directed *to* the divine. Phrased more succinctly, Smith argues that to participate *properly* in the creator is to also be *directed to* the creator. In light of his theological creation-fall-redemption framework, Smith argues that the directional participation in the Spirit—for which humans were originally made—is not what is now being experienced by the majority of human beings; rather they are participating in a mere structural manner, experiencing a less intense form of participation due to the state of (theological) fallenness, having broken relationship with their divine creator. However, though being in this fallen condition, in the God-given gift of redemption a human is re-orientated by the restoring work of the Spirit who *intensifies* that person's participation; as such that person is restored back from mere *structural* participation in the Spirit to *directional* participation in the Spirit—the participation humans were designed to know and enjoy from the beginning.

Smith then further develops this model—with a specifically Pentecostal mind-set—by contending that a believer (in her directional orientation) can experience greater and deeper participation through further intensifications of the Spirit as she continues to live and participate in (directional) relation to God. This latter development of his work—advanced into his Pentecostal "enspirited creation ontology"—is philosophically-theologically revealing in that, on the one side of the coin, Smith wants to argue that *creation participates in the Spirit*, then on the flip side of that coin, that *the Spirit fills creation*; related, as creation can intensify in its participation in the realm of the Spirit, Smith argues that the Spirit intensifies his presence at times and at places in creation. So, in returning to his (full) quote above (indicative of his enspirited creation ontology) such a Pentecostal ontology allows Smith to regard the world as primed by the Spirit for his (on-going) work in the world.

This gives Smith an interesting angle to address the (on-going) debate concerning God's relation to his world and how he acts in/upon his world; Smith's making the case that the world is enspirited means that a unique contribution is brought to the debate. With the Spirit's dwelling in creation, Smith's model provides a solid ontological basis for affirming the Spirit's more regular work of his creating and sustaining creation according to its natural rhythms and order, so facilitating a solid base for the endeavor of the natural sciences. Yet at the same time as providing this foundation, Smith's ontology also gives a basis for the Spirit's more "miraculous" manifestations (such as healing, prophecy, etc.)—these being due to "more *intense* instances of the Spirit in creation" or "'sped-up' modes of the Spirit's more 'regular' presences."[23] Smith's Pentecostal ontology, therefore, facilitates both the regularity of the laws of natural science whilst leaving room for miracles—providing space for Pentecostal spirituality whilst also the order of science.[24]

There is much of value in Smith's Pentecostal ontology. It provides a rich renewal pneumatology and articulation of the worldview inherent in Pentecostal worship practices. It also offers an interesting basis for the natural order of the physical world whilst also affirming the possibility of the miraculous. It further bifurcates naturalistic views of the universe and more "interventionist" views of theism—whilst also managing to bypass more panentheistic views of the God-world relation.[25] And with this ontology being unreserved in its Pentecostal color and nature, it provides a substantive basis and model in general to serve as a suitable Pentecostal start-point and worldview from and within which to build an anthropology. That said, it does suffer something of a lacuna in that it gives no attention to *other* spirits; in giving such a (Holy) Spirit-full ontology, Smith

---

23. Smith, *Thinking in Tongues*, 104. At this point, the specifics of the place of "naturalistic" science might arise and the question be put to Smith of *how* his idea of Enchanted Creation would engage/facilitate the scientific method. Although Smith's answer cannot be fully articulated here, he is very aware of such discussions and devotes much of his chapter to the relevant (and often underlying philosophical) issues of metaphysical and methodological naturalism, defining categories such as supernaturalism, anti-supernaturalism, and (what he calls) supernaturalism, and elaborating how science is born out in his proposal. As stated above, he is clear that his Enspirited creational ontology would *facilitate* the regular workings of science (as well as allowing the place of miracles within creation) and is keen, with Yong and others, that Pentecostals engage thoroughly with the scientific arena (see further his "Is There Room for Surprise in the Natural World? Naturalism, the Supernatural, and Pentecostal Spirituality" in Smith and Yong, *Science and the Spirit*, 34–49 [cf. the compendium as a whole]). For an overview of how Pentecostals have engaged with science generally from the beginning of the twentieth century, see Yong, *Spirit of Creation*, chapter 2 (and in the wider discussion, the literature surrounding the relationship [and complementarity] between theology and science is becoming very substantial [cf. works by Paul Davies, Alister McGrath, John Polkinghorne, Arthur Peacocke, Francis Collins, Owen Gingerich, to name but a few]).

24. Which he relevantly also titles an enchanted/enspirited "*naturalism*" (Smith, *Thinking in Tongues*, 97–99).

25. See Churchouse, "How Could (Some) Pentecostal Theology Be Analytic Theology?"

gives no explanation to the nature of any of the "other spirits," or their relationship to creation.

This lacuna in pneumatology (though common in western Pentecostal theology) is unfortunate given that such a discussion would be of value for Pentecostal theology in general.[26] But specifically for the development of anthropology it is also a lamentable gap due to its downplaying of a key facet of Pentecostals' understanding of the world. Remembering Smith's own description of the world as being enchanted/*populated* by spirits—spirits plural not just singular—such an articulation would have been of benefit for considering the topic of the human soul/spirit.[27] As such, this lacuna in Smith's ontology will therefore be partially addressed in the following section by providing an apposite understanding of angels which would be fitting of Pentecostals' and Smith's ontology.[28] This will allow for the desired progress of this book by filling out more of the world's Spirit *and spirit*-filled nature, displaying the reality all the more clearly that the world Pentecostals believe in is a *spirit and* physical world; the significance of this spirit-filled world, for the topic of theological anthropology, is then explored as the section progresses with its implications being unfurled.

Filling Out Smith's Enchanted/Enspirited Creation Ontology with a Doctrine of Angels

Similarly to the ontology of Smith (and as was seen in chapter 3), Yong affirms the spirit-filled reality of the world Pentecostals believe in. He states:

> belief in a spirit-filled cosmos is *endemic* to Pentecostal spirituality. . . . [This spirit-filled cosmos is a world] that includes not just the Holy Spirit but also angels, demons, and other spiritual beings and powers.[29]

26. See Churchouse, "Angels."

27. The two terms will be used synonymously, through the course of this chapter, to refer to the (immaterial) spiritual aspect of a human. On the rare occasions Smith refers to this entity, he opts to employ the language of the human "spirit."

28. An entirely comprehensive articulation of *all* the "other spirits" might include ghostly beings and demons; but given the scope of this book, whilst these types of spirits are given cursory consideration at relevant points, the focus in this chapter (and book) will be specifically on *angels*.

29. Yong, *Spirit of Creation*, 174–75 (emphasis mine). Yong has elaborated this point much more fully in his *Discerning the Spirit(s)*, 127–32, 234–55 and 294–308. However, it is only in his more recent book that he has sought to give a full interpretation of these phenomena.

Biblical Holistic Dualism

Whilst not having received much scholarly attention,[30] Pentecostals have tended to follow the classical understanding of angels (and demons), which has been embraced throughout most of church history, viewing them as spirit beings. Defined more fully, and influenced by the Augustinian model, the angels that Pentecostals believe in are aptly defined as a type of heavenly being; they are:

> Created,[31] spiritual,[32] (self-) conscious beings,[33] who joyfully worship God,[34] and function as servants in the carrying out of God's plans and purposes[35]—"angels" often being a specific term to refer to those heavenly beings who from time to time take on a visible or physical form to carry out some of those purposes in the material world.[36]

Although not necessarily using such language, a similar type of definition is what most Pentecostals have in mind when reflecting on angels within their theology (and the related topic of demons)—classic expositions of such being given, for example, by C. D. Baker and Macchia, or Grudem in the 1990s.[37] In Pentecostal thought, these beings populate or (to use Smith's phraseology) "enchant" the world—there being multitudes of these self-conscious spiritual agents inhabiting the world (Neh 9:6).

Expanding the work of Smith, it might be said that the world is *Enspirited* by the Holy Spirit but is also *enspirited* by angelic beings (the Spirit as an infinite being Enspirits the whole cosmos, angels as finite

---

30. Cf. Churchouse, "Angels."

31. Neh 9:6; Ps 148:2,5; Col 1:16; Rev 4:11.

32. Acts 12:5-10; Col 1:16; Heb 1:14; cf. Num 22:31; Judg 13:8-20; 2 Kgs 6:8-20; Luke 2:13.

33. Under the term "(self)conscious," it is worth explicating more fully that they are: rational beings (2 Sam 14:20; Matt 24:36; Eph 3:10; 1 Pt 1:12; 2 Pt 2:11), moral agents, (Ps 103:20-21; Mark 8:38/Luke 9:26; Acts 10:22; Rev 14:10), and those with significant causal powers (Ps 103:20-21; Dan 10:13, 20; 2 Thess 1:7; 2 Thess 2:9).

34. Neh 9:6; Ps 103:20-21; Ps 148:2,5; Isa 6:3; Heb 12:22; Rev chapters 4,5,7,15.

35. Heb 1:14; Ps 103:21.

36. E.g., Gen 18; Judg 13:8-20; 1 Kgs 19:5-6; Matt 1:20-21; Acts 1:10; Acts 12:5-10. With both Hebrew and Greek words for angel meaning "messenger" it is not surprising that some of the purposes these beings are given—to carry out in the material world—are to convey messages.

37. See for instance C. D. Baker's exposition followed by that of F. D. Macchia's on demons as a joint chapter entitled "Created Spirit Beings" in Horton, *Systematic Theology*, 179-94 and 194-213 respectively; or Grudem's chapters 19 and 20 "Angels" and "Demons" in his *Systematic Theology*.

beings enspirit *parts* of the cosmos); the world in Pentecostal theology is abundantly spirit-inhabited, enchanted by manifold spirits not just the Holy Spirit. The particular significance at this point, and reason for expanding Smith's work, is not just to show the fullness (and intimacy) of the spirit-physical world in the Pentecostal worldview but also to highlight that all these self-conscious beings Pentecostals believe in are *spiritual (immaterial)* beings. In approaching the doctrine of the constitution of a human, this ontology highlights that the world Pentecostals believe in is one populated by myriads of spiritual self-conscious beings—indeed, beyond the human realm, *every* self-conscious being a Pentecostal believes in is a *spiritual/spirit* being. This is a backdrop worth keeping in mind when approaching an anthropology of constitution.

Towards the Construction of an Enhanced Pentecostal Doctrine of Human Constitution

As has been seen, Pentecostal spirituality carries within it a dualistic understanding of reality—a view which very much affirms the physical realm whilst also accentuating the spirit realm. This dualistic (physical-spirit[ual]) world is integral to Pentecostal ontology and theology and so it would therefore seem appropriate to keep this dualism (prominently) in mind in the constructing of an enhanced Pentecostal doctrine of human constitution. Remembering, in addition, the (high) view Pentecostals hold concerning their understanding of Scripture, and their desire for theology that is exegetically rooted, it would be appropriate for this anthropology to be constructed in a similar manner—holding Scripture as the final authority and indeed rooting the model in exegesis. It would likewise be prudent to heed the admonishment of Yong and Kärkkäinen to avoid the notorious pitfalls of the two dualisms rightly rejected (the Platonist and Classic Cartesian varieties) and indeed build an anthropology that affirms a *holistic* view of a human. But having learned from the philosophical missteps of both thinkers in chapter 3, it would be helpful, along with these insights, to approach the topic with a fuller philosophical rigor and construct the anthropology to follow in a *philosophical-theological* manner. As such, a helpful dialogue partner to advance the constructive project is John Cooper.

Whilst not identifying as a Pentecostal and so his approach to Scripture is not identical hermeneutically,[38] Cooper's Evangelical approach is sufficient and comparable to Pentecostals' high view of Scripture—similarly holding this high view of Scripture so exegetically rooting his anthropology. Whilst his background is in philosophy (with specialism in philosophical anthropology), his training in the Evangelical tradition has meant that he is additionally strong in biblical studies, enabling him to bridge both these disciplines—of philosophy and biblical studies—so enabling him to rigorously engage with the constitutional topic at hand. (As regards the *holistic* nature of a human as desired by Pentecostals, this will likewise become clear from expounding his work in the pages that follow.) Indeed, there appears much to commend John Cooper as a dialogue-partner for this project of constructing an enhanced doctrine of constitution so his work will be fully expounded and followed by evaluative critique. The chapter will then conclude at a point of having given a biblical foundation—in accord with the (fourth) Pentecostal emphasis and worldview of a spirit-filled cosmos—for the subsequent work to follow of developing the enhanced constitutional model.

John Cooper's Holistic Dualist Proposal

Cooper affirms that Scripture is the final authority in matters of life and doctrine, so he predominantly approaches his work as a philosophical-theological exegete—one aware of the philosophical discussions of the mind-body relation (which feed into the exegetical work) but primarily rooting his anthropology in the teaching of Scripture.[39] Given his approach and exegesis, Cooper arrives at his understanding of human constitution particularly through exegeting the relevant verses pertaining to personal survival beyond a human's physical death. Similar to most Pentecostals—as expressed through their theological history[40]—Cooper

---

38. Though see footnote in the Introduction for the closeness of Pentecostal hermeneutics to *contemporary* Evangelical hermeneutics (as displayed for instance by Evangelical Kevin Vanhoozer).

39. Cooper, *Body, Soul, and Life Everlasting*, xvi.

40. Cf. Pearlman, *Knowing the Doctrines*, 370–71 (Pearlman specifically disavowing the soul sleep hypothesis on the basis of Isa 14:9–11; Ps 16:10; Luke 16:23; 23:42; 2 Cor 5:8; Phil 1:23; Rev 6:9); Also Williams, *Systematic Theology*, 3:178; Arrington, *Christian Doctrine*, 238; Horton, "Last Things," 606–13 (who argues on the basis that Moses and Elijah appeared with Jesus at the transfiguration that there has to be some kind of existence between death and final resurrection) and Grudem, *Systematic Theology*, 816–24.

deduces his theology of constitution from a recognition of Scripture's contention that an aspect of a human survives death and continues into the intermediate state. The deduction that follows this insight is that if such an aspect survives and so exists in the intermediate state, then humans cannot be monistic beings; rather, there has to be an aspect to them that is ontologically distinct from the body, which survives into the intermediate state whilst the physical body decays in the grave. Supported by the interpretation of the consensus of Christians throughout church history,[41] he contends that humans must be dualistic entities—to survive their physical death—suggesting the terminological use of the word(s) "soul"/"spirit" for articulating this (non-physical) aspect.

Building his argument on the revelation of Scripture—and indeed the *progressive* revelation of Scripture—Cooper makes his case for anthropological dualism by beginning with the anthropology of the Old Testament, followed by that of the Intertestamental period writings, before proceeding to the teaching of the New Testament on the topic. This case from progressive revelation enables him to argue decisively that Scripture is dualistic in its theology of constitution. The sections that follow below expound his scriptural case.

Old Testament

In accord with the scholarly consensus, Cooper affirms the *holistic* nature of the anthropology taught in the Old Testament [O.T.] writings. Summarizing the O.T. meanings of the terms, *nephesh, rūach, bāsār, qereb,* and *lēb* (translated very roughly and initially as "soul/life-force," "spirit," "flesh," "inner parts/bowels," and "heart" [respectively]),[42] he states that the O.T. teaches:

> the functional integration or unity of the psychophysical totality rather than the compartmentalization of the soul's functions and the body's functions.[43]

He then, however, identifies a mistake that is commonly made in O.T. scholarship—that of equating this *functional* holism with *ontological*

---

41. See Cooper, *Body, Soul, and Life Everlasting,* xv, 15, 31 (and chapter 1 of this book).

42. Cooper, *Body, Soul, and Life Everlasting,* 39–41.

43. Cooper, *Body, Soul, and Life Everlasting,* 44 (this being in distinction from the Platonist and Classic Cartesian ideas as expounded in the preceding excursus).

monism. In addressing this (category) error, Cooper points to the limited O.T. verses which address the topic of personal eschatology. Whilst recognizing the scarcity of such verses in the O.T., Cooper identifies the consistency of these handful of verses and the impact that they had on the beliefs of O.T. Israelite readers; he argues that these verses had the effect of bringing the Israelites to believe in the continued existence of a person beyond the death of her body and that such (disembodied) people continued to exist as "*rephaīm*" in *Sheol*. Given the meaning of "*rephaīm*"—translated by Kaiser as meaning "shades"[44]—Cooper argues his case that the belief of the O.T. Israelites was that an individual continued to exist, beyond her physical death; yet this continued existence was as a "shadowy, ghostly" form—a limited version of her former holistic self.[45]

Related to this understanding, Cooper points to the O.T. teaching of the forbiddance of necromancy. For Cooper, this forbiddance of the occultic practice (of calling up the dead) implies that continued existence is likely—in this shadowy form after death—an idea given substance by Saul's calling up the ghost of Samuel (1 Sam 28). This idea is not unique to Cooper, in fact he cites the writing of Wolff (a leading O.T. scholar of the last century with specialism in anthropology) who affirms that "The Old Testament itself is able to report a successful case of conjuring up the dead. . . . Samuel does actually rise up in ghost-like form."[46] Indeed, from this necromantic account, he contends that the story gives further evidence of personal survival after death in the O.T. Whilst recognizing that most of the descriptions of the *rephaīm* in *Sheol* depict these beings as either sleeping or in a more dormant state,[47] he makes the case that Samuel is a *typical* resident of *Sheol*[48]—able to communicate with the world of the living—meaning that *rephaīm* in the realm of the dead must experience a *conscious* existence, even if existing as a ghostly shadow of their former earthly selves.[49] So rather than mere extinction, Cooper ar-

---

44. The language comes from Kaiser, *Death and Life*, 34 which Cooper affirms (*Body, Soul, and Life Everlasting*, 53n3).

45. Cooper, *Body, Soul, and Life Everlasting*, 52–56.

46. Cooper, *Body, Soul, and Life Everlasting*, 58; affirmed in this understanding by Wolff, *Anthropology of the Old Testament*, 104.

47. Cooper, *Body, Soul, and Life Everlasting*, 55–57.

48. Cooper, *Body, Soul, and Life Everlasting*, 58–59.

49. He further interestingly notes that these *rephaīm* in the realm of the dead are *not* just Platonist/Classic Cartesian minds, rather they are "shades"/"shadows"/"ghosts." Taking into account the bodily dimension of the ghost of Samuel (in contrast to the non-bodily nature of Plato's/Descartes's view of the soul) he makes a nuanced

gues that this practice of necromancy gives further reason to think the O.T. gives indication of conscious existence after death (as *rephaīm* in the world of *Sheol*.)[50] Cooper further expounds that these *rephaīm*, which exist in *Sheol*, are awaiting the final judgment (of Dan 12:1–2 [cf. Isa 26:14, 19]) where the faithful will receive their reward—of eternal and resurrection life—and the unfaithful will receive their due—the punishment of eternal destruction. The implication he draws from this exegesis is that if some aspect of a person survives the death of her physical body, then a human must be *more than* a body, and the language of dualism is apt for describing this bipartite nature. Whilst making this deduction, Cooper continues to affirm that, in normal embodied condition, a human is a *holistic* being whose body and spiritual aspect are those that function *together*—as a union of body and "soul"/"spirit."[51]

Intertestamental Period

True to the approach he employs—making his case from progressive revelation—Cooper's ultimate reason for investigating the teaching of the O.T. Scriptures is that they give the (Hebraic) background for understanding the New Testament [N.T.] texts. The understanding of progressive revelation is that the N.T. (doctrinally) fills out what is indicated in the O.T., and so for his seeking to ascertain the scriptural doctrines of anthropology—and indeed the associated doctrine of eschatology—Cooper investigated the O.T.'s teaching as the context for the N.T.'s teaching, giving a clearer picture and full understanding as regards the constitution of humanity. But in seeking to make such a case, Cooper recognizes that the O.T. hints on these subjects are also expanded through the writings of the *Intertestamental period*, which likewise provide the backdrop for understanding the N.T. texts on these doctrines. Aware of this contextual backdrop, he illumines the common and popular misstep of assuming

---

distinction, affirming "the dead are thought of as ethereal bodily beings whereas the living are fleshly bodily beings. The contrast is between fleshly and non-fleshly, not between bodily and non-bodily." (Cooper, *Body, Soul, and Life Everlasting*, 67.)

50. Recognizing the argument that certain O.T. passages (such as Eccl 9:10; Isa 38:19; Ps 88:10–12) imply that the there is no conscious existence in *Sheol*, Cooper argues these have to be read in light of the necromancy passages, as well as related passages such as Gen 35:18; Lam 1:1; Ps 30:3; 86:13 and Isa 14:9–10.

51. These words being used at this point in a way not particularly evident in the O.T. understanding of *nephesh* and *rūach*, but as a helpful contemporary term for expressing the spiritual (immaterial) aspect of a human.

that the terms "soul" and "spirit" are employed in the same way by each biblical author. By contrast he clarifies that the meaning of these anthropological terms—and indeed the related doctrines—need to be read in the light of their context(s), with a recognition that their meanings developed through the period of progressive revelation. As such, from the time of the O.T. writings through to that of the N.T. writings, the terms "spirit" and "soul" gathered fuller meaning—and indeed a variety of fuller meanings. The different biblical writers, therefore, use these anthropological terms with related-but-differing meanings, so there is no one definitive meaning of these terms as employed in the writings of the biblical authors.

Keeping this recognition in mind when making his dualistic case, Cooper includes a section on how these terms and doctrines developed through the *Intertestamental Period* [I.P.]; this gives him a full contextual background, which enables him then to progress and understand these terms and doctrines in the N.T. writings.[52]

Cooper identifies that the (Jewish) writers of the I.P. were much more interested in the afterlife than were the O.T. writers. Yet, he also makes very clear that the thoughts of the I.P. writers (though influenced *to a certain degree* by Hellenistic ideas on the topic) were primarily derived from—and expansions that were rooted in—the O.T. concept of *Sheol*. Although such "developments" on the theme led to a wide variety of views concerning what happens to a person after death, Cooper derives from his study that the views of the I.P., on the topic of the afterlife, can be roughly summarized into three recognizable positions:

1. After a person's death, there is nothing that lies beyond—there is no life after death (being the view of the Sadducees).
2. After a person's death, she lives on eternally in a spiritual/non-physical form (being more a view of the Greeks).
3. After a person's death, she awaits the final judgment, the righteous awaiting their resurrection and eternal life in bodily form.[53]

The latter group sub-divides into a further three positions:

a. Those who thought that the person, following death, would be *immediately* raised with a transformed resurrection body.

---

52. Cooper, *Body, Soul, and Life Everlasting*, 73–74.
53. The unrighteous awaiting judgment and everlasting destruction.

b. Those who thought that the person, following death, would await the final resurrection in an intermediate state (the view of Pharisees).

c. Those who thought that the person, following death, would be raised—immediately or later—as some kind of "heavenly being" (by which there was a range of interpretations [ranging from transformation into a star or planet, to becoming like a super-spiritual physical person {possibly something akin to a kind of angelic being}])—with some of these interpretations being compatible with what is espoused in view [b]).[54]

Acknowledging the variety, Cooper recognizes a consistency and correlation—among all of these categories and views—between the person's *mode of existence* in the afterlife, and her *location of existence*.[55] Moreover, in categories 3b and c, there is further consistency displayed, in that those in the intermediate state, whilst at times being described as "asleep,"[56] are also described in language that implies conscious awareness.[57] Such "persons" in the intermediate state are referred to in those writings as "souls" and "spirits,"[58] that is, they are not holistic human persons (in that they are without a physical body) but continue to exist spiritually whilst awaiting the final judgment.

Cooper is keen to make clear that this language of "souls" and "spirits" is not (as is sometimes assumed) a jettisoning of O.T. Hebraic holism in exchange for a view more akin to Greek idealism.[59] He delineates, more

---

54. Cooper, *Body, Soul, and Life Everlasting*, 76–80.

55. With the exception of the view of the Sadducees. Whilst it could be argued that the mode of the dead person on the Sadducees' view fits with the "location" (i.e., complete extinction), the Sadducees would likely have objected to the use of the term "existence" because the person, on their view, has gone out of existence.

56. Cf. 1 En. 22:3–9; 102:4–5; Jub. 23:31; 2 Esd. 7:78–80; 2 Bar. 36:11 (Cooper, *Body, Soul, and Life Everlasting*, 83–84.)

57. Cf. 1 En. 100:5 and 102:4–5; with the passages in the footnote above.

58. Citing Russell who finds the usage of "soul" in this sense in the books of Enoch, Psalms of Solomon, 2 Enoch, Testament of Abraham, 2 Baruch; and the usage of "spirit" in this sense in 1 Enoch, Assumption of Moses, and 3 Baruch (Russell, *Message and Method of Jewish Apocalyptic*, 151. Cited in Cooper, *Body, Soul, and Life Everlasting*, 82n19).

59. Similarly to Joel Green, Cooper notes that this standard rhetoric/narrative—that Greek dualistic ideas influenced and polluted the Hebraic holism of the Jews—is one that is far too simplistic; Among Greeks of the period themselves, there were those who espoused anthropological monism [and anthropological holism too], and some of *that* thought was of influence among groupings of Hellenized Jews (examples of such influence being the Stoic ideas that can be found in Ben Sirach, and the materialistic

accurately, that the way the anthropological terms are used by the I.P. writers, in regard to the intermediate state, is actually an augmentation of their O.T. meanings and usage. The, now, familiar O.T. terms, i.e., *nephesh, rūach, bāsār,* and *lēb,* are translated in the Greek I.P. writings as *psuchē, pneuma, sarx,* and *kardia*—having the same connotations they previously did from the O.T. writings. But in the I.P., the meanings of these terms are subsequently developed and filled out, meaning that, at times in the I.P., the terms *psuchē* and *pneuma* are used in reference to a person in the intermediate state—in her *discarnate form*.[60] In their O.T. usage, none of the anthropological terms are given specifically "physical" or "spiritual" functions; so the references in the I.P. writings—to a *psuchē* or *pneuma* existing in the intermediate state (without its physical body)—are a natural extension and development of how the terms are used in their O.T. context.[61] Whilst these beings are truncated versions of their former holistic selves, these ethereal (yet bodily) spirits,[62] in the I.P. writings, are portrayed as able to function—functioning consciously, morally, religiously—whilst missing their physical bodies.[63]

The writings of the I.P. further developed the eschatology of the O.T.—particularly concerning the contours of the intermediate state. They did so by depicting the spirits/souls of the dead in a further delineated *Hades* (the Greek translation of *Sheol*). In this further delineation of *Hades*, these spirits/souls are depicted as abiding in differing quarters or chambers—with separation between these abodes; some being quarters

---

ideas evident in the thought of the Sadducees [Cooper, *Body, Soul, and Life Everlasting,* 85]). However, Cooper maintains that, even recognizing the influence of Hellenistic culture "most Jews continued to think of the soul as retaining bodily form after death and included the notion of bodily resurrection in their eschatologies" (86). So, the commonly assumed rhetoric/narrative—of "a Hebraic holism vs. a Greek dualism"—is an inadequate understanding and one that needs to be re-considered (cf. Green's discussion of the topic in the footnotes of this book's chapter 3).

60. The words *rūach* and *nephesh* were used synonymously in that context, weakening the case for a trichotomous understanding of humanity (Cooper, *Body, Soul, and Life Everlasting,* 82n20).

61. Whilst there are only hints (and so a debate among scholars) as to whether there is a direct linkage between the use of *nephesh* (*/nephāshōth*) and *rephaīm* in the writings of the O.T., the I.P. writers bring clarity to the debate, being content to use the terms *nephesh* and *pneuma* in reference to "persons" in the intermediate state.

62. That is, they do not have *physical* bodies but are depicted with ethereal, non-fleshly bodies (Cooper, *Body, Soul, and Life Everlasting,* 83).

63. Cooper, *Body, Soul, and Life Everlasting,* 83, 93.

for the "blessed" (/the faithful) and others assigned for the "cursed" (/unfaithful).[64]

Due to their differing interpretations of the writings of the I.P., there was variation amongst Jewish groups as to the depiction of the intermediate state's *topography*; there was likewise variation in the *terminology* such groups employed when describing this world of the dead. However, Cooper contends that the view which regarded the intermediate state as *synonymous* with the realm of *Hades* (a place containing the deceased, those awaiting the final judgment) was a view consistent with the O.T. and became the view of the group known as the Pharisees (cf. the gospels and Acts 23:8). By the time of the N.T. writings, this view had come to be one that was held likewise by a number of ordinary Jews; endorsing this I.P. understanding and development of O.T. thought, these everyday Jews preferred this view of the Pharisees to the (Hellenized) views of the Sadducees or Herodians.[65] Having documented this contextual backdrop—up to the point of the N.T. writings, Cooper then naturally turns to address how this anthropology and eschatology further developed in the *N.T.* writings.

New Testament

In approaching the N.T.'s anthropological teaching, Cooper is particularly aware of the previous mistakes that have been made by a number

---

64. Cooper, *Body, Soul, and Life Everlasting*, 86–88. Passages such as 1 En. 22 suggest different chambers in *Sheol*, with some being reserved for the righteous, certain others for the wicked—with the same being depicted in 2 Esd. 4:41. Or 2 Bar. 21:23 and 30:2 speak of "storehouses" and "treasuries" or a place of "many mansions" being described in Jewish Apocalyptic. 2 Esdras 7 suggests that the blessed find rest in these dwellings (1 En. 60:8 extending this description to depict the righteous as in a [edenic] "garden," otherwise described as "paradise"), whereas the cursed must roam around (Cooper, *Body, Soul, and Life Everlasting*, 87–88).

Some of these quarters in the intermediate state are what some might, today term "heaven" and "hell," a usage that might be legitimate if remembered that "heaven" and "hell" in these texts are (mainly) descriptions of the *intermediate state*. In (some) contemporary Christian circles, these terms are used (possibly capitalized) to refer to the *final destination* of the righteous and unrighteous after the resurrection. However, such an understanding should not be read into the I.P. texts, which (for the specific Jewish groups that interpreted the passages in this way) refer to the intermediate state as a place of *awaiting* the final judgment (either in joyful or lamenting anticipation of the final Day) (Cooper, *Body, Soul, and Life Everlasting*, 88–89).

65. Cooper, *Body, Soul, and Life Everlasting*, 90 (cf. Cavallin, *Life After Death*, 194 and Bonsirven, *Palestinian Judaism in the Time of Jesus Christ*, 163).

of dualistic forebears. He recognizes that many Christian dualists of the past have read (Platonist) metaphysical thinking *into* the N.T. terms, mistakenly *eisegeting* terms like "soul," "spirit," and "body" (etc.) instead of *exegeting* these terms. Countering this mistaken approach, Cooper admonishes that the N.T.'s anthropological terms are just as diverse as the O.T. terms—the words *sarx, sōma, psuchē, pneuma,* and *kardia* being used in a variety of ways. He identifies that the N.T. writers often drew upon the terminology and meanings that were familiar to their original intended reader(s), both using and modifying such language to suit the writers' intentions. Related, he identifies their regular employment of devices such as synecdoche,[66] synonyms, and parallelism,[67] devices which are missed and often bypassed by those seeking to draw metaphysical conclusions from their chosen anthropological texts. A classic instance of such would be the metaphysical reading of 1 Thess 5:23—drawing a trichotomous anthropology from this verse.[68] In fact, a synecdochical reading of the verse may be a much more appropriate reading, one which recognizes this stacking together of terms as seeking to emphasize the fullness and scope of Paul's prayer—namely, that the Thessalonians *in their entirety* might be kept blameless at the coming of Christ.[69]

Other verses such as Matt 10:28, 1 Cor 14:14 or Heb 4:12—verses often taken to support metaphysical conclusions—could also be read in such ways,[70] written not to distinguish anthropological parts, but written

66. The literary figure of speech in which a word that is sometimes used to refer to a *part* of something / someone is used to refer to that thing/person in their entirety (/as a whole) (e.g., Luke 12:19).

67. For example, Heb 8:10b (quoting Jer 31:33b) "I will put my laws in their *minds* and write them on their *hearts*" (NRSV). Heb 10:16 later goes onto quote identically except that "minds" and "hearts" have changed places in this latter verse.

68. The verse stating: "May the God of peace himself, sanctify you entirely; and may your spirit and soul and body be kept sound and blameless at the coming of our Lord Jesus Christ" (NRSV).

69. Cooper argues that the device used may be similar to that used by Jesus, where he teaches people to love God with all their heart, all their soul, all their mind and all their strength (Mark 12:30) (Cooper, *Body, Soul, and Life Everlasting,* 103–4). The fact that Matthew and Luke use different anthropological terms in their equivalent narrating of this pericope suggest that this synecdochical stacking is exactly what is happening in the latter example.

70. Matt 10:28 stating "Do not fear those who kill the body but cannot kill the soul; rather, fear him who can destroy both soul and body in hell." 1 Cor 14:14 "For if I pray in a tongue, my spirit prays but my mind is unproductive" (NRSV). Heb 4:12 "Indeed the word of God is living and active, sharper than any two-edged sword, piercing until it divides soul from spirit, joints from marrow; it is able to judge the thoughts and intentions of the heart" (NRSV).

in reference to the whole of the person.⁷¹ Cooper wants to beware the problem of anthropological eisegesis and suggests that the fluidity of the usage of terms, displayed in the N.T. writings, points more in the direction of *holism* (the holistic functioning of a human) than giving grounds for assuming a position such as dualistic (or trichotomous) viewpoints.⁷² So he circumvents the word studies approach in order to avoid the eisegetical mistake. But having recognized this potential problem with the case some dualists have made in the past, Cooper then identifies the mistake that monists then want to deduce.

Recognizing that a dualistic case based on word studies can potentially be precarious, he highlights the related mistake of deducing, then, that the N.T. must assume monism as its anthropological viewpoint instead.⁷³ Even if there is nothing in the word studies approach to suggest a metaphysical anthropological position, Cooper illumines that this does not justify monism; rather, one would be unable to tell—from the exegeses of these passages alone—whether their authors are monists or dualists (or indeed, whether they are, in fact, neither). Whilst underlining a *functional holism*,⁷⁴ if verses such as the preceding selection give no grounds for assuming dualism, they neither give grounds for assuming the alternative—ontological monism. Cooper is willing to admit that if there were nothing in the N.T. texts that pointed in the direction of dualism, then monism would be a reasonable guess, but he exposes the monistic *assumption* as one that is certainly not valid. But he thinks that there *are* certain verses that point to their authors being anthropological dualists. He argues that these verses (to be addressed below) relate to and affirm his overall thesis—that the anthropological viewpoint of Scripture, and indeed of those who *authored* the Scriptures, is related

---

71. Cooper, *Body, Soul, and Life Everlasting*, 98. For a slightly different perspective—one that draws on Matt 10:28 (and scholarly exegesis thereof, of both traditional and contemporary scholars) to contribute to a case for dualism, see Churchouse, "Healthier Anthropology."

72. In similarity to what he argued concerning the O.T. anthropological terms, he comments "Numerous examples could be given demonstrating that heart, soul, spirit, and mind are each used to refer to the seat of emotions, the source of thoughts and actions, and the deep self which knows and is known by God" (Cooper, *Body, Soul, and Life Everlasting*, 97).

73. Cooper, *Body, Soul, and Life Everlasting*, 99–103.

74. That is, humans are "single, functionally integrated entities" (Cooper, *Body, Soul, and Life Everlasting*, 103n14).

to the eschatological question, namely "what (in the N.T.) happens to a person after her physical death?"[75]

Cooper contends that a N.T. scholar has three possible options or answers that could be given in response to the question (focussing specifically, in the list here that follows, on the eschatology of a Christian believer):

1. A person dies and is resurrected immediately,
2. A person dies and goes out of existence, only to be re-created on the day of resurrection,
3. A person dies and whilst awaiting resurrection a non-physical part of her survives and awaits in some kind of intermediate state.[76]

In considering these three possible options, Cooper implies that if 1 or 2 is correct, then there are no grounds for advocating dualism. However, if 3 is correct, then monism cannot be correct and dualism most likely is.[77] He goes about seeking the answer—concerning the view of the N.T. writings—by way of turning to the non-Pauline books, followed by examination of the corpus of Paul, to examine theological themes of both groupings, to determine the N.T.'s answer.

Regarding the grouping of non-Pauline books, Cooper advances a philosophical-exegetical case that if anthropological terms such as "soul" or "spirit" can be identified in reference to human persons *but who lack an earthly or resurrection body*, then this gives cause for thinking that humans have a part that is separable post death—giving grounds for anthropological dualism. Cooper finds clear examples of such (when focussing on the anthropological term "spirit") in Heb 12:23,[78] as well as

---

75. Cooper, *Body, Soul, and Life Everlasting*, 108–9.

76. In terms of how he narrows the options from those discussed in the I.P., Cooper is able to eliminate the "complete annihilation" view of the Sadducees in that all (conservative) scholars are agreed that ultimate resurrection is the goal of the N.T.—that there *is* life after death. This also sheds light on his declining the Greek view—the "spiritual existence" option—because, in the N.T., ultimate life after death is resurrection, it is embodied *physical life*. One can also understand why (though it is not specifically commented on in his chapter on the I.P.) Cooper gives the extinction-re-creation view as one of the options above; given that some scholars bypass the I.P. and its views of the afterlife entirely due to its wide variation of views (such scholars opting solely for the O.T. as background), this "O.T.-only" background has led a number of scholars to the extinction-re-creation view.

77. Cooper, *Body, Soul, and Life Everlasting*, 110–78.

78. Cooper, *Body, Soul, and Life Everlasting*, 113–14.

passages which speak of Jesus's death and his "giving up his spirit" (e.g., Luke 23:46).[79] (A third possibility of such, he suggests [but being less clear than the other examples {so not used in support of the argument}] is 1 Pet 3:19–20.) Further, and in use of the term "soul," he argues that Rev 6:9–11 might also be an example of such, and (whilst arguing the verse is not explicit) Matt 10:28 would suggest an assumed dualistic anthropology.[80] So, there is evidence in the non-Pauline literature of people being described as "souls" or "spirits" in the afterlife, post-physical death.

As regards the Pauline literature,[81] Cooper contends that Paul's eschatology gives a strong indication that some aspect of the human person survives beyond her physical death; but Paul *does not* describe that aspect in the language of "soul" or "spirit."[82] Rather, Paul prefers the use of pronouns—such as "we" or "I" or "he"—to refer to this personal aspect which survives the death of the body (cf. 2 Cor 5:1–10; Phil 1:21–23; Acts 23:6–8 and 1 Thess 4:13–18).[83]

So, from this selection of N.T. findings, option 3 of the list seems most cogent—that the N.T. writers were of the belief that some part of a person continued, beyond the death of her body, into the intermediate state, awaiting her resurrection. But in further support of his case, Cooper draws from wider N.T. teaching to *counter* the other two options. For instance, Luke's reference to the resurrection as occurring specifically *in the age to come* (Luke 20:35) is considered by Cooper as counting against the *immediate* resurrection view.[84] He finds support for this particular interpretation in Paul's regular eschatological teaching—that the resurrection will occur at the moment when Christ returns at the end of the age (e.g., Rom 8, Phil 3:20–21, and particularly 1 Cor 15).[85] And he argues that the second of the options above—the *extinction*-resurrection position—is refuted on numerous lines: Jesus's comment that the patriarchs are *living* (though of course not physically alive) (Matt 22:32), the

---

79. Luke 23:46 needing to be read in conjunction with Luke's use of pneuma in Luke 24:37—the verse in which Jesus differentiates between a spirit/ghost and himself as a physical/fleshly being.

80. Cooper, *Body, Soul, and Life Everlasting*, 112–19.

81. Cooper regards all 13 letters as Pauline.

82. Cooper, *Body, Soul, and Life Everlasting*, 156.

83. Cooper, *Body, Soul, and Life Everlasting*, 156.

84. Cooper, *Body, Soul, and Life Everlasting*, 120.

85. Cooper, *Body, Soul, and Life Everlasting*, 152–54.

appearance of Moses and Elijah with Jesus at the transfiguration,[86] the story of the rich man and Lazarus in the intermediate state (Luke 16:19–31),[87] and Jesus's comment that the thief would be with him in paradise *today* (Luke 23:43), all undermine the extinction-resurrection view as a rival or viable option.[88]

Given the N.T. reasons for holding to option 3, and the N.T. counters for rejecting 1 and 2, Cooper derives the consistent position that the N.T. authors were of the belief that a part of a human continues, beyond her physical death, existing in the intermediate state, awaiting the return of Christ. This is consistent with what he has argued throughout the course of his book. It would seem appropriate, here, to term the aspect that survives the death of the body as the "core"/"essential" person—given that Cooper is very careful with the language of "soul" or "spirit";[89] he is willing to use "soul" and "spirit" in more of a *conceptual* sense but after the biblical meanings have been fully and carefully examined. As such, to re-state the view of Cooper, using this terminological nuance: the "core"/"essential" person survives the death of her physical body, and awaits the return of Christ in the intermediate state; on the last day when Christ returns, she will be raised to face judgment, and if believing in Christ as her savior will receive eternal, resurrection life. Given the O.T. and N.T. teachings, he draws his definite conclusion that, in regard to human function, Scripture is *holistic* in its view, in regard to human ontology it is *dualistic* in its view. In sum, he terms his view holistic dualism (or dualistic holism) affirming both holistic function and dualistic ontology.

Evaluation

Cooper has gained the accolade of being *the* lead advocate and defender of biblical holistic dualism—demonstrated by the attempts of various scholars to critique and refute his position. The exegete Joel B. Green has made the fullest attempt at critiquing the holistic dualism of Cooper. So, his critique will be used as the basis of the evaluation of Cooper's

---

86. In their ethereal/ *rephaīm* bodies—comparable to that of Samuel (1 Sam 28) (Cooper, *Body, Soul, and Life Everlasting*, 123).

87. Read in light of Jesus's comment in Luke 23:43.

88. Cooper, *Body, Soul, and Life Everlasting*, 120–31.

89. The phrase "core person" is my own, the phrase "essential person" is drawn from Swinburne (c. *Evolution of the Soul*, and *Mind, Brain, and Free Will*)—see discussion to follow in chapter 5.

position, to establish the rigor of holistic dualism for establishing a doctrine of constitution.

In responding to the proposal of Cooper, Green thinks that Cooper's eschatological approach to anthropology is problematic for three reasons. First, the issue of personal eschatology was not particularly rampant in *Greco-Roman* antiquity, and that those who *did* hold beliefs on the matter show variety in what they believed. Second, the first century *Jewish* believers showed varied beliefs on the topic. Third, the N.T. writers themselves had no knowledge or first-hand experience that they could draw on concerning the matter, so their writings were necessarily speculative when it came to this particular issue.[90] Green thinks it better, instead, to build anthropology from the scriptural teaching that focusses on human nature *before* the boundary of death before gleaning some subsequent insights as to what happens *beyond* one's physical death.

Whilst being *the* lead critic of Cooper,[91] Green's lines of counterargument, above, are not substantial when examined more closely. Contra his first attempt critique, the issue of whether personal eschatology was rampant (or varied) in the first century mindset *of the Greco-Roman society* does nothing to undermine the contention that Jews *within* that society might have held views on this pertinent issue. Indeed, remembering Green's own understanding that the N.T. writers were influenced primarily by their Hebraic and O.T. background,[92] his comments regarding the beliefs held by the Greco-Roman culture do not particularly impact the proposal put forward by Cooper. If Green is wanting to argue that the beliefs of the surrounding culture had *colored* (maybe "tainted") their Jewish beliefs (bringing limits and variation to their O.T. views on the topic), this is already acknowledged by Cooper and accounted for in his case. Green's second attempted critique—concerning the varied Jewish beliefs at the time of the N.T. writings—is already acknowledged and accounted for in Cooper's constructive case (above). Green's third attempt at critique—that N.T. eschatology (and hence anthropology) can only be that which is speculative due to its writers being limited in knowledge or first-hand experience of the matter—is one that seems somewhat

---

90. Green, *Body, Soul, and Human Life*, 60.

91. Cf. Green, *Body, Soul, and Human Life* as just one example of this contention, but from the (on-going) back and forth between the two scholars—from the year 2000 through to the present—Green is recognizably *the* leading scholar who has devoted most time to critiquing Cooper's viewpoint.

92. See previous chapter.

curious. Were the N.T. writers simply proposing their own thoughts or views on the matter, there might be some merit to Green's contention, but given that the N.T. writings were authored by Jesus's *apostles*, and those associated with the apostles, the thesis that they had limited knowledge and experience of the matter seems rather unlikely. After three years of physically following Jesus as rabbi and master and Lord, the apostles then propagated Jesus's teaching—as subsequently did their associates; so, like with the rest of their N.T. teachings, they were drawing upon the teaching of *Jesus*, and his interpretation of the O.T. Scriptures, with a specific authority to expound *his* teachings. Therefore, they had plenty of knowledge to draw upon concerning life and life-after death.

Whilst being unsuccessful in his attempt at a counter of Cooper's position from a N.T. perspective, Green also attempts to refute Cooper's viewpoint based on a case from the *O.T.* writings. Green denies the argument given by Cooper concerning the O.T. *rephaīm*; he agrees that necromantic practice occurred in O.T. Israel but thinks that the practice does not require an intermediate state, nor a disembodied person. He admits that the deceased, in such encounters, were "called up," but seemingly follows in the footsteps of Arnold in saying that these raising(s) are *physical resuscitations*—the person being raised up *embodied*.[93] As was implied in the previous chapter, this is the view Yong espouses; both he and Green are apparently drawn to Arnold's position, and specifically his understanding derived from his work on 1 Sam 28.[94] But Arnold's view on this passage is problematic for a variety of reasons and does not give a basis for this resuscitation view.[95] So whilst acknowledging the reality of the "calling up" of Samuel, Green provides no cogent explanation for that event; Cooper's viewpoint is more convincing.

93. Green, *Body, Soul and Human Life*, 156n32.

94. See Arnold, "Soul-Searching," 75–84.

95. In that work, Arnold states that it could have been a *resuscitated*, physical Samuel that spoke to Saul as opposed to the *spirit/ghost* of Samuel. But rather than arguing the case, Arnold merely asserts that, with both readings being possible, the resuscitated view is more likely because the worldview of the O.T. was Hebrew holism (cf. the exposition of Cooper above); he comments "... the socio-historical background of the text makes it unlikely that a disembodied 'soul' of Samuel could be involved" (81) and then "Recent studies have admitted the Hebrew Bible's purely physical perception of human personhood, acknowledging the impossibility of developing a Christian dualistic anthropology on the basis of these data" (83). But re-exposing the error of equating Hebrew Holism with ontological monism, once this has been removed from the "case" Arnold puts forward, it is seen to be just built on assertion rather than any argument being presented for the conclusion he affirms.

Further to his attempts at critiquing Cooper's position based on O.T. exegesis and the *context* of the N.T. writers, Green additionally seeks to refute Cooper's holistic dualism on the grounds of actual *N.T. exegesis*—particularly with regards to Luke 16:19–31. He argues that this passage does not refer to the intermediate state as Cooper wants to maintain, rather, the parallel passage concerning the afterlife in Luke 23:42–43 implies that Luke, in both passages, is more realistically referring to the time of "the last day" (i.e. the time of ultimate paradise [/resurrection life] or final destruction).[96] Green thinks this suggestion is made further likely by the physicality of the events described in Luke 16, plus the finality of the torment/bliss.[97]

Cooper's N.T. understanding is built on a cumulative succession of passages, so refutation of his exegesis concerning one or two of these would not negate his position. However, in responding to Green's immediate critique above, concerning the focus on Luke's eschatology, Cooper's views regarding Luke 16 actually take into account—and indeed *are based upon*—his exegesis of Luke 23:42–43. Cooper's work on this latter passage gives superior exegetical reason for thinking that the "paradise" being referred to—in Luke 23:42–43—is in fact the intermediate state, so giving grounds for thinking that Luke 16 is referring to that location too.[98] As regards the question of the physicality of the story in Luke 16, Cooper anticipates the objection and argues that the *bodily* suffering of the rich man in the passage is consistent with the I.P. depictions of the nature of the intermediate state. Drawing attention to the narrative of the story, he reminds that the rich man's brothers are still living on earth during the episode (the rich man pleading that someone would warn them about what is to come), and highlights that the place is described as *Hades* (remembering the terminology from the I.P.) as opposed to being termed as *Gehenna*. These points of counter-refutation give better reason for thinking that the story of Luke 16:19–31 is depicted in the intermediate state, not in the final state.[99]

---

96. Green, *Body, Soul, and Human Life*, 164–65.

97. Green, *Body, Soul, and Human Life*, 144, 157–65.

98. Cf. Cooper, *Body, Soul, and Life Everlasting*, 126–29 and the theological reasons Cooper gives (articulated in the exposition above) for thinking that the immediate resurrection view is incorrect.

99. Cooper, *Body, Soul, and Life Everlasting*, 124–29.

So, whilst Green has attempted most fully to refute the position of Cooper, his critiques are unconvincing, and Cooper's holistic dualism presents as an exegetically strong position.

Further Evaluation

Cooper's holistic dualist position is deeply rooted in Scripture, but his philosophical background has informed the position as well. He carefully exegetes the Scriptures but is aware of the need for inference to obtain an accurate anthropological *ontology* given that none is *explicitly* taught in the Scriptures. He has therefore been clear exegetically, but then carefully philosophically *inferred* his (ontological) dualistic position. What *is* explicitly taught in the Scriptures is a person's functional holism, an emphasis highlighted by Cooper in his exposition of biblical anthropology. But rather than making the error of equating this functional holism with ontological monism, Cooper resists this blurring of categories; he maintains the philosophical distinction between ontology and function. His work is a helpful analysis of whether monism or dualism is preferable in light of the explicit scriptural teaching(s); and in light of his full exegesis, and nuanced philosophical inference, his argument that Scripture assumes an implicit *dualistic* anthropology is more persuasive and cogent than alternative monistic views. His key argument for holistic dualism is that the (essential) person continues, after physical death, and awaits the final judgment in the intermediate state. Whilst the reader is left, at times, wondering whether Cooper has actually started with the N.T.'s teaching and worked backwards to the O.T. texts, his progressive revelation approach enables him to focus on the N.T. passages as illumining the O.T. texts (and those of the I.P.); this particular methodology means he avoids a "word studies" approach, and enables him to proffer a strong case for holistic dualism.[100]

---

100. Concerning the issue of word studies, it might be helpful to illumine that Cooper's work is apologetic in nature and, as such, he *appears* willing to concede a lot of ground for the sake of allowing his (key) argument to shine. Recognizing the potential mistakes that have been made by the "word studies" approach, he distances himself from any such approach to clear the way for his key argument—so that his case is not written-off early by monistic biblical scholars. But, in fact, Cooper is quite coy in the language he uses when referring to such word studies arguments. He does not entirely rule them out but instead cites how a *monist* would respond to such—using terms such as "might," "could," "may" when giving his own opinion of the validity of such arguments. Such arguments play no part in Cooper's case, and he does not reveal

Due to his scope and the goals of his project, Cooper deliberately limits his aims—seeking to identify the scriptural understanding of what constitutes a human being. Given this particular goal, he arrives at his conclusion that the teaching of Scripture affirms a *general* holistic dualism. Because of his focus and scope, he makes no attempt to advance beyond this general description; he does not intend to offer a specific philosophical version of the holistic dualism he espouses. This discernibly apologetic approach—with its limited goals and intentions—is commendable in making its case; Cooper is content to finish the project having ascertained from the teaching of Scripture a holistic dualism that is general. But a more delineated viewpoint—within the parameters of holistic dualism—could be helpfully advanced from this point onwards, from the point at which Cooper *ends* his anthropological task. Indeed, whilst accepting Cooper's holistic dualism—recognizing its strong exegetical grounding—the questions of the soul's nature, and its relationship to the body, would benefit from further exposition than Cooper's deliberately limited work. So, as this book proceeds from here, it will seek to move beyond the work of Cooper but within the biblical holistic parameters to articulate a more specific understanding of the soul and its relation to the body.

Summary of the Chapter

In summary, the chapter has begun the project of constructing an enhanced Pentecostal doctrine of human constitution. It began in dialogue with Smith to give a Pentecostal start-point and worldview from and within which to commence the work of construction. Through filling out a theology of angels, within the second element of Smith's Pentecostal social imaginary, the emphasis Pentecostals put on the *spirit-filled* nature of reality was illumined in the opening half of the chapter. This focus brought forth a new pointer for advancing the constructive project as to

---

where he stands on a number of these "word studies" verses, however, given that he initially *appears* to concede Matt 10:28 on a monistic reading but then rehabilitates the verse recognizing its dualistic implications, one wonders whether he would actually be open to further work investigating terms such as "soul" and "spirit"—even if they play no role in his case. Clearly, he has circumvented such questions in not wanting his main argument to be clouded; but whilst granting these terms' *functional* purposes in Scripture (underlining his holistic contention), it seems plausible that certain of these anthropological terms could actually be referring to the spiritual entity he infers from the passages concerning the intermediate state.

who might appropriately serve as a next dialogue-partner for the project. Combined with the insights of the book's previous parts—parts I and II of the work—these pointers combined to suggest that Cooper would be a fitting dialogue partner to provide a biblical foundation for the enhanced Pentecostal doctrine. His biblical holistic dualism has been seen to be one that affirms the physical-spiritual realm(s), through an understanding that is rooted in Scripture, giving place for the human spirit (through his work on eschatology), and of course affirms Pentecostals' desire for a holistic understanding of a human. As such, whilst not claiming himself to be a Pentecostal (so not *majoring* on the renewal pneumatology) the biblical holistic dualism he proffers is concordant with the four Pentecostal theological emphases—in a way that is superior to the monistic anthropology of Yong and Kärkkäinen. Adding to its preferable theological status, it is additionally more persuasive in its handling of the philosophy entailed. Whilst continuing with the insights gleaned, then, from the first four chapters of this book, this holistic dualism will be taken as the biblical foundation for the following chapters—those that will advance this *general* holistic dualism into a *specific* holistic dualism, on route to constructing the desired enhanced Pentecostal doctrine of human constitution.

5

Advancing a Contemporary (Holistic) Substance Dualism

IN LIGHT OF PENTECOSTAL pneumatology, chapter 4 initially made the case that the world that Pentecostals believe in (and inhabit) is one that is populated by spiritual self-conscious beings. Indeed, beyond the human realm, but throughout this spirit-filled world, *all* the self-conscious beings that Pentecostals affirm and believe in are (immaterial) spiritual beings—namely God, angels, demons (and many Pentecostals worldwide would want to add to the category ghosts and ancestral spirits too[1]). In light of this realization, it was suggested that it would not be a surprise, therefore, for Pentecostals to discover that self-conscious *humans*, likewise, are also beings with a spiritual aspect to their ontology/constitution. Further, with human bodies being thoroughly affirmed in this pneumatologically-charged creation ontology, and indeed the spirit and physical world(s) being very intimate, this gave grounds for seeking an *anthropology* that similarly affirms the closeness of relation between the spiritual and the physical aspects of a human being's constitution.

Proceeding from this Pentecostal pneumatology—and the directions it suggests for anthropology—the latter part of chapter 4 then disclosed that the inferred scriptural understanding of the constitution of a human is that of a holistic dualism; humans are an intimate union of

---

1. See the conclusion for a brief consideration of this topic.

body and soul. The teaching that some aspect of a person—what from here shall be termed the "soul"[2]—survives her bodily death and awaits the final resurrection in the intermediate state gives evidence of a human's dualistic nature, even if in ordinary, embodied condition that soul functions in holistic union with its body.[3]

Drawing together these insights, gained from the work of the preceding chapters, the book is now at a point of being able to define the soul. The (human) soul is:

> a spiritual entity that is the bearer of (a Subject's self-) consciousness, which in ordinary (embodied) condition functions in holistic union with the body.[4]

Reached in light of Pentecostal pneumatology and the anthropological teaching of Scripture, this holistic dualist understanding of the soul (and body) gives a framework for proceeding in this and the subsequent chapter.

At this point in the overall project, because the holistic dualism arrived at in the previous chapter was quite a general position, the definition of the soul above is also quite general; for the purposes of proposing a specific understanding of the soul for Pentecostal theology, it would benefit from philosophical refinement and advancement. But the soul has been deliberately defined in this manner, and at this point, in order to give space and ancillary credence to a range of different understandings of the soul—those that could potentially be adopted and employed with benefit in Pentecostals' philosophical-theological anthropology, and all of which are ably encompassed within the definition of the soul just given. As this chapter proceeds towards its goal, therefore, of articulating a *specific* understanding of the soul and indeed *a* holistic dualist model in particular—now in dialogue with the philosophy of mind—these varying understandings of the soul and models of holistic dualism will be

---

2. The preference for the term "soul" is due to its familiarity in the philosophy of mind (with additional reason for this preference being highlighted in chapter 6).

3. It is to be clarified that the term "soul" is being used in a *conceptual* sense of the word, heeding the lessons that were learned from Cooper concerning the term's range of meanings in Scripture.

4. Note "Subject" is capitalized to underline its referring, not just to a "topic" but, to an *individual* with *first-person* perspective. (In expansion of the term "bearer," it might be alternatively put that a soul is the spiritual entity that is the "seat" of [a Subject's self-] consciousness.) For a complimentary variation of the definition of the soul given above cf. Churchouse, "Healthier Anthropology," 26–27.

touched upon and highlighted as potential alternative avenues for the development of other Pentecostal theological anthropology. Whilst highlighting these interesting avenues, this will be on route to achieving the primary aim of the chapter—that of adopting *a specific* view of the soul and indeed a particular holistic dualist model for the Pentecostal theological anthropology being constructed in this book.

Holistic Dualist Models within the Philosophy of Mind

The engagement with Yong and Kärkkäinen's anthropology highlighted that whilst Pentecostals are keen to emphasize embodiment and the *value* of the body, the issue of the human *mind* needs thorough attention as well when constructing Pentecostal anthropology. As well as affirming the material body, Pentecostals need to give an account of the human mind/center of (self-) consciousness—so integral to anthropology. As was seen in the models critiqued, in chapters 2 and 3 of the book, the philosophy of mind provides an important complement and counterbalance to Pentecostals' theology of the body, giving scholarly focus on the mind—the center of (self-) consciousness—to facilitate a credible account of a human. For Pentecostals, then, wanting to seek an appropriate theological anthropology, it is not sufficient to simply affirm the body, there needs to be engagement with the (philosophy of) mind (/soul).[5] However, because the book has arrived at a holistic dualist understanding of a human being, the parameter of this expansive field has been already narrowed and set, so only views from the philosophy of mind that lie within this holistic dualist framework will be considered as avenues of potential exploration for development of the desired Pentecostal anthropology.

The limited selection of mind/soul–body dualisms that lie within this holistic dualist parameter can be grouped under three headings (or categories): Emergent dualism(s), Aristotelian-Thomistic dualisms,[6] and contemporary Cartesian substance dualisms. The intricacies of these positions I have expounded in detail elsewhere,[7] however, these dualisms can be overviewed and summarized by way of the following short synopsis.

---

5. Recalling that the "mind" in the discipline is used—in certain dualistic views in the field (see below)—as synonymous with the term "soul" (hence this chapter's being content to refer to it as the mind/"soul"-body relation).

6. These have been termed "dualism(s)" in the sense that they espouse the separation (and survival) of the soul from the body at the point of the human's death.

7. See Churchouse, "Renewing the Soul," chapters 5 and 6.

In the first of these categories, William Hasker has championed the "emergent dualist" position, a viewpoint which argues that (at a certain point in evolutionary history) a unique ontological substance—i.e., the "mind"/"self" (/"soul")—emerged out of the human brain; (in ordinary embodied condition) humans are now, therefore, those with an emergent self which supervenes on the brain.[8]

In the second of these categories, Brian Davies, Eleanore Stump, and Brian Leftow are leading proponents of the classic Thomistic position[9]—with thinkers such as Robert Pasnau and J. P. Moreland defending related, hylomorphic or Thomistic-like views[10]—all of these views contending (in their particular ways) that the soul *animates* or enforms the body (the soul being the body's "principle of organisation").

In the third of these groupings, John Foster, Charles Taliaferro, and Richard Swinburne have defended contemporary (Cartesian) substance dualist positions which affirm that soul (/mind) and brain are ontologically distinct entities—responsible for mental and brain states respectively—which mutually interact; indeed, these contemporary substance dualists affirm that the soul's mental states are *correlated* with the (physical) states of the brain.[11]

Each of these groupings can be termed "holistic dualist" positions in that they affirm: (1) the (ordinary) functional union of soul and body, (2) the survival of the soul (/mind)—beyond the death of the body, and (if pushed *theologically* [on what are otherwise philosophical positions],) (3) the ultimate goal of the human is resurrection embodied life—with the (re-)union of body and soul occurring at that eschatological climax. With these holistic dualist features in mind, and with the general definition of the soul given above, it seems a Pentecostal theological anthropology could be constructed by drawing on *any* of these philosophical positions—each of which being consistent with the Pentecostal pneumatology and scriptural exegesis given in chapter 4.

---

8. Hasker, *Emergent Self*.

9. These thinkers hold to the classic Thomistic position but with certain contemporary modifications. Cf. Davies, *Thomas Aquinas*; Davies and Stump, *Oxford Handbook of Thomas Aquinas*; Stump, *Aquinas*; Leftow, "Souls Dipped in Dust"; Leftow, "Soul, Mind, and Brain."

10. Cf. Moreland and Rae, *Body and* Soul; Moreland, *What Is the Soul?*; Pasnau, *Metaphysical Themes*; Pasnau, "Philosophy of Mind."

11. Foster, *Immaterial Self*; Taliaferro, *Consciousness and the Mind*; Swinburne, *Evolution of the Soul*; Swinburne, *Mind, Brain, and Free Will*.

However, in wanting to choose *a* particular model for advancing the goal of this book, group one of the categories above (Hasker's emergent dualist position) is not the position opted for due to the philosophical problems of emergence already highlighted in chapter 3. Whilst sympathetic to the Aristotelian-Thomistic metaphysics of group two, because corpuscularian metaphysics underpins most academia of the present, and indeed is the metaphysic most scholarly Pentecostals are accustomed to (/assume), to make a case for a theological anthropology that is already new for Pentecostal theology—but itself built on top of a metaphysic to which Pentecostals are unaccustomed—would not, here, be preferable either. And so, choosing the contemporary substance dualist grouping, the book will proceed with group three, and within that particular grouping will focus on Richard Swinburne's eminent model.

The reason for the specific focus on Swinburne's renowned substance dualist model is due to its having been defended by Swinburne over a period of forty years of critique (and in the process of such critical dialogue its arguments have been subsequently strengthened)—being still widely regarded currently as *the* dualist position to beat.[12] As such, his view will be explored and the levels of critique examined to consider how viable it might be as a model—as potentially an *advanced* holistic dualist model—for furthering the Pentecostal doctrine being developed in the course of this book.

Keeping the desired Pentecostal doctrine in mind as the overall goal of the project, once Swinburne's position has been expounded and critiqued—predominantly on a conceptual level—focus will subsequently turn to his view's understanding of the *body*, in relation to the human soul, to address the on-going concern of Pentecostals that a substance dualist position might unfittingly down-play the body (as per the problematic varieties of dualism). Whilst the *Classic* Cartesian dualism has already been elucidated in the excursus—to distinguish this former view from (contemporary) substance dualisms of a stronger variety—these

---

12. Swinburne's credence as Professor of the Philosophy of Religion at the University of Oxford (followed by his subsequent role in retirement as Emeritus Professor of Philosophy at the same institution) has no doubt been a contributing factor in keeping his work under full and on-going scrutiny throughout those forty years; his dualist interactionist model continues, in the current, to be the position scholars are particularly drawn to when considering a contemporary form of substance dualism. Through the critical dialogue of the past four decades, Swinburne has sharpened the *arguments* he makes for his view, but his view as a whole remains the same—his distinctive substance dualist position.

questions of the place of the body will be very much the focus of this chapter's latter examination. Recognizing the holistic and anthropological emphasis as prevalent in Pentecostal theology, Swinburne's view will be fully considered in light of this particular emphasis, and so the validity and applicability of his model—for Pentecostal theology in particular—will be considered in that examination, allowing the chapter to then be brought to its goal at the point of the conclusion that follows.

Swinburne's Contemporary Substance Dualism

Richard Swinburne's substance dualism has recognizable roots in the Cartesian tradition yet advances a significant distance beyond the Classic Cartesian position. Remodelling the position with an eye to philosophical and scientific development, from and since when Descartes originally penned his position, Swinburne has advanced (what might be termed) a substance dualist model of a "Contemporary Cartesian" variety that is in accord with the best and most recent science and philosophy of mind (and, indeed, theology[13]).

Resulting from his period of research which gave rise to his Gifford Lectures of 1983–84, Swinburne subsequently wrote his book *The Evolution of the Soul*,[14] and has since advocated his substance dualist position over the period of the following forty years. Whilst refining details of his argument during that period in response to on-going critique and the development of knowledge, his thesis has remained substantially the same since he originally authored the work. Subsequent works on the issue—such as his second edition of *The Evolution of the Soul* (1997) then *Mind, Brain, and Free Will* (2013) (and on a slightly more popular level *Are We Bodies or Souls?* [2019])—have clarified, expounded, and furthered his original view on the topic but the thesis has remained largely the same throughout those four decades; and (now in his late eighties) Swinburne continues to advocate this same position today as he expounds his substance dualist view in academic lectures across the world.

---

13. Whilst his view is argued philosophically throughout, in an appendix to the second edition of his work *The Evolution of the Soul* Swinburne indicates accord with the related developments in theology.

14. Swinburne, *Evolution of the Soul*.

The Difference between Mental States and Brain States

In exposition of his view, Swinburne argues that for any comprehensive description of the world—a story of the world which seeks to describe *all* the goings on in the world (past, present, and future)—that description would have to consider the reality of *mental events* as well as physical events.

As an example of the latter, *brain* events are the *physical* firings of a person's neurons when that person has a conscious experience; such physical activity is "public" in the sense that any interested member of the public could be made aware of what is happening in that person's brain through the benefit of neuroscience.[15] In this sense, knowledge of brain events—or (more specifically, knowledge of) brain "states"[16]—are readily available to anyone from a third person perspective because they are physical/empirical events that can be scientifically observed.

In differentiation to brain events, the *mental* events of a person (more specifically the mental "states" of a person) are those that a person has *privileged* knowledge of, and indeed has privileged access to. For instance, in the mental event of experiencing the sensation of pain, the person has privileged (first-person) access to the feeling of "what it is like" to be having this sensation[17]—a privileged access not available to anyone beyond that person (/"Subject"). This suggests, in the thinking of Swinburne, that mental events/states are different to brain events/states and that the former are a property of the mind, whereas the latter are a property of the brain.

---

15. Swinburne, in his earlier exposition(s), uses the term "man" as a noun synonymous with (and designating) a human being, so derivatively uses the pronouns "he" and "his" in reference to such. In his later books, he adjusts the terminology to speak of both "he or she" (so "his or her") in reference to a human being. Whilst, in previous chapters, I have tended to employ the terminology of the author being engaged with, because in summarizing Swinburne's position there is variation between the former and the latter expositions, I will retain the pronouns "she" and "her"—as used through the course of this book—when referring to a person in summary of his view, recognizing that there will be times (when quoting his work directly) when the "he" and "his" of his quote stands out from the "she" and "her" of my own summarizing of his position.

16. A "state" being a type of "event." Swinburne defines "events" succinctly as "occurrences at particular times, which consist in substances having or changing their properties" (Swinburne, "Precis," 1). (Cf. Moreland who defines *"Events are states or changes of states of substances. An event is the coming or going of a property in a substance at a particular time, or the continued possession of a property by a substance throughout a time"* [Moreland, What Is the Soul, 8 (emphasis his)]).

17. Philosophers of mind sometimes using the word "qualia" to designate such a property.

Elaborating on these states of the mind, Swinburne contends that there are five types of foundational mental states, namely: sensations, thoughts, desires, beliefs, and "purposings" (or "volitions"/"intentions").[18] All the rest of a person's mental life (e.g., one's emotions, fears, longings) are built on top of these five, and the person experiencing these mental states has privileged first-person knowledge and access to their content, beyond the mere third-person knowledge acquirable from neuroscience.[19]

Differentiating an "Essential" Person from Her Physical Brain (+ Body)

On the basis of this philosophical groundwork, Swinburne argues that an essential *person* (or "Subject")—one who experiences these mental states—is a *different* thing/entity to her physical brain (+body). He argues and develops this case, first, by proposing a distinctive thought experiment, and then having stressed its implications, he proceeds to make an argument for substance dualism—highlighting the logical and metaphysical possibility of personal survival beyond the death of a person's brain and body.

Swinburne sets up the thought experiment with certain neurological findings. He highlights that, for a regular human being, neuroscience has shown that the right hemisphere of the brain controls much of what occurs on the left side of the body, and the left hemisphere of the brain controls much of what happens on the right side of the body—but *both* hemispheres are used for processing memory and forming character, and both (if the other were damaged) are able to adapt to carry out the function of the other hemisphere. He further highlights the reality that a current day neurosurgeon can successfully and safely cut the corpus callosum—which joins the two hemispheres of the brain—and so sever the connection between both hemispheres without the human suffering serious deleterious effects. Swinburne therefore conceives of the advancement of neurosurgery to the point where brain *transplants* of regions of the brain might become a possibility, to then propose the following thought experiment:

---

18. Sensations being non-propositional events (Swinburne, *Mind, Brain, and Free Will*, 72–74), the other four being propositional events (74–87).

19. Swinburne, *Evolution of the Soul*, 2, expounded in chapters 2–7. Cf. Swinburne, *Mind, Brain, and Free Will*, 67–68 and 95. (From this point on, all references to Swinburne's *The Evolution of the Soul* will be from the revised edition of 1997.)

A brain surgeon operates on a Subject—a Subject called "Alexandra"—and in the surgical procedure removes each of the hemispheres of Alexandra's brain, putting the left hemisphere into the skull of a new body ("Alex") and the right hemisphere into the skull of a new body ("Sandra")—the new bodies successfully accepting each hemisphere respectively. Given that both hemispheres are able to carry out the function of the other (now absent) hemisphere, and both display the memories and character of Alexandra, Swinburne asks: which of the brains and bodies is the person Alexandra?[20] Swinburne acknowledges that it could be either Alex, or it could be Sandra, or it could be that neither is Alexandra—(assuming the indivisibility of persons[21]) all three of these answers are logically possible. So, through empirical investigation of the matter—of the brains and bodies of Alex and Sandra—the observer would not know who the *person* Alexandra is; and through hearing of the memories of Alex and then Sandra, or by witnessing their characters, the observer would still not be able to acquire that knowledge. This reveals that personhood (and personal identity) is something different and beyond the (empirical) brain (+body), and so personhood is something different, and cannot be reduced to the physical brain (+body).[22] The grounds are therefore provided for thinking that the "essential" person is something beyond the human physical brain; the "essential" person/"mind" (to draw on the term from the philosophy of mind) being distinct from the physical brain (+body).

Swinburne's Argument for Substance Dualism

So far, Swinburne's argument demonstrates that mind and brain are different entities, but to make it into an argument for a fully-fledged *substance*

---

20. The names Alexandra, Alex and Sandra are a development of the original argument (where the designators P, P1, P2 etc. are used). Cf. Swinburne, *Are We Bodies or Souls*, 61.

21. Swinburne assumes this on the grounds that a person has experiences of the world. Even if Alex and Sandra both had exactly the same memories and character as Alexandra, from that point on, their experiences of the world would be different, so the question remains, which one (if either) is Alexandra. That said, even if persons *are* divisible—giving a fourth option in his thought experiment (i.e., that Alexandra is identical to Alex *and* Sandra)—his argument still holds in that the observer would not know which of the four options Alexandra was.

22. Swinburne, *Evolution of the Soul*, 9–10, 147–50.

Advancing a Contemporary (Holistic) Substance Dualism

dualism, he recognizes it requires further development;[23] his brain transplant thought experiment only shows that a level of brain continuity is *insufficient* for personal identity but does not rule out the possibility that a person needs some kind of bodily matter to survive as a person. So, to argue that a person is not essentially her body, (in his book *The Evolution of the Soul*) he gives further thought experiments to highlight a vital premise to his argument, the premise *it is logically possible that a person could survive even when her body is annihilated.*[24] Whilst helpful in highlighting this premise,[25] he upgrades these thought experiments with another that is particularly specific and clear in his subsequent book on the topic, *Mind, Brain, and Free Will*.

In this latter book, Swinburne upgrades his earlier thought experiment by considering another surgical procedure in which, every year for a period of ten years, a person has a tenth of her brain removed and replaced with a new part. This happens consistently and consecutively—a tenth of the brain every year—until, over the course of the ten-year period, the whole of that person's brain has been removed and replaced. Recognizing, in that instance, that it seems both logically possible that that person is still the same person as she originally was—just with an entirely new brain—but that it also seems logically possible that it is *not* the same person—given that her entire brain has been replaced—then this likewise underscores the thought experiment expounded in the section above but advances it to indicate the logical possibility of the survival of a person with *no* brain continuity whatsoever.[26]

So, with these thought experiments supporting, he lays out his philosophical argument for substance dualism as follows:

---

23. It could, as it stands, just be seen as validating a *property* dualist view—but one that is espoused and contended by an (ontologically) substance monist.

24. See argument to follow below.

25. Swinburne, *Evolution of the Soul*, 150–51. The conceivability of a person's swopping bodies with someone else (or indeed a different animal [cf. Kafka's Beetle]) is often used as a conceivability argument to make this case—though Swinburne uses alternative thought experiments to make a case of his own. (Swinburne prefers the thought experiment of a husband's finding himself gradually losing the ability to have causal influence on and within his body [through mental purposing] but simultaneously finding himself developing the ability to exert causal influence on and within the body of his wife]).

26. Swinburne, *Mind, Brain, and Free Will*, 155–57.

(where & = and, ~ = not, ◊ = it is logically possible that)

p = "I am a conscious person and I exist in 1984" [or any year after one's birth]
q = "My body is destroyed in the last instant of 1984"
r = "I have a soul in 1984"
s = "I exist in 1985"

x ranges over all consistent propositions compatible with (p & q) and describing 1984 states of affairs
"(x)" is to be read in the normal way as "for all x"

So, in formal logic terms, the argument proceeds:

p   ...Premise 1

(x) ◊ (p & q & x & s)   ...Premise 2

~ ◊ (p & q & ~r & s)   ...Premise 3[27]

Articulating the argument further,[28] (and clarifying in his *Mind, Brain, and Free Will* that logical possibility entails metaphysical possibility in the argument he is proposing,[29]) Swinburne's main argument for substance dualism proceeds as follows: if it is (logically and metaphysically) possible for me (a person) to exist even when my brain and body are destroyed, then I am (essentially) not my body, and can exist without my body; therefore, I have to be a (non-physical) substance distinct from my (brain and) body, i.e., I have to be essentially an immaterial/spiritual soul.[30]

27. See Appendix C of (his revised edition of) *The Evolution of the Soul* (323–32).

28. His argument being laid out in formal logic as an appendix to confirm its validity.

29. Swinburne, *Mind, Brain, and Free Will*, 14–22, 54, 158–59. In the argument (which follows in the main text above) Swinburne contends that it is metaphysically possible (not just logically possible) because "I" is a (rigid) informative designator. He defines an informative designator by stating: "anyone who knows what the word (the designator) means (that is, has the linguistic knowledge of how to use it) knows a certain set of conditions necessary and sufficient (in any possible world) for a thing to be that thing." (12). This stronger metaphysical claim means that the critique given of Descartes's view (in the excursus) (that the thinking mind and the body could be the same thing—the thinking mind just being ignorant of that fact) is an objection that fails (against Swinburne's contemporarily-enhanced Cartesian model).

30. ("Immaterial" is Swinburne's terminology [which will be used in expounding his argument further], "spiritual" is my preferred terminology as expounded in the book's introduction.)

On Swinburne's thinking, each immaterial soul possesses the philosophical property of "thisness," giving each soul (/person) her own individuation,[31] and this soul is the substance that experiences unified consciousness at *a* time, and indeed unified consciousness *through* time[32]—being the essential bearer of consciousness. Progressing quite a distance beyond the Classic Cartesian view, Swinburne maintains that there is a very intimate relationship between the essential person (/soul/mind) and her brain (+ body),[33] and that the person's mental events are clearly *correlated* with brains events.[34] So, in his dualist interactionist soul-body model, the brain (and hence body) is the *instrument* of the soul to exert action on the outside world,[35] and reciprocally, the soul is affected by what is experienced in its physical (body +) brain.[36] Underlining and confirming, therefore, the intimacy between the soul and brain (+ body),[37] Swinburne describes the soul as *functionally dependent* on the brain (though not *causally* dependent); that is, the two are not separate

---

31. Swinburne, *Evolution of the Soul*, 152–53 and Swinburne, *Mind, Brain, and Free Will*, 33–38, 149, 165.

32. As has been implied, Swinburne rejects the notion that memory and character provide the necessary persistence conditions for a person through time—these not being fundamental (cf. Swinburne, "Personal Identity," 231–47). For his argument regarding the "unity of consciousness," see Swinburne, *Evolution of the Soul*, 160 and Swinburne, *Mind, Brain, and Free Will*, 144–48. (In the latter he states ". . . it is an evident datum of human experience that conscious mental events of different kinds [visual sensations auditory sensations, etc.] are co-experienced, that is, belong to the same substance, both at one time and over time" [142–43]).

33. Swinburne, *Evolution of the Soul*, 10, 174–76. In rather straight forward terms, Swinburne comments "A person has a body if there is a chunk of matter through which he makes a difference to the material world, and through which he acquires true beliefs about that world" (146).

34. Swinburne acknowledging that the neuroscientist would likely be able to see the correlated firings of the neurons in the brain (when a person experiences a mental event) and thinks that neuroscientists, in time, would be able to make a long list of such correlations (Swinburne, *Evolution of the Soul*, 188).

35. For instance, a "purposing" of the soul to write a letter is carried out by means of the soul's exerting causal influence on the brain and body to bring about the hand picking up the pen and writing.

36. For instance, the eye might see a green tree, which is translated through neurons in the brain, giving the mind the sensation of "being appeared to greenly"—and it is this awareness of such things, as brain and mind interact, that brings about consciousness.

37. From here onwards, "brain (+body)" will be shortened (as per the common philosophical usage) and the human body will be assumed when employing the term "brain."

entities that have individual and differing functions, they are intimate and functionally united in the usual operating of a human.

At this point, the question, again, arises as to the *mechanism* of interaction between a person's soul and her brain. Swinburne is at ease with not being able to give or propose a scientific mechanism, speculating that humans may not *ever* have the intelligence to enable them to know what such a mechanism would be.[38] He sees that as unproblematic for his substance dualist view, simply and unashamedly stating that the mental and the physical states clearly *do* interact (giving agent causation as an example[39]) and contends that to not know *how* such entities interact in no way undermines the reality that they *do* interact.[40]

The Difference(s) between Swinburne's Model and the Substance Dualism of Descartes

It has already been shown how the view of Swinburne is quite a distance beyond the Classic Cartesian position; it becomes additionally apparent when Swinburne's model is applied to the mental lives of animals and so when considering animal souls. Unlike the viewpoint of Descartes—who thought that animals are merely automata (with humans being alone in possessing souls), Swinburne's model recognizes that animals—from a certain point in evolutionary history[41]—display evidence of experiencing

---

38. Swinburne, *Evolution of the Soul*, xii (reflecting on McGinn, *Problem of Consciousness*).

39. Swinburne, *Mind, Brain, and Free Will*, chapter 5.

40. Cf. Discussion in chapter 3 of this book. Whilst a similar line of reasoning to the above might be argued regarding the origin of a human soul (namely, one does not need to know when or how it originated to affirm that it is in existence), in an appendix added to the revised edition of *The Evolution of the Soul* (and so not being fundamental to his argument) Swinburne, in fact, conjectures that the (immaterial, personal) soul has a personal (as opposed to scientific) cause, namely it came (and comes) into existence as a direct creation from God. Whilst entertaining the possibility of the traducian understanding of its existence, given his argument that the soul is ordinarily functionally dependent upon the brain, he conjectures it would be unsurprising if the soul came into existence at a similar time to the foetus's nervous system, created directly by a personal cause—namely, created by God. However, whilst asserting that the soul clearly needs the brain to function and experience consciousness, he highlights that function is different from existence, so it is possible that God created this new entity at conception and then it existed without functioning until the development of the brain (Swinburne, *Evolution of the Soul*, chapter 10, see specifically the appendix, 198–99).

41. Where exactly this point in evolutionary history is, Swinburne does not specify (though he is very clear that mammals experience a conscious mental life)—but see his argument from inference that follows.

mental lives, so he thinks it is legitimate to draw the conclusion that animals have conscious souls too.[42]

Arguing throughout that (human) consciousness is functionally dependent on the brain, Swinburne argues that inference to the mental life of animals is legitimate but only as far as to the extent that their brains are similar to human brains. (For instance, it could not be legitimately inferred that an animal could be in possession of long-term memory beliefs due to their not being in possession of the necessary limbic circuit). And whilst affirming that certain higher primates display evidence of a full and vibrant mental life, he argues that human consciousness is yet more advanced (and so derivatively, so is the human soul [the bearer of human consciousness]); he argues it is more advanced and superior in four distinctive areas.

The first way in which human consciousness is more advanced and superior to that of animals is its capacity to reason, or to think in a rational way. Using such concepts as truth, negation, universals, particulars, etc., humans think in logical terms and employ rationality—and they communicate that rationality in *language*. Whilst certain higher animals might show evidence of thought, such thought is not of a *rational* nature and indeed (whilst they show evidence of *communication*) animals do not speak in *language*.[43]

Second, humans have *moral* beliefs.[44] Whilst a crocodile might *kill* a wildebeest, it does not *murder* it, whereas humans have moral beliefs—about what is ethically right and wrong—and they act upon (or against) what they believe to be right.

Relatedly, the third area that is distinctive (specifically to the consciousness of humans) is the possessing of the capacity to exercise (libertarian) free will.[45] An animal will act out of *instinct* (for example, to kill the wildebeest and to eat it) whereas humans have the conscious capacity to freely choose to do A or not to do A.

Fourth, Swinburne argues that the human soul and consciousness is distinct and more advanced than that of animals in that, contra the souls

---

42. (Whilst Swinburne would start lower down the evolutionary tree.) It being apparent that dogs and cats, for instance, display evidence of conscious awareness (e.g., having sensations [of pleasure or pain for example], thoughts [potentially about people], purposings [to eat and drink] etc.).

43. Swinburne, *Evolution of the Soul*, chapter 11, in particular 203.

44. Swinburne, *Evolution of the Soul*, chapter 12.

45. Swinburne, *Evolution of the Soul*, chapter 13.

of animals, human souls have a particular *structure*.[46] This fourth of these distinctive traits will take more exposition but it helpfully draws out the place and nature of *character* in Swinburne's model of the human soul.

Consciousness and Character

To clarify the nature of *consciousness* and its relationship to mental states, consciousness is the mind (/person)'s *awareness* of her mental states at any given time. The mental states of sensations, thoughts, and purposings are all temporary and *episodic* states in which the person experiencing them cannot help but be consciously aware of these states at the moments that they occur (and then is not aware of these states after these episodic states disappear). By contrast, a person's beliefs and desires (in the view that Swinburne espouses) are mental states that *endure* in the mind even when the Subject has no conscious awareness of them.[47]

In exposition of the enduring nature of a person's beliefs and desires, Swinburne details that that person might become more aware of certain beliefs and desires at times when these enduring beliefs and desires become "prominent" (or they "come into the sun" of the person's consciousness)—as opposed to the times when they are "less prominent" (/"in the shade" of that person's consciousness).[48] When a person is knocked-out, for example, and in a deep state of sleep[49]—or in some other unconscious mode—she still retains her desires and beliefs but they are not consciously prominent to her.[50] But even when fully conscious, a person still retains her mental states of beliefs and desires, even if not consciously aware of these enduring beliefs and desires at a particular moment in time (moments in which her beliefs and desires are less prominent/"in the shade").

---

46. Swinburne, *Evolution of the Soul*, chapter 14.

47. Swinburne, *Evolution of the Soul*, chapters 6 and 7—Swinburne espousing the "categorical" view of the enduring nature of such mental states. (Of course, whilst beliefs and desires endure [on this view]—whether the person is aware of them or not—such beliefs and desires can *change* over time.)

48. Swinburne, *Evolution of the Soul*, 108–13, 134, 279–82, 286–92.

49. So not dreaming in this state of sleep.

50. Neither, of course, at that point, are any of the other mental states (e.g., sensations, thoughts, or purposings. (Swinburne, *Evolution of the Soul*, 18–19 and 174–75.)

As regards a person's character, Swinburne follows in the footsteps of Quine to contend that everyone has a "net" (or "web") of beliefs.[51] In this "net" (/web) of beliefs, a person's beliefs about her apparent experience of the world are at the periphery/edge of the net, her beliefs about particular facts concerning the world being closer towards the center; the closer to the center of the net, the more fundamental are these beliefs to the person (and so one's core metaphysical and moral beliefs often lying close to the center of the net).[52] But Swinburne then advances an additional step further (advancing beyond the thinking of Quine) to articulate that a person has a comparable net for their *desires* (as well as beliefs).[53] This net is similarly arranged (for instance, having desires for food or drink at the periphery/edge of the net, desiring to have a stable marriage being closer the center) but, since in order to have a desire about something one has to have certain *beliefs* about that thing, Swinburne contends that these two nets of beliefs and desires are those that are interrelated.[54] The more consistent a person's beliefs (one with another and indeed with her desires), and the more consistent a person's desires (again, one with another and indeed with her beliefs) the more integrated that person will be; a person's character, therefore, in this matrix of beliefs and desires, is:

> A matter of his [moral] beliefs about the worth of actions and their centrality in his system of beliefs; his strong long-lasting and more intrinsic desires; and whether he has or lacks the desire to control the short-term [extrinsic] desires which frequently occur.[55]

Such an understanding receives clarification from Swinburne's later work on the topic in which he further elucidates a person's character as:

> A matter of what . . . [a person/man] thinks worth while [sic], how he naturally directs his life, and how he is inclined to cope with his pangs and urges when they come. A man's character is a central element of his belief-desire set.[56]

51. Swinburne, *Evolution of the Soul*, 263.
52. Swinburne, *Evolution of the Soul*, 263.
53. Swinburne, *Evolution of the Soul*, 263–65.
54. He comments "You cannot just desire something, you need some beliefs about it in order to desire it" (Swinburne, *Evolution of the Soul*, 264).
55. Swinburne, *Evolution of the Soul*, 268–69.
56. Swinburne, *Evolution of the Soul*, 269. Again, phrased elsewhere, he comments "A person's character is a matter of how he or she behaves and thinks. This in turn depends on what that person has the power to do, what he or she believes about, how

Further related to the topic, Swinburne clarifies that a person's character does not *determine* the choices she makes but does make certain choices easy, whilst making other choices hard.[57]

This integration of (enduring) beliefs and desires indicates that the soul—as the bearer of consciousness—has a unique structure, which affects the physical functioning of the soul's correlated brain. Whereas animals might have beliefs and desires, they do not have (second order) desires about their desires,[58] or beliefs about their beliefs,[59] and so do not have an integrated character or indeed structure to their soul; so, this expounds the fourth of the four particular senses in which the human soul (and consciousness) is distinct and more advanced than those of animals.

Life after death?

Finally, in expounding Swinburne's contemporary substance dualist view, it is valuable to consider his (philosophical) thoughts on the continued life of the soul after the death of the brain, and indeed what might follow (from and) beyond this bodiless existence of the soul after physical death.

Though not persuaded (in 1997) of any of the philosophical arguments for life after death (for instance, from claims of re-incarnation, medium-spiritualism, or near-death experiences), integral to Swinburne's argument for substance dualism is that it is logically (and hence metaphysically) possible that the soul survives after physical death—something all the more likely, he argues, if God exists.[60] For Swinburne, the most likely circumstance for the soul, beyond the death of its body, is that, having left its physical brain (and so no longer experiencing sensations, thoughts, and purposings—in the natural embodied manner), the soul carries with it its enduring desires and beliefs. As such, the *character* of the person is carried into life after physical death (whatever that disembodied

---

to attain goals, what he or she desires to do and have (and so what kind of behaviour comes naturally), and what that person believes about what is morally good and bad. While there may be limits (different for each of us) to what we can achieve in these ways, nevertheless (helped or hindered by others) we can to a significant extent for our own characters—if we choose to do so" (Swinburne, *Mind, Brain, and Free Will*, 228).

57. Swinburne, *Evolution of the Soul*, 269.

58. For instance, the desire to control their urges.

59. I.e., rationality.

60. As a work of *philosophy*, and specifically philosophy of mind, Swinburne does not assume the existence of God for his substance dualist position; his arguments are independent of whether God exists or not.

Advancing a Contemporary (Holistic) Substance Dualism

existence is like and however that disembodied condition lasts). Highlighting the soul's (ordinary, embodied) functional dependence on the brain, plus illumining the possibility of the soul's being later re-embodied, Swinburne's conclusion to *The Evolution of the Soul* (his revised edition of) is highly explicatory of his position, and worth quoting in full:

> The view of the evolved human soul which I have been advocating may be elucidated by the following analogy. The soul is like a light bulb and the brain is like an electric light socket. If you plug the bulb into the socket and turn the current on, the light will shine. If the socket is damaged or the current turned off, the light will not shine. So too, the soul will function (have a mental life) if it is plugged into a functioning brain. Destroy the brain or cut off the nutriment supplied by the blood, and the soul will cease to function, remaining inert. But it can be revived and made to function again by repairing or reassembling the brain—just as the light can be made to shine again by repairing the socket or turning on the current.[61]

Recognizing that his analogy breaks down a little, he furthers,

> [But] [h]umans can repair light sockets . . . [whereas] there is a practical limit to the ability of humans to repair brains; the bits get lost. Humans can move light bulbs and put them into entirely different sockets. But no human knows how to move a soul from one body and plug it into another; nor does any known natural force do this. Yet the task is one involving no contradiction and an omnipotent God could achieve it; or maybe there are other processes which will do so. And just as light bulbs do not have to be plugged into sockets in order to shine (loose wires can be attached to them), maybe there are other ways of getting souls to function than by plugging them into brains. But investigation into the nature of the soul does not reveal those ways. And humans cannot discover what else is needed to get souls to function again, unless they can discover the ultimate force behind nature itself.[62]

---

61. Swinburne, *Evolution of the Soul*, 310.
62. Swinburne, *Evolution of the Soul*, 310–11.

Evaluation of Swinburne's Contemporary Substance Dualism

Review of the Analytic Critique of Swinburne's View

Having been a (/the) leading substance dualist view for the last forty years, not surprisingly Swinburne's work has attracted a lot of attention and critique. Whilst his distinguishing between a human mind (/soul) and brain is quite commonplace amongst *property* dualists—in the discipline of philosophy of mind—much attention has been focussed on his argument for *substance* dualism in particular. For instance, following his original *The Evolution of the Soul* (penned in 1986), Alston and Smythe sought to expose that Swinburne's modal argument—for the logical possibility of the soul's survival after death[63]—depends on a "modal confusion"; they sought to show that Swinburne had confused the premises "It is not logically possible both that I am only a body and that I continue to exist in a disembodied form" and "*If* I am only a body it is not logically possible that I continue to exist in a disembodied form."[64] Dean Zimmerman likewise called into question the strength of the modal argument (along similar lines to Hatfield's critique of Descartes's argument), stating:

> Although I may recognize the logical possibility of a psychological subject with a mental life like mine surviving its death, and though I may be able to conceive of myself as unextended [/spiritual/immaterial], I may still be an extended thing *for all I know.*[65]

In reply to these potential objections, Swinburne responded to these selections of critique in his article "Dualism Intact,"[66] by re-laying out his argument for substance dualism in its logical well-formed

---

63. An argument, which, at that time, was being employed *just* to make a case for the *logical* possibility of the soul's survival after death (it being subsequently modified in *Mind, Brain, and Free Will* to also entail metaphysical possibility).

64. Alston and Smythe, "Swinburne's Argument for Dualism," 127 (emphasis theirs).

65. Zimmerman, "Two Cartesian Arguments," 225. He continues: "Conceivability provides only defeasible evidence for possibility. And if one assumes (as Descartes does) that whatever is extended is essentially extended, and whatever is unextended is essentially unextended, then it also follows that I may for all I know be *necessarily* an extended thing."

66. Swinburne, "Dualism Intact," 68–77.

formula.⁶⁷ By detailing the argument in modal logic and tightening up some gentler introductory sentences to the work, he counter-refuted the objection from Alston and Smythe, displaying that he had not slidden from the *de dicto* form of the premise into the *de re* form (as alleged by their suggested "confusion").⁶⁸ Likewise, this tightening-up/clarifying of his argument went a distance in refuting the suggestion of Zimmerman that it was based on fallacious reasoning—the distance being completed by work that followed in his *Mind, Brain, and Free Will*.

In this latter work (of 2013), Swinburne went on to clarify (and so completing the response to Zimmerman⁶⁹) that the "I," in his particular argument, is a "rigid informative designator." To clarify what he means by this, Swinburne initially refers to the work of Saul Kripke who states that

---

67. To remind, his well-formed formula for the argument uses the following representation:

$\&$ = and $\quad \sim$ = not $\quad \lozenge$ = it is logically possible that

With the premises

p = "I am a conscious person and I exist in 1984"
q = "My body is destroyed in the last instant of 1984"
r = "I have a soul in 1984"
s = "I exist in 1985"
x ranges over all consistent propositions compatible with (p & q) and describing 1984 states of affairs"(x)" is to be read in the normal way as "for all x"

So in formal logic terms, the argument proceeds:

p $\qquad$ ...Premise 1

(x) $\lozenge$ (p & q & x & s)...Premise 2

$\sim \lozenge$ (p & q & ~r & s) ...Premise 3

Taken from Swinburne, *Evolution of the Soul*, (Appendix C,) 322 (with further defence on pages 323–32) but additionally penned in his (response) article Swinburne, "Dualism Intact," 69.

68. Swinburne, "Dualism Intact," 70–71.

69. The objection that "I may still be an extended thing for all I know" (Zimmerman, "Two Cartesian Arguments," 225). (Hatfield also highlights such an objection against Descartes's original position [cf. Hatfield, *Descartes and the Meditations*, 246], so Swinburne's model showing further evidence of being a substantial distance beyond the Classic Cartesian model).

a rigid designator is a word which "in every possible world, designates the same object."[70] Then in his own extension of this, Swinburne furthers that:

> For a rigid designator of a thing to be an *informative* designator it must be the case that anyone who knows what the word means (that is, has the linguistic knowledge of how to use it) knows a certain set of conditions necessary and sufficient (in any possible world) for a thing to be that thing (whether or not he can state those conditions in words.)[71]

Later in the book he advances:

> What sort of designators are "I" or "Richard Swinburne" as used by me? These seem to be informative designators. If I know how to use these words, then—when favourably positioned, with faculties in working order, and not subject to illusion—I can't be mistaken about when to apply them . . . and when I am considering applying these words to a person in virtue of that person being the subject of a present experience, no mistake at all is possible. . . . My knowledge of how to use "I" . . . means that I know the nature of what I am talking about when I use the word."[72]

As such he stipulates that "I" is a rigid informative designator, giving him the additional means of counter-refuting Zimmerman's refutation.[73]

Whilst additionally responding to critiques from Moser, Vander Nat,[74] and Shoemaker,[75] in his "Dualism Intact" (of 1996), Swinburne further countered the critiques of Smythe and Alston and Zimmerman—in that article of widely-refuting defence—by highlighting the following principle:

> Like all worthwhile arguments, mine purported to start from premises which many an opponent might grant—viz. (1), (2), and (3) as they stand—to establish a conclusion which he did not previously recognise. I suggested that most people not already having a firm philosophical position on the mind-body issues will grant my premises. But someone already having a firm

---

70. Saul Kripke, *Naming and Necessity* (Oxford: Blackwell, 1980) 48, cited in Swinburne, *Mind, Brain, and Free Will*, 10.

71. Swinburne, *Mind, Brain, and Free Will*, 12 (emphasis mine).

72. Swinburne, *Mind, Brain, and Free Will*, 158.

73. He furthers "Two informative designators are logically equivalent if and only if they are associated with logically equivalent sets of necessary and sufficient conditions." (12)

74. Moser and Vander Nat, "Surviving Souls," 101–6.

75. Shoemaker and Swinburne, *Personal Identity*.

> philosophical position contrary to mine can challenge [in this particular argument] premise 2 [highlighting the approaches of Alston, Smythe, and Zimmerman by way of example]. . . . Now it is true that my argument will not convince anyone who claims to be more certain that the conclusion is false than that the premises are true. But then that does not discredit my argument—for no argument about anything will convince someone in that position. My argument was designed for those prepared to set aside philosophical dogma concerned explicitly with the mind/body issue and rely only on philosophical theses and intuitions about logical possibility relating to other or wider issues.[76]

Whilst being applicable to philosophical argumentation as a whole, this reminder will be of importance when considering subsequent additional critics, and when considering the modal argument he defended (and still defends today) (in particular premise 2)—the comment highlighting that critics should be aware of premises commonly presumed such as "I am purely material in year X" or "I am identical with my body or some part of it."

Further critique of Swinburne's work followed from Eleanore Stump and Norman Kretzmann who additionally sought to refute the targeted premise 2 in their "An objection to Swinburne's Argument for Dualism."[77] This time their critique was argued on the grounds of the philosophy of time; in short, the claim of these thinkers was that Swinburne's argument entailed an "implausibly stringent understanding of a hard fact about a time as one whose truth conditions lie solely at that time."[78] In his "Reply to Stump and Kretzmann," Swinburne countered that the examples to which Stump and Kretzmann appealed—to counter his second premise—concerned *instants* and not *periods* of time, so, given that the relevant facts of his argument concerned *periods*/intervals of some duration, Stump and Kretzmann's refutation was also unsuccessful.[79]

William Hasker then also attempted refutation of Swinburne's argument—again with focus on premise 2—by claiming it to be a circular argument;[80] Swinburne then refuted this attempt at critique by clarifying that one can accept premise 2 of the argument without ever

---

76. Swinburne, "Dualism Intact," 71.
77. Stump and Kretzmann, "Objection to Swinburne," 405–12.
78. Swinburne's words from the abstract to his response: "Reply to Stump and Kretzmann," 413–14.
79. Swinburne, "Reply to Stump and Kretzmann," 414.
80. Hasker, "Swinburne's Modal Argument," 366–72.

understanding the conclusion (or without accepting Premise 3)—making the claim of circularity implausible.[81]

By this point, Swinburne had published the revised edition of *The Evolution of the Soul* with supplementary appendices added to respond to the objections that had been drawn since the publishing of the earlier edition. Following that revised edition of the book, further critiques were made by Hasker and then more latterly from Nicholas Everitt and from Yujin Nagasawa.[82] By now, Swinburne had refrained from counter-refuting every article that appeared in response to his work, but he subsequently penned *Mind, Brain, and Free Will* to strengthen his earlier arguments.[83]

81. Swinburne, "Argument is not Circular," 371–72.

82. Hasker, *Emergent Self*, 152–60; Everitt, "Substance Dualism and Disembodied Existence," 331–47 and Nagasawa, "Review of Evolution."

83. He describes the arguments of this latter work as "deeper and stronger . . . based on a full discussion of underlying philosophical issues (e.g., the criteria for the identity of events and substances, and the grounds for asserting that a certain state of affairs is metaphysically possible"). (He further clarifies in the work that the soul he espoused [by 2013] was simple/indivisible [an advancement beyond the Bonaventurian view he had formerly entertained] [Swinburne, *Mind, Brain, and Free Will*, preface].)

As regards the critiques of Everitt or Nagasawa, whilst not responding directly to their critiques in this 2013 work, Swinburne's responses are *entailed* in *Mind, Brain, and Free Will* (as well as in previous work[s]). (Nagasawa's first attempt at critique—seeking to draw a distinction between the "original" body and the "current" body on Swinburne's argument—is unsuccessful given Swinburne's "Quasi-Aristotelian assumption" (that a substance has to have some continuity with itself in order for it to be the same substance [See Swinburne, *Evolution of the Soul*, 153]. Nagasawa's second attempt to refute the argument was the standard "problem of interaction," which has already been responded to in chapter 3 of this book [and see further the developments of Swinburne's counter to this objection in *Mind, Brain, and Free Will*, chapter 4]. Everitt seeks to refute Swinburne's modal argument epistemologically—questioning the reality of a person's *perceiving* in a disembodied state, and second by critiquing the validity of the argument giving [what he sees as] an analogous invalid argument based on the possibility of his plastic chessboard surviving into a world without plastic. As will be seen in what follows, Swinburne's first premise entails metaphysical possibility [as well as logical possibility] because the "I" in the premise is a genuine rigid [informative] designator [meaning that Everitt's second critique concerning the "parallel" argument fails because the chessboard in his critique is a *non*-rigid designator]; and in response to the objection of the *perceiving* of a disembodied person, this is not necessary to or part of Swinburne's modal argument—it being an argument of the logical possibility of *ontological* survival. [Whilst an interesting subsequent question, the person's epistemological capacity of perception does not give grounds for refuting an *ontological* argument.] As for the specifics of the critiques made by Hasker—concerning the *origin* of the soul [both humans' and animals']—a number of these were actually responded to by J. P. *Moreland* in "Origin of the Soul in Light of Twinning, Cloning and Frozen Embryos," 1–12. The relevant remainder to his argument—not addressed in *Mind, Brain,*

Following the publication of that work, in 2013, further critique of his argument arose (against his argument from modal logic) as the *European Journal for Philosophy of Religion* devoted an edition of the journal to Swinburne's *Mind, Brain, and Free Will*—encouraging critiques from philosophers of mind and then inviting Swinburne to respond.[84] Whilst additionally focussing on mental and composite substances, and free will and moral responsibility, not surprisingly, much of the discussion centered around informative designators—a key facet in Swinburne's (making the) case for metaphysical (not just logical) possibility. In a similar manner to the discussion in *Faith and Philosophy* through the 1990s, refutations were met with counter-refutations from Swinburne—rebutters struggling to find holes in his modal logic—but the issue of metaphysical possibility remaining where a lot of the attention has been focussed.

In regard to metaphysical possibility, the case that Swinburne makes for this position might be strengthened by the contemporary work on near-death experiences (NDEs)—particularly the work published in 2018 by researcher Gary Habermas.[85] Swinburne previously chose to refrain from employing this line of argumentation—due to the absence of evidence (at the time [when he was originally penning his argument]) that the brain, in such NDEs, had definitively ceased to function;[86] but given that the research of Habermas purports to demonstrate exactly that

---

and *Free Will*—Swinburne addressed when the three of them interacted [he, Moreland and Hasker] at a live conference at Biola in 2013 entitled "Neuroscience and the Soul." [For more details of the intricacies of these arguments see Churchouse, "Renewing the Soul," chapters 5 and 6]).

84. Swinburne, *Are We Bodies or Souls?* (penned in 2019) was then similarly followed by a round table discussion—followed by Swinburne's counter response(s)—in an edition of the journal *Roczniki Filozoficzne* (69.1 [2021]).

85. Habermas, "Evidential Near-Death Experiences," 227–46.

86. At the time of consideration, Swinburne was drawing upon the work of Paul Badham—from 1982. Being forty years previously, he commented "[Although there was evidence in the instances of NDEs that the patients' *hearts* had stopped beating during the time of their conscious experience] I do not know of any evidence that at these moments their *brains* had ceased to function. And if the brain was still functioning then, what the evidence would show is not that the soul may function when the brain does not, but only that its perceptual experiences (i.e., sensations and acquisitions of belief about faraway places) are not dependent on normal sensory input" (Swinburne, *Evolution of the Soul*, 304 [emphasis mine]). Swinburne appears justified in his caution at the original time of writing, but with the neuroscience and medical technology having developed in the subsequent forty years to the point of now being able to acutely monitor a patient's brain, see argument above.

premise, Swinburne's case might be additionally strengthened through drawing on this contemporary research.

In brief, these accounts of NDEs reveal that, with the brain of the patient being demonstrably "offline" during the time of clinical death (shown by a flat line on the electroencephalogram [EEG]), the patient—narrating each account—had experienced a (conscious) NDE and been able to acquire knowledge from that experience which would have been impossible to acquire had the patient not had that conscious experience.[87] The research of Habermas reveals that these conscious NDEs, and the knowledge which was gathered during such periods, occurred for each of the patients surveyed whilst his or her brain was flatlined during the time of clinical death.

Regardless of whether or not Swinburne opts to employ the argument from NDEs, enough has been seen in this review to show the robustness of Swinburne's modal argument and that attempts to critique the validity of the argument—at least on the grounds of modal logic—have always been met with vigorous counter-rebuttals; Swinburne continuing to advance and defend the argument in the present.

But whilst recognizing the analytical strength of the argument from this discussion of Swinburne's modal logic above, Pentecostals will be of particular concern to consider the *body* on his contemporary substance dualist view (remembering the concerns of Yong and Kärkkäinen as expressed in chapter 2).

Critique of Swinburne's View based on the Relationship of the Soul to the body?

Swinburne's argument received particular focus, concerning the body-soul relationship, from J. P. Moreland in his 2000 work *Body and Soul*;[88] it then received further comment from Stephen Evans in a 2014 review of *Mind, Brain, and Free Will* in the journal *Faith and Philosophy*.[89] Each of these reviews help to highlight the issues concerning the body that may

---

87. For instance, giving accounts about what was happening on the hospital roof, what was occurring back home—even acquiring knowledge of deceased relatives—all experienced during the time the patient was clinically dead.

88. Rae and Moreland, *Body and Soul*. The particular critique came from Moreland—who contributed the philosophy of mind to the book (with Rae contributing the section on ethics to the work).

89. Evans, "Swinburne," 105–8.

be of concern to Pentecostals (whilst also elucidating the relationship of the soul to the body in the specific model that Swinburne espouses).

Moreland is glad to affirm much of Swinburne's substance dualist position, however, he critiques the place of the body, recognizing that it becomes, on Swinburne's model, merely a "property thing." Preferring a more Thomistic(-like) understanding—in which the soul *animates* the body, so giving the body a specifically human identity—he critiques that, for Swinburne's substance dualist position, the contingency of the body makes it difficult to establish what makes a human body specifically the body of a *human*.[90] Moreland is correct in his understanding that the body, on Swinburne's view, is contingent—something Swinburne himself affirms in the following passage:

> ... each human is a pure mental substance, having a soul as their one essential part and a body as a non-essential [contingent] part; physical properties belong to humans in virtue of belonging to their bodies, and pure mental properties belong to them in virtue of belonging to their souls.[91]

Indeed, elaborating on the body's contingency (before assessing the actual *critique* of Moreland) allows for an important nuance to be identified in Swinburne's dualistic position. In a passage which deserves full citation to avoid caricaturing the model of Swinburne (into the Classic Cartesian mould) (and indeed, in a passage which further brings insight as to the *presumable* viewpoint of Descartes [but which Descartes found difficult to convey with the clarity that would have been helpful]), Swinburne elucidates the meaning of "person" on his view:

> Some dualists, such as Descartes, seem sometimes to be saying that the soul is the person; any living body temporarily linked to the soul is no part of the person. That, however, seems just false. Given that what we are trying to do is to analyse the nature of those entities, such as men, which we normally call "persons," we must say that arms and legs and all other parts of the living body of a man are parts of that person. My arms and my legs are parts of me. The crucial point that Descartes and others were presumably trying to make is not that (in the case of men) the living body is not part of the person, but that it is not essentially, only contingently part of the person. The body is separable from the person and the person can continue even if the body

---

90. Rae and Moreland, *Body and Soul*, 201.
91. Swinburne, *Mind, Brain, and Free Will*, 2.

is destroyed. Just as I continue to exist wholly and completely if you cut off my hair, so, the dualist holds, it is possible that I continue to exist if you destroy my body. The soul, by contrast, is the necessary core which must continue if I am to continue; it is the part of the person which is necessary for his continuing existence. The person is the soul together with whatever, if any, body is linked temporarily to it."[92]

This highlights that Swinburne does not want to downplay the body, but that it *is* contingent on his view—the soul being the only *essential* aspect of the (holistic) human being. Indeed, if the soul survives the death of the body and is the only part of a person to persist through the event of death,[93] then it *has* to be the case that it is specifically the *soul* that is the *essential* person[94]—the body being contingent. So, Moreland is right that Swinburne's view holds that the body is contingent, and, with the body being a physical substance, it is likewise apt to label it a physical "property thing."

But the actual *critique* of Moreland (which will be common among philosophers of an Aristotelian-Thomistic persuasion[95]) is that such a view makes it difficult to establish just what makes a human body specifically the body of a *human*. This is a thought-provoking critique, and one Swinburne seems not to answer directly (being more interested in the question "what makes a body *my* body?"). However, Swinburne holds the viewpoint that the present day human body has evolved to its current form and that it is sufficient, in its modern day form, for the functioning of the immaterial soul,[96] and he sees the human body as "a chunk of matter

---

92. Swinburne, *Evolution of the Soul*, 146.

93. See the discussion in chapter 4.

94. The soul that could subsequently receive a renewed temporal body *after* the period of the intermediate state.

95. Cf. Dew "Swinburne's New Soul," 29–37 who (preferring a Thomistic view of the soul) comments "In my view, substance dualism seems to diminish the important role of the human body" (30).

96. Remembering that, whilst advocating the evolution of the body, he is of a creationist view of each individual human soul (See Swinburne, *Evolution of the Soul*, 199). Recognizing that certain animals also have conscious minds/souls too, it would seem plausible to infer that Swinburne believes that their souls are directly created too (though he does not explicitly state this). Swinburne does not specify at what point, in the evolutionary lineage, that animals began to exhibit consciousness—and so which animals have conscious souls. (At times he muses that invertebrates might be conscious but [along with the rest of the philosophical and scientific community] acknowledges that it is a question on which it is difficult to be precise.) Whilst behavior might give some indication, it is to be reminded that he thinks that the mental life of animals is

through which ... [an essential person] makes a difference to the material world, and through which he acquires true beliefs about that world."[97] As such (whilst each human soul has the property of "thisness"—giving each a distinct individuation), it would appear that, on Swinburne's view, a body gets its *human* identity from its relation to its human *soul*, i.e., what makes the body distinctly a *human* body is its being the chunk of matter through which a (defining) (human) soul interacts with the world.

If the understanding above is a correct deduction of Swinburne's view, then a response is necessitated to an anticipated objection to this view, namely, would it not have the implication that, were a human soul re-embodied in the body of a lower animal, e.g., in the body of an antelope, that that would make the antelope's body, by definition, a *human* body? In response, (though such are useful as thought experiments for illustrating the possibility of the soul's being dis/re-embodied) Swinburne would likely argue that this scenario would be an impossibility given that the human body *alone* is endowed with the faculties for the functioning of the human soul. When articulating the capacities unique to the human soul, he argues that the *structure* of each human soul—specifically each person's unique integration of beliefs and desires—means that (were the latter thought experiment actually possible) only certain (very similar) brains to that of the soul's (original) resident body—i.e., specifically its *human* brain—could possibly house the soul. So, whilst Kafka's Beetle and related fairy-tale examples are engaging, the event of the human soul's being re-embodied in the body of another animal would actually be impossible, so the objection does not stand or hold.

If the above deduction of Swinburne's viewpoint is correct, it would also carry the implication that a deceased human body would not actually be a *human* body in that the soul is no longer present to give it that human identity. This is interestingly similar to Aquinas's attitude that (with its defining form no longer present) it is inaccurate to describe a deceased human body as still a *human* body—both Swinburne and Aquinas would regard it as "matter" but not, in fact, *human* matter. (In application, further, to a debate within the philosophy of mind) It would

---

that that has to be inferred from the degree of similarity of the animal's brain structure to that of the human brain. So, whilst in cats and dogs (for instance) it is an easier task to affirm that they have conscious souls (demonstrated by their behavior [expressing beliefs, desires, intentions etc] and the requisite brain structure) for animals lower down the evolutionary scale it becomes a lot less clear (cf. Swinburne, *Evolution of the Soul*, 180–89).

97. Swinburne, *Evolution of the Soul*, 146.

also have the implication that a zombie (i.e., a body without any self-consciousness) could likewise not be called a human. It is the human *soul*, on Swinburne's view, according to the above deduction, that gives its physical body the identity of being a *human* body.

By this point one can anticipate a possible level of discomfort amongst certain theologians—particularly of a Pentecostal spirituality—for whom the body is essential to human identity. Thinkers like Yong and Kärkkäinen are adamant that the body is paramount to a person's identity and any indication of the body being contingent—even with the advancements that Swinburne has made—might well be met with accusations of the view's being comparable to the problematic forms of dualism, such as the Classic Cartesian/Platonist models which de-value and downplay the body. Indeed, both scholars were definite in maintaining that "human identity = embodied." With these sentiments being markedly strong, and in seeking to allay some of these fears, it is important to say that, for Swinburne (as indeed for contemporary dualists), the body is highly important—it is good and to be affirmed. Swinburne clarifies his belief on this matter in three definitive passages. He states:

> Some of the modern hostility to substance dualism arises from the feeling that it leads to the view that having a body and bodily well-being are unimportant. But substance dualism in no way entails that; . . . having a body is necessary for a worthwhile human existence, and . . . pleasure arising from bodily causes is a good thing.[98]

Then, further, in a summary of his view:

> Bodies keep us alive and, by enabling us to interact with each other and the world, they make our lives greatly worth living; but our soul is the one *essential* part of each of us.[99]

And in light of the doctrines of creation, incarnation, and (re)new(ed) creation,[100] Swinburne underlines the value of the body, stating:

> [The view] I have been advocating . . . is, I believe, that of the Bible. Both Old and New Testament hold that a man is a thing of flesh and bone. (Because the Jews believed—see Genesis 1—that all material things were good, they could set a high value on

98. Swinburne, *Mind, Brain, and Free Will*, 2.
99. Swinburne, "Summary," 7.
100. Cited in a theological appendix included in the revised edition of *Evolution of the Soul*.

> man without denying his materiality.) When . . . the Christian religion arose within Judaism affirming life after death, the life which they affirmed was not a natural immortality, but a resurrection—God intervening in history to give to Christ or all men new bodies and thereby new life. The Nicene Creed affirms belief in 'the resurrection of the body.' Christian theology has always affirmed that the reunion of a soul with a body in the General Resurrection requires a divine act. . . . [Certain Platonist-coloured Christian views seem] to me to be out of line with the Christian emphasis on the embodiedness of men as their normal and divinely intended state, and also to fall foul of the arguments of . . . [his chapter concerning the future of the soul]. If souls exist in purgatory or elsewhere without their bodies or with totally new bodies, they do so by special divine act, not under their own natural powers.[101]

These extended sections are worth citing in full as they directly refute the claim that Swinburne's view downplays the body. Yet, whilst his position stands up against such critiques, it is also worth asking the question of Pentecostal theologians—if still feeling potentially uncomfortable with the substance dualist view(s)—as to what might be underlying such discomfort. Whilst recognizing that Pentecostal theology has a particular theological emphasis on the holistic nature of a human, might it be, in its contemporary scholarly era, that an (over?-) *exaggerated* emphasis on the body (and on the correlative theme of embodiment) has arisen in Pentecostal theology—due to an underlying driver or ideology distorting the holistic emphasis? In particular, might a post/late-modern ideology (that has reacted to Descartes's anthropology) have exacerbated the holistic anthropological emphasis, turning it from a healthy holistic emphasis into an *over*-emphasis on the body?

Current academic literature is full of lament concerning Descartes's anthropology and his regarding human beings as primarily "thinking (/ [self-]conscious) things." Whilst Descartes could/should have been stronger in his regard for the human body, as part of the reaction to his anthropology (which is often equated with modernism), the body and its materiality—celebrating, for instance, a human's gender, race, and sex— is affirmed again and again in a *post*-modern reaction to the modernistic Cartesian view.[102] Indeed, entailed within such an ideology is a related

---

101. Swinburne, *Evolution of the Soul*, 311–12.

102. Whilst "late-modern" is a helpful and nuanced description, because "postmodern" is more commonly used, so more familiar in contemporary discussion, from this

"materialism" of the age—which has no place for the existence of self-conscious spirits/souls.[103] So, it is worth asking the question as to whether the discomfort of some Pentecostals, towards a contemporary substance dualism, might be as a result of having unconsciously joined that reaction and so are now *over*-affirming the body (and the popular emphasis on embodiment). Comparable to what was seen in the analysis of chapter 1, are certain Pentecostals unwittingly absorbing (in this instance) the materialist postmodern ideology, so having implications for their theology and specifically anthropology? Whilst postmodern thought stimulates further interest in the related doctrines of creation, incarnation, and (re)new(ed) creation (which is certainly a positive thing), when viewing these important doctrines *through the postmodern materialist lens*, the potential of this approach is that it results in the downplaying or out-right rejection of the (self-conscious) spirit realm, and the over-emphasizing of the body.

Whilst Pentecostals need to entertain the suggestion described above, the status of the human body on Swinburne's contemporary substance dualist view might have its language helpfully modified by one further review comment, this time from Evans. His following question is helpful, both in the sense of giving language to Pentecostals still feeling discomfort with Swinburne's substance dualist view, but also in its allowing Swinburne to further allay the fear(s) that are obviously felt when regarding a human person as essentially a soul (with a contingent body). In a very appreciative review, Evans asked the nuanced question:

> If, like Swinburne and Descartes, we take the [essential] human person to be a pure mental substance, rather than a composite of body and soul, could we nevertheless think of the body as in some way the *mode of existence* the mind takes in this life, rather than a separate "entity" or "part" of the person? This might allow us to agree that the person is distinct from his or her body, but still see the person and body as intimately fused.[104]

(Whilst the term "distinct" would be preferable to that of "separate," and it being important to remind that the *human being* as a whole is a composite of body and soul [see chapter 4]—even if the essential human

---

point on in the chapter this latter term will be used in reference to the modern-day context/ideological climate.

103. See the following chapter for further discussion of the use of the terms "soul" and "spirit."

104. Evans, "Swinburne," 108 (emphasis mine).

person is an immaterial soul,[105]) To think of human beings as souls that are in a particular embodied mode—or, put another way, that humans are "embodied souls" (which after death become temporarily disembodied)—might help allay the concern of Pentecostals with this idea—that an essential person is a mental substance (soul) with her body being contingent.[106] But to take heed again of an important clarification laid out by Swinburne, Pentecostals need to remember that "substance dualism is a doctrine about what is necessary *for our existence*, not about what makes a full and worthwhile life."[107] This distinction is vital for Pentecostals to understand (and perhaps is often not grasped as fully as would help the wider theological discussion). As such, Swinburne's view puts forward a helpful view of the soul and its relation to the body.

Conclusion

This chapter has expounded Swinburne's contemporary substance dualism in exploration of its potential and capacity to serve as an *advanced* holistic dualist model (within the Cooper holistic dualist paradigm) for the book's overall goal of proposing an enhanced Pentecostal doctrine of human constitution. Whilst not the only view of the soul-body relationship to which Pentecostals might be beneficially drawn,[108] the philosophical rigor of Swinburne's model and its concordance with the

---

105. Using the analogy of the Apollo rocket might help convey what is being contended. The majestic rocket stood ready for lift-off endowed with major fuel cells as the *whole* rocket. As the mission continued (and once out of the earth's atmosphere) those fuel cells gradually were jettisoned until all that remained of the rocket was the lunar capsule containing the astronauts for landing on the moon. This might be called the "essential" rocket as it enabled the astronauts to land and then fly back to earth, but on its own it was just the essential rocket which was re-awaiting re-embodiment as a whole rocket for another mission. (As with all analogies, this has its short-fallings but hopefully illustrates the full/whole version of the human being as embodied, even if it is possible for the soul—the essential human person—to survive temporarily without the body.)

106. And as a further distinction worth considering, if one used the language of "enfleshed" as opposed to "embodied" the interesting distinction made by Cooper (that the souls/"shades" in the intermediate state are implied as being bodily but not fleshly beings) would allow for this feature of the contemporary substance dualist soul to be likewise—immaterial yet bodily, whilst not being "fleshly." (This would give grounds for considering the soul to be consciously present and causally active throughout the human body.)

107. Swinburne, *Mind, Brain, and Free Will*, 2 (emphasis mine).

108. See the other holistic dualist models articulated at the start of the chapter.

Pentecostal accent on holistic anthropology reveal it to be a particularly strong and suited model for the development of the Pentecostal doctrine. This contemporary substance dualism views humans in their (ontological) constitution as beings that are embodied (self-conscious) souls. The soul, on this model, is the core/essential person which can survive the death of the body, but the ordinary and desired condition (of this essential and spiritual soul) is its being fully and gladly embodied—in union with its physical body.

Recognizing that Pentecostal potential objections to this model would be focussed on the place of the body—given Pentecostals' theological emphasis on holistic anthropology—the chapter has given sustained and focussed attention to the body on Swinburne's view. Through closely considering the model, it has disclosed itself as being fully concordant with this accent—the third of the quadrant of emphases (more commonly pronounced in Pentecostal theology). Given that Swinburne's model is clearly concordant with Pentecostals' eschatological emphasis, as indeed it is concordant with their "supernatural" dualistic emphasis, it has not been necessary to consider these accents during this present chapter. It is also, in its current form, concordant with the distinctive renewal pneumatological accent, even if at this point in its development, it might be regarded as a little "under-dynamic" concerning this first theological emphasis. More will be said, in this respect, in the pages of the following chapter. But having advanced, by this point, a specific holistic dualism—a model that has been constructed in light of Pentecostal pneumatology and biblical studies (chapter 4), and philosophy of mind (chapter 5)—the book will progress to its last and final chapter in which the (philosophical) spiritual soul established, at the core of the model expounded, will be further enhanced in dialogue with the pneumatological spirituality at the core of Pentecostal theology.

Part IV

A Pentecostal Enspirited Proposal for Enhancing the Doctrine of Human Constitution

6

The (Theological) Spiritual Soul and an Enspiritable Holistic Dualism

IN LIGHT OF PENTECOSTAL pneumatology, and the anthropological teaching of Scripture, the holistic dualism of Cooper was highlighted in chapter 4 as a suitable foundational model for the constructive work of this book. Given that Pentecostals are keen to emphasize the physical but spirit-filled world, and they desire to ground their doctrine in the final authority of Scripture, the holistic dualism of Cooper has been commended as an apt and healthy foundation upon which the following work of construction has been seeking to build and develop.

Building onto the biblical anthropology of Cooper and advancing within-but-beyond his general holistic dualist model, chapter 5 then proceeded to highlight Swinburne's contemporary substance dualism as a further development in the project. This contemporary dualistic model—with the nature of the soul entailed—provides a philosophically robust understanding of the soul in relation to the body. As well as being philosophically strong, the model is also concordant with the quadrant of Pentecostal emphases (even if [currently] being somewhat "under-dynamic" regarding the renewal pneumatological emphasis). It is therefore a preferable model to the emergent monism of Yong and Kärkkäinen. But whilst being initially enhanced in this sense, this model might be further developed—indeed *Pentecostally*-enhanced—through additional engagement and dialogue with the spirituality of Pentecostalism.

In order to arrive at the ultimate goal of proposing an enhanced *Pentecostal* doctrine of human constitution, the model that has been so far constructed will initially be tested for "fit," in relation to and within the (spirit-inducing) anthropology of Pentecostal spirituality. This testing the model for "fit," in dialogue with Pentecostal spirituality, will bring supplementary theological insight for additionally enhancing the model. Following this focus in the first half of the chapter, the second half of the chapter will then proceed to *make* the theological enhancement, leading to the desired enhanced Pentecostal model of constitution being attained by the end of the chapter.

So, checking the model for "fit," the chapter will begin by engaging with Steven Land's celebrated work *Pentecostal Spirituality*,[1] from which the chapter will proceed to constructive *theological* enhancement of the model—specifically a *pneumatological* enhancement—one advanced and stimulated by that engagement with Land's Pentecostal spiritual theology.[2]

Trying the Model for "Fit" in Dialogue with Land's Pentecostal Spirituality

To check the contemporary substance dualist model for "fit" with(in) Pentecostal theology and spirituality, this section will proceed with a brief description of the thesis of Land's *Pentecostal Spirituality* followed by an exposition of the anthropology of his spirituality; a review will then ensue which will consider the strength of Land's anthropology and whether it could be surpassed. This process will provide the means of testing the "fit" of the contemporary substance dualist model in relation to and within (current) Pentecostal theology and spirituality.

In a definition that has been etched in the minds of Pentecostal scholars since he originally wrote it in 1993,[3] Land defines spirituality as:

---

1. Land, *Pentecostal Spirituality*.

2. "Spiritual theology" is actually a phrase coined by Simon Chan to describe theology integrated with spirituality; (see Chan, *Pentecostal Theology*, 31–32) but as the exposition to follow will show, it is a very apt description of Land's integrated thesis—the thesis he contends for in his *Pentecostal Spirituality*.

3. The definition being quite possibly the most oft-cited sentence in Pentecostal scholarship to date.

> The integration of beliefs and practices in the affections which are themselves evoked and expressed by those beliefs and practices.[4]

Describing the affections more fully as "construals of" or "concerns for" the world,[5] or one's "dispositions" or "reasons for action,"[6] Land roots the beliefs and practices of Christians in these integrating affections; the result of this (re-)rooting is that the *theology* of believers (their "understanding of God") becomes rooted in their *spirituality* ("their lived experience of faith").[7] What therefore follows from this thesis is that Pentecostals (embracing the definition[8]) contend that their theology arises from and flows out of their distinctive spirituality.[9] As regards what is distinctive to *Pentecostal* spirituality, and hence Pentecostally-coloring their theology, Land's work is a carefully nuanced proposal that draws from the history of the *Classical* Pentecostal tradition to then contend a thesis for the contemporary Pentecostal era.

For specifically *Classical* Pentecostals (of a Wesleyan-Holiness heritage), and from the defining "heart" of this movement's spirituality,[10] Land identifies a distinctly (Classical) Pentecostal affection—a *passion* and *ruling* affection—that shapes and integrates of all the other Christian affections. From the beliefs and practices of (Classical) Pentecostals—during that specific decade and heart of their history—he identifies a distinctive "Apocalyptic Vision," that is, an eschatological worldview-hence-longing for the coming of the Kingdom of God (this "Apocalyptic Vision" [of the time] carrying a dispensational theological flavor). Land argues that this key and ruling affection, distinctive of Classical Pentecostal spirituality, shapes and colors the other Christian affections of a believer and her related beliefs and practices. However, in recognizing among contemporary Pentecostals that dispensationalism has patently waned, and arguing that the related eschatological fervor has therefore also considerably

---

4. Land, *Pentecostal Spirituality*, 13.

5. Land, *Pentecostal Spirituality*, 136.

6. Land, *Pentecostal Spirituality*, 136. Examples being compassion, gratitude, and courage.

7. Definitions taken from Albrecht and Howard, "Pentecostal Spirituality," 235.

8. And (as seen in the introduction) this being the majority consensus of Pentecostal scholars.

9. See introduction to this book.

10. Land draws from the first ten years of the Classical Pentecostal movement but wanting to affirm that this first decade of the movement forms the "heart" not the "infancy" of the spirituality (Land, *Pentecostal Spirituality*, 13).

waned, Land has suggested that the spirituality of *contemporary* Classical Pentecostals (but now applicable to Pentecostal spirituality more widely) still exhibits a distinctive Pentecostal affection—namely a *passion for the Kingdom*—but now viewed through a Trinitarian lens.[11] This Pentecostal yearning for the Kingdom of God is the (one) distinctive Pentecostal affection that frames the other Christian affections;[12] for Land, it is the ruling and central affection—distinctive of Pentecostal spirituality—that shapes all of the other (Christian) affections, and indeed Pentecostally-colors the theology that flows from this distinctive Pentecostal spirituality.

Land's work has had a substantial impact on ensuing Pentecostal scholarship. Whilst the Pentecostal distinctive affection has been subsequently discussed and honed by Pentecostal scholars,[13] Land's thesis of wanting to root Pentecostal theology within the affections of Pentecostal spirituality *per se* is very much a pattern that has been followed and celebrated by Pentecostal scholars since he originally authored the work. Indeed (as was stated in the book's introduction) the consensual majority of Pentecostal scholars (of all varieties [not just of the Classical persuasion]) want to affirm this ground-breaking thesis that Pentecostal theology flows out of this distinctive spirituality.

The (Theological) Anthropology of Land's Pentecostal Spirituality

Expounding his work a step further, Land attempts to locate the *anthropology* of Pentecostal spirituality in the concept of the human "heart"; he identifies this biblical term as denoting the center or "I" of a human—being the person's integrative center of mind, will, and emotions.[14] As the

---

11. That is, Pentecostals exhibit a distinctive passion for the kingdom of the *Trinitarian* God (Land, *Pentecostal Spirituality*, 197).

12. Land, *Pentecostal Spirituality*, 66. This "yearning" for the kingdom of God is manifested in Pentecostals' longing to "see" God, to experience his kingdom, to be filled with the eschatological Spirit, to "taste" the life of that new creation (Land, *Pentecostal Spirituality*, 60–66, 174–78).

13. See for instance this book's introduction for a discussion of the distinctive Pentecostal spirituality. The discussion does not use the term "affection" but employs the language of the Pentecostal "worldview"/"social imaginary" when articulating what is distinctive about Pentecostal spirituality and so theology.

14. Land, *Pentecostal Spirituality*, 132. Though in an earlier passage, he comments on how, for Classical Pentecostals, the heart was seen as the seat of the mind, will and the *affections* (105) giving an indication of the difficulty he exhibits in seeking to locate (anthropologically) the spirituality within the human "heart" (see exposition to follow in main text).

title of his book spells out, his is a work of *spirituality*, not *systematic* or *philosophical* theology, however, remembering his spiritual-theological thesis (as articulated in the paragraphs above) it is not surprising that Land's anthropology of the "heart" has since been adopted and subsequently assumed by Pentecostal theologians. Such assimilation is illustrated by Vondey in his (global) *Pentecostal Theology*,[15] in which he affirms that:

> The integrative centre of human spirituality is the "heart" composed of human affections, beliefs and practices. Recognisably dominant in Pentecostal anthropology is human affectivity, the passions and desires, or "abiding dispositions" of the heart, which play a central role in Pentecostal accounts of human spirituality and the transformative encounter with God.[16]

Summative of the thought of many,[17] this highlights the prevalent influence of Land's theological anthropology; Land's emphasis on the heart and its affections has become integral to Pentecostal anthropology. In sum, for him—and for Pentecostals following—their Pentecostal encounters with God (and additionally with one another) are those they gladly affirm and regard as being encounters of the "heart."[18]

On many accounts, this language and concept of the "heart" might be helpful for expressing the "I" and center of a human—indeed it is a term employed in this way throughout the teaching of Scripture. However, when carefully considering Land's thesis concerning spirituality in relation to the (biblical) meaning of the "heart" he establishes, it becomes apparent that there are issues contained therein; the (language and concept of) "heart"—though biblical and exegetically helpful—is not adequate to contain *theologically* everything that Land (and Pentecostals) desire of it, and there appear conceptual holes and cavities in this theological anthropology.

In elucidating Land's understanding (which draws on a biblical understanding historically accepted by Pentecostals), his definition of the

---

15. An award-wining work that both draws on and reflects Pentecostal scholarship historically and globally.

16. Vondey, *Pentecostal Theology*, 183–84.

17. See further Costello, "Tarrying on the Lord," 31–56; Smith, *Thinking in Tongues*, chapter 3; Smith's Cultural Liturgy trilogy—in particular *Desiring the Kingdom*. See also Coulter and Yong, *Spirit, the Affections*; Yong and Studebaker, *Pentecostal Theology and Jonathan Edwards*.

18. Vondey, *Pentecostal Theology*, 187.

human "heart" as the center/the "I" of the person is one in which he accommodates the mind and the will (and indeed also the emotions). He then affirms that beliefs arise from the mind, and practices from the will, but wanting to assert that these beliefs and practices are rooted and integrated in the *affections,* he then gives no equivalent location from which the affections arise. Such affections, in Land's understanding, just arise from "within the heart" and then these location-less affections are where, he asserts, the beliefs and practices are "evoked and expressed." This leads to anthropology that is, unfortunately, conceptually unclear. In diagrammatic form, Land's anthropology might be pictured as the following:

(The circle on this diagram = the "heart"—the center/"I" of a person)

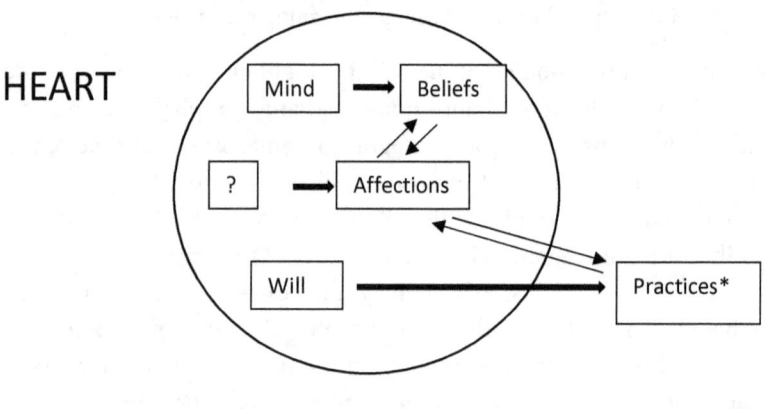

Figure 1[19]

In Land's anthropological thinking (and within the center/"I" of a person), it is not conceptually clear where the affections are actually located, and it is therefore further unclear as to the location in which the beliefs and practices are supposed to be integrated—the affections are nebulously left as located as somewhere "within the heart." From Land's articulation, the missing location for the affections would *appear* to be "in the heart" (out of which the affections arise)—as pictured in the diagram below:

---

19. These practices arise from within the "heart"—specifically, they flow from the will—and are then carried out (/put into action) in the external world.

The (Theological) Spiritual Soul

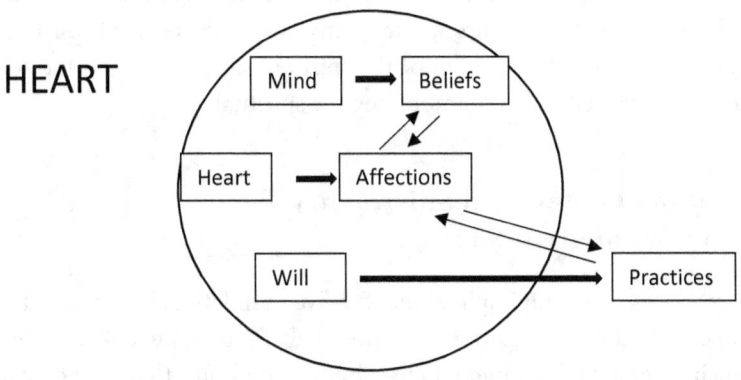

Figure 2

but this would fall into equivocation in the sense of viewing the "heart," on the one hand, as the "I"/center of the person—in which the mind and the will are contained—but also using the term "heart" more specifically to be the location out of which the affections arise. His anthropology is conceptually unclear and the language and concept of the "heart," on this model, appears inadequate for explicating the (wider) anthropology of Pentecostal spirituality.

In addition to this lack of conceptual clarity, there is no anthropological means in his model by which the beliefs-affections-practices tripod may under-go Pentecostal renewal. Of course, Land would argue that the beliefs-affections-practices are renewed by the Holy Spirit and by spiritual practices such as prayer,[20] but the *anthropological* means of this renewal is unclear on his understanding of the heart. Put differently, on Land's anthropological model, the thinker is left with the question: What is the human location of the Divine-human (Pentecostal) encounter? Better, *where* is the human location, and point of S/spiritual interface, in (or at) which the human experiences the pneumatological encounter? This is likewise unclear on Land's model.

In contrast to Land's limited anthropological suggestion, a clearer and fuller location for both accommodating the spirituality's anthropology and so for expounding the human interface (/"pole") of the Divine-human encounter—a location able to contain Land's model of spirituality whilst additionally enhancing it spiritually—would be to locate the human "I" not in the heart, but in the *spiritual soul*. The second half of the

---

20. Land, *Pentecostal Spirituality*, 165–73.

chapter will focus on the latter of these two benefits, but the first will be addressed at this point through mapping Land's Pentecostal spirituality onto the spiritual soul (or "into" the spiritual soul)—showing the soul's superior capacity for accommodating the spirituality.

Mapping Pentecostal Spirituality into the Spiritual Soul

In chapter 5 it was highlighted that the five foundational mental states—namely thoughts, sensations, desires, beliefs, and purposings (upon which all of a person's mental life is built)—are states that are possessed and experienced by the (immaterial) spiritual *soul*. To deepen this understanding, and to map the model of Land onto/into this view of the soul,[21] the additional (expository) terminology of Moreland helps to clarify the *nature* of this spiritual soul.

In short, Moreland's terminology explicates that the soul is endowed with certain *capacities* which enable it to experience its mentals states, and these capacities can be helpfully grouped into *faculties* of the soul.[22]

The soul's ability to experience the sensation of the color blue serves as an example of a *capacity* of the soul. Whilst not always (consciously) *experiencing* the color blue, the spiritual (/immaterial) soul has *capacity* for experiencing the sensation of blue—indeed it has numerous capacities for experiencing a wide range of sensations.[23] Beyond the mental state of sensation, it further has multiple capacities for experiencing its other mentals states (for instance the capacity to make a decision, to think about food, to desire freedom). Within the soul these capacities can be "roomed" into compartments or *faculties* of the soul[24]—each faculty containing a natural grouping of related capacities. As examples of specific faculties, the capacity to experience the sensation of the color green, or the sensation of the color red, are capacities that can be roomed into the soul's faculty of sight; the capacity to hear music (for instance) into the soul's faculty of hearing.

---

21. Preferring, from here, to employ the latter preposition—mapping Land's model *into* the spiritual soul.

22. Moreland, *What Is the Soul*, 39–41.

23. Further examples of capacities for sensation would be the capacity to see green, hear sounds, feel glad etc.

24. Because the term "housed" (or "accommodated") is used to speak of the *soul's* "housing" or "accommodating" the spirituality, when referring to where capacities abide—within that overall "house" of the soul—they will be spoken of as being "roomed" within the relevant faculty.

The (Theological) Spiritual Soul

Augmented by this further terminology, Land's faculties of the "will" and "mind" can be now mapped into the *spiritual soul*, giving early signs of the soul's potential for better "housing" the anthropology of Pentecostal spirituality. If the terms "will" and "mind" are employed in the everyday sense in which Pentecostals tend to employ them (that is, using "mind" in the regular sense of the word [as opposed to the specific disciplinary meaning of the term as used in the philosophy of "mind"][25]), it can be said that a person's capacities for willings/"purposings" are contained within the *faculty* of the "will" (with one's *actions* and *practices* then proceeding from the will's capacities for purposings). It can further be stated that the second component of the tripod—this time the Pentecostal (oral/narrative) beliefs—can be sourced, as per the thinking of Land, in (the faculty of) the mind. In considering this latter faculty, Land's designation (that the beliefs occur in the mind) is helpful to an extent, although, being more philosophically specific, a person's capacity for *thoughts*—as well as their capacity for *beliefs*—should also be roomed in the mind.[26] But indeed it is right to say that a person's capacities for belief can be placed within the faculty of the mind, giving a soul that so far looks like the diagram below.

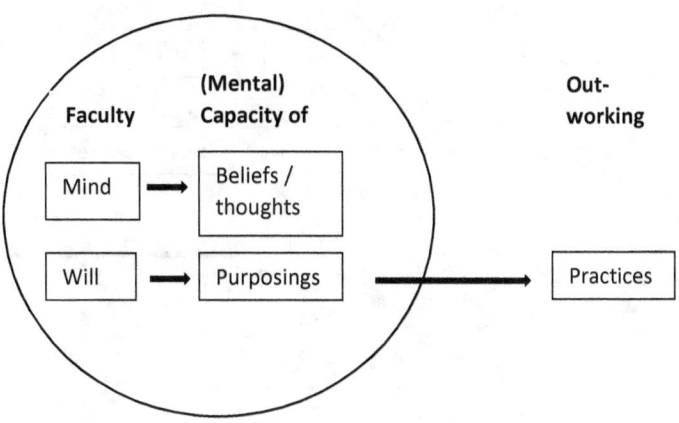

Figure 3

---

25. It is to be remembered that philosophy of mind uses the language of "soul" as synonymous with the language of "mind," whereas the (more regular and) Pentecostal usage would see the "mind" as part of the human "I" (or, in the language just espoused, a *faculty* of the soul).

26. Cf. Moreland, *What Is the Soul?* 40.

In considering the Pentecostal usage of the anthropological term "heart," and the related "desires/affections," it might appear tempting initially to room those capacities of "desire/affection" within the faculty of "heart"; however, (whilst a human's desires certainly have a place within the spiritual soul as one of the five foundational categories of mental states) for two significant reasons this mapping of the desires into the faculty of "heart" would be overly hasty and, in fact, facile. The first of these reasons is the slipperiness of the term "heart" which was highlighted in the review above in the critique of Land's anthropology. Given the lack of clarity concerning the relationship of the "desires/affections" to this understanding of the "heart," to attempt to describe the heart as a "faculty" of the soul—which contains the capacities of human desires/affections—might not seem particularly precise or wise. Second, although recognizing that the terms "desires" and "affections" are sometimes used synonymously in the Pentecostal scholarly literature,[27] they are not, in fact, synonymous. Therefore, any overly hasty attempt at mapping Pentecostal spirituality into the soul—to look (anything) like figure 1.4—would be facile.

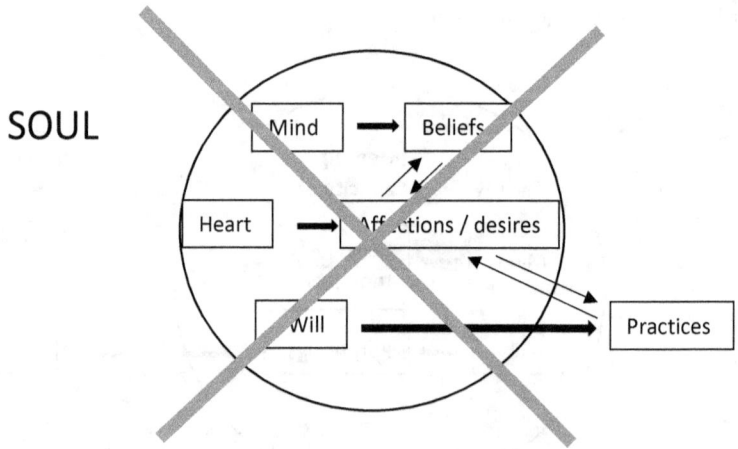

Figure 4

In fact, the "affections" (as Land himself describes them) are actually "cares"/"motivations"/"dispositions"/construals" of the soul, and Land gives compassion, courage, and gratitude as specific examples of such

---

27. See for instance Vondey's quote above or cf. Smith's usage in his *Desiring the Kingdom*.

affections.²⁸ So, affections/dispositions are *more than* just desires, they are based and "supervene" on both the desires *and beliefs* of a person,²⁹ but they are not merely synonymous with the desires.

To understand the relationship of the affections, the beliefs, and desires, it is helpful to recall (from chapter 5) Swinburne's exposition of the mental states of beliefs and desires to understand how it is that they give rise to the affections. First, it will be recalled from his exposition that a person's desires and beliefs are like two inter-related "nets" (with one's net [or web] of desires entailing certain underlying beliefs to give content to the desires).³⁰ Second, it will be remembered that beliefs and desires *persist* (that is, whilst they are not always "prominent" [in a person's {self-} conscious awareness], one still retains these beliefs and desires [even at the times when they are "in the shade" of the mind's conscious awareness]). Third, it is to be recollected that a person's *character* is given rise to by a combination of her moral beliefs and her desires—Swinburne defining the character of a person as:

> A matter of his [moral] beliefs about the worth of actions and their centrality in his system of beliefs; his strong long-lasting and more intrinsic desires; and whether he has or lacks the desire to control the short-term [extrinsic] desires which frequently occur.³¹

With these three pertinent factors being recalled as the backdrop to the present discussion, it becomes evident that desires *and* beliefs are the bases from which affections/dispositions arise (they "supervene" on the two "subvenient" bases of the beliefs as well as the desires). As such, a more nuanced and accurate depiction of the relationship of a person's mental states to that of the affections would be the following:

---

28. Land, *Pentecostal Spirituality*, 136–41.

29. The word "supervene" has here been employed in the philosophical sense—as used in previous chapters. Given that those previous chapters rejected the philosophical position(s) that advocate the mind supervening on the brain, the use of "supervene" above is simply borrowing the term to state that the affections are given rise to by a combination of the beliefs and desires—beliefs and desires which are mental states, that is, states of the (immaterial) spiritual mind.

30. In this paragraph, the words "one" and "a person" are being used synonymously.

31. Swinburne, *Evolution of the Soul*, 268–69.

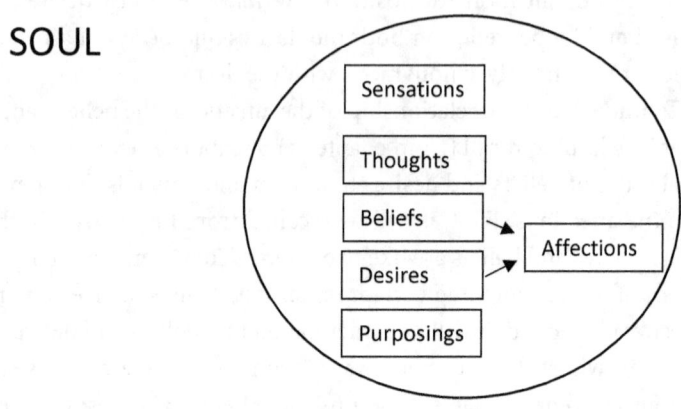

Figure 5

This provides a clearer, more nuanced understanding of the affections than merely equating them with desires, and as such, also avoids the facile understanding (highlighted in figure 4) of conceiving the "desires/affections" as rooted in the "heart," which are then evoked and expressed by the beliefs and practices.

By this point in the chapter, it should now be becoming clear that the (immaterial) spiritual soul has superior resource and capability for accommodating the components of Pentecostal spirituality—due to its fuller delineation of mental states, capacities, and faculties. If employing the same diagrammatic form, an attempt to visually depict the anthropology of Pentecostal spirituality—as mapped "into" the spiritual soul—might look something like the following:

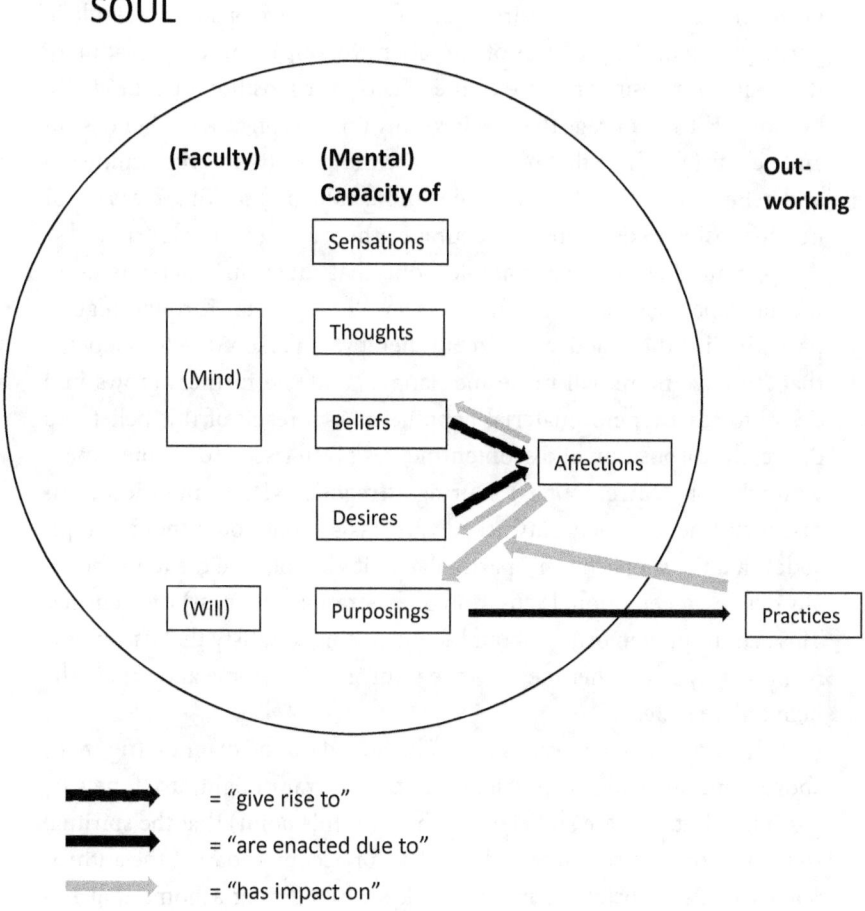

Figure 6

Whilst quite a full depiction, the diagram intends to convey that a person's affections are given rise to by (combinations of) her beliefs and desires. A person's desires are impacted by the practices in which she participates—practices which themselves are enacted due to her purposings. But the affections which have been given rise to then in turn *impact* (some of) the beliefs and desires that the person currently holds—or subsequently *comes* to hold; they also impact, as a result, her purposings and hence subsequent actions and practices.

The following example illustrates what is depicted on the diagram above. A person believes that this world is not final, and that a (re)new(ed) creation awaits, and longs/desires to experience the reality of that (re) new(ed) creation. (This desire is one that has developed as a result of participating in the practices of Christian worship). This combination of the belief and desire give rise to the affection/disposition of courage (in her soul).[32] That courage then reciprocally impacts on other of her desires and beliefs (she finds that her love of the things of this world diminishes and believes that the ultimate goal is more valuable) making it easier for her purposing to develop, to encourage others along on the journey.[33]

Or another possible example—one that draws in a person's other mental capacities too—may further serve to elucidate. Through regular partaking in (the practice of) "retail therapy," a person develops a belief that "to have more will make me happy;" and she furthers grows in a desire for that type of material happiness. As a result of this belief and desire, the disposition of discontentment is given rise to (discontentment with what she currently has). During a (regular) visit to the shops, this discontentment is then outworked; she has a (conscious) thought (episode) that the shops, on this particular visit, do not have the item she really desires; an emotional sensation of frustration (or angst) then ensues. This sensation then brings about her purposing to satisfy the discontentment by way of another means—she returns to her home and orders the item online instead.

The arrows and relations might be honed on the diagram (figure 6) above—and indeed, it is possible that the diagram might, itself, be surpassed[34]—but they are sufficient to show (at this point) that the spiritual soul has thorough resource and expanse for accommodating the anthropology of Pentecostal spirituality. Indeed, by offering a home that has *superior* capability for accommodating the anthropology of Pentecostal spirituality (preferable to Land's conception of the "heart"), it shows not only to "fit" with Pentecostal theology and spirituality but that both Pentecostal theology and spirituality might be enriched through accepting this offer of a new anthropological home.

Having offered Pentecostal spirituality and theology this superior location and home for its anthropology, might the spiritual soul,

---

32. A disposition being particularly notable in the face of affliction and persecution.

33. As examples of the impact that the above affection might have on her other beliefs and desires, her desire for the things of this world might diminish or take less priority, or her belief that the goal is more valuable might subsequently increase and mature.

34. See discussion below.

in addition, have capability for addressing the second and pertinent issue—potentially providing resource for the (S/)spiritual *renewal* of the anthropology of Pentecostal spirituality? This question may be helpfully modified in a way which seeks the mutual benefit of Pentecostally-enhancing the soul; so, rephrasing the question, (and having dialogued with Land's spiritual-theological thesis,) can the spiritual soul *be enhanced* to provide an *anthropological* means by which the Holy Spirit brings renewal to the components of Pentecostal spirituality? The argument of the second half of this chapter is that it can, and in a way that *pneumatologically* enhances the model so far established—giving a theological injection to the meaning of the soul's being a "spiritual" soul.

Means of Pentecostally-Enhancing the Soul

The remainder of chapter 6 sets out to provide the desired anthropological center and means of S/spiritual renewal for the components of the Pentecostal spirituality—seeking to proffer (within the [immaterial] spiritual soul) the human interface (/"pole") of the Pentecostal Spirit-human encounter(s). In order to do this, and stirred by Land's spiritual theology, the chapter will return to Pentecostals' interest in the concept of the *human spirit*; it will consider the possibility of this spirit's serving as the anthropological interface and means by which the Holy Spirit renews the beliefs, affections, practices of Pentecostal spirituality, indeed being the possible means of the Spirit's renewing *all* the soul's mental capacities. Through implementing this process, the "spiritual" nature of the soul—established so far in this book—will be injected with additional *theological* meaning, and an enhanced *Pentecostal* model of the human soul will be proposed as a result. This will lead to the chapter's concluding with the desired goal of this book—an enhanced Pentecostal doctrine of human constitution.

The model that has been so far constructed—and will be completed by the end of the chapter—is one that is ultimately *philosophical-theological* in nature. Having been constructed (so far) in light of Pentecostal pneumatology, biblical exegesis, and philosophy of mind, in order to provide the final constructive enhancement of this model this chapter will return to all of these components (whilst inverting the order in which they are taken) to provide a Pentecostal philosophical-theological model of the soul and hence doctrine of constitution.

Recognizing the Pentecostal desire that theological models are biblically rooted (or consistent), this second half of the chapter will proceed exegetically, initially, to explore what Scripture reveals about the human spirit. It will begin by interacting with the work of two Pentecostal biblical scholars—John Levison and Gordon Fee—to draw out the scriptural teaching concerning the human spirit (in relation to the Holy Spirit); Levison's work on the Spirit and spirit in the Old Testament and Fee's work on the Spirit and spirit in Paul will be employed to ascertain a sufficient understanding of what Scripture says on this issue.

After ascertaining, from this exegetical work, an understanding of Scripture's anthropology of "spirit," these insights will be taken and conceptualized through interacting with a particular idea of Moreland—specifically from his philosophy of mind—that can likewise be drawn upon to develop a Pentecostal (philosophical-theological) understanding of the human spirit.

After modifying Moreland's philosophical-theological idea and applying it to the model of the soul being constructed in this book, the resultant model of the soul will then be enhanced in a Pentecostal manner through returning once more to the ontology of J. K. A. Smith and applying his "Enspirited Ontology" specifically in the direction of this newly constructed model. This will result in the proposing of a "spiritually"-enhanced model of the soul—one that is now *theologically* "S/spiritually"-enhanced—engendering the desired enhanced Pentecostal model. Moreover, this (theologically-) enhanced spiritual soul will serve as a renewed locus for both understanding and articulating the anthropology of Pentecostal spirituality, serving as an anthropological means of (the Holy Spirit's) renewal of the components of the spirituality.

Biblical Pneumatology

Levison: Spirit and spirit in the Old Testament

The biblical pneumatology of Levison is somewhat controversial, diverting from the consensual understanding of what is being referred to by the Old Testament term *rūach* ("spirit"). But critical engagement with Levison's work allows the drawing out of Scripture's Old Testament [O.T.] pneumatology and brings particular insight to its understanding of the *human* spirit.

Standardly, scholars adopt a position similar to Wolff's, which asserts that *rūach* in the O.T. refers predominantly to "the divine Spirit, ... the principle of life, [the] life-force."[35] As a specialist in O.T anthropology, Wolff's understanding conveys and leads the consensus—his definition above being expounded in chapter 2 of his *Anthropology of the Old Testament*.[36] There, he elaborates that the originating sense of *rūach* is that of the moving wind or air. (As with the related term *nephesh*) Wolff expounds that *rūach* is associated with "breath" and most often refers to the breath of God (though referring sometimes to the breath of a human). Further, this "breath" is the God-given and animating power (or the enlivening God-given energy/force) which vitalizes living beings (cf. Ezek 37), animating but also enabling such beings to carry out their purpose in life. So, in application to a human, *rūach* empowers one's thought, gifting, and will (for instance) and so empowers the person to carry out her God-given vocation. Knowing that this is the representative view, Levison agrees with much of the consensus's *meaning* (of *rūach*) but disagrees with the term's *referent*.

As a summary of his *Filled with the Spirit*,[37] Levison argues that theologians mistakenly read the *Holy Spirit* back into the O.T. passages when reading its references to "the spirit/breath of God." He argues that this approach is incorrect because there is no indication given in O.T. passages that the *rūach* of God is the person of the Holy Spirit, it is simply "the spirit of God" (or "spirit of life") which inhabits and vitalizes all living things.[38] For Levison, this *rūach* (breath/spirit) of God—breathed into every living being—is the same spirit that charismatically endows people for certain roles (for instance, charismatically gifting Bezalel), or gives wisdom and godly character to his people (for instance, to Elihu, Micah, Daniel); Levison argues that this divine spirit which animates a person is the same spirit of a person that empowers their virtue, knowledge, and skill—the divine and human spirit being in fact one and the same thing.[39]

---

35. Wolff, *Anthropology of the Old Testament*, 22.

36. Wolff, *Anthropology of the Old Testament*. The summary to follow comes from this second chapter of Wolff's book. (Note, either English spellings *rūah* or *rūach* are appropriate due to trying to give the phonetics of the Hebrew term.)

37. Levison, *Filled with the Spirit*.

38. Levison, *Filled with the Spirit*, 422.

39. Levison, *Filled with the Spirit*, 34–86.

On the understanding Levison proposes, it is up to the individual person whether she rejects or nurtures the divine spirit within her—whether she develops her God-given gifts and character, and how she responds when called by God.[40] So, rather than anachronistically reading "the Holy Spirit" into certain references in the O.T., Levison contends that all the references to "spirit," there, should be non-capitalized as they all refer to the holy breath of life.[41] The implication is that the O.T. does not distinguish between the concept of a human spirit and the divine spirit, a human is alive because of the (vitalizing) spirit/breath of God in her.

In terms of how this relates to the coming of the S/spirit in the New Testament [N.T.], Levison argues that, because of the imbalanced work of Gunkel (who argued that after the time of the last O.T. prophet the Spirit stopped being among Israel until the time of the N.T.),[42] most theologians think the "coming of the Spirit" is something new, and unique to Christians who have received the redemption offered in Christ. However, given the teaching of the O.T., this coming is not something entirely new but rather an additional endowment—an "expansion" of the spirit of God in a human.[43] Levison contends that Luke, Paul, and John's pneumatology (as well as that of the Intertestamental period with its emphasis on charismatic endowment) complement and fill out the pneumatology of the O.T.,[44] which assumes that the spirit of God is in everyone/everything, thus enabling creatures to be alive.

Such an account is intriguing, and not surprisingly garnered much interest from Pentecostals. And the interaction between Levison's work and Pentecostal scholars' (mainly appreciative) critiques give fuel for considering the place and nature of the *human* spirit as delineated in Scripture. For instance, Max Turner, in his critique, helpfully clarifies Levison's controversial premise, highlighting that this (non-capitalized) holy spirit—that has been planted in a person—is the means "by which YHWH orchestrates human activity to enhance creation and accomplishes his particular historical purposes with Israel."[45] He further highlights that, for Levison, a lot of the references to the *rūach/pneuma* of God in a human person are speaking not about: "the transcendent divine

---

40. Levison, *Filled with the Spirit*, 118–53.
41. Levison, *Filled with the Spirit*, 87–103.
42. Gunkel, *Wirkungen des heiligen Geistes*.
43. Levison, *Filled with the Spirit*, 423.
44. Levison, *Filled with the Spirit*, 253–421.
45. Turner, "Levison's *Filled with the Spirit*," 195.

Spirit (the Holy Spirit), occasionally on loan to humans . . . [but of the] immanent God-given *anthropological spirit*—the living heart, mind and soul, ever open to, and influenced by, the Lord himself."[46]

This key contention of Levison has not surprisingly received critique; representing the views of many,[47] Donaldson and Buchanan see an "ambiguity of 'spirit,' 'a spirit,' and 'the spirit' . . . inherent in Levison's thesis."[48] Of course, this is something Levison would like to maintain, but the majority of Pentecostals disagree with him on exegetical grounds. Gabriel, for instance, points to Numbers 16:22 and Psalm 32:2 as clear references to a (human) spirit differentiated from the S/spirit of God.[49] When developing this critique further in light of N.T. pneumatology, Turner advances that in Luke's pneumatology (as well as that of Paul and John), if a person has not received the Holy Spirit (in a soteriological sense) she has not got the Spirit at all, so Levison's talk of "expansion" or "greater endowment" or "redirection" cannot do complete justice to the N.T. texts.[50]

Anticipating such a reaction, Levison wrote his own rejoinder to the Pentecostals' responses to his work—at the end of the editions of *Pneuma* and the *Journal of Pentecostal Theology* devoted to his work on the topic.[51] Unsurprisingly, he sought to defend his position, in the process helpfully elaborating that:

> The original Hebrew and Greek words for 'spirit' were used to convey concepts as diverse as a breath, a breeze, a powerful gale, an angel, a demon, the heart and soul of a human being, and the divine presence itself.[52]

Such a full understanding of the possible meanings and referents of *rūach* is helpful, as is his underlining of the *very* close association between the Holy Spirit and the human spirit. Whilst Pentecostals' exegetical critique needs to be maintained regarding the distinction made in the O.T.

---

46. Turner, "Levison's *Filled with the Spirit*," 195 (emphasis mine).

47. See also the responses by A. T. Wright, J. B. Shelton, J. M. Everts, and F. D. Macchia in the edition of *Pneuma* devoted to the topic—*Pneuma* 33.1 (2011).

48. Donaldson and Buchanan, "Filled with the Spirit," 34.

49. Gabriel, "Intensity of the Spirit," 367.

50. Turner, "Levison's *Filled with the Spirit*," 199.

51. See footnotes above for the specific editions devoted to Levison's work.

52. Levison, "Conversation," 221.

between the Holy Spirit and the human spirit,[53] what certainly *can* be affirmed is that the human spirit has a very close and intimate relationship with the life-giving Holy Spirit. This intimate relationship between the Holy Spirit and the human spirit described in the O.T. may go some way in possibly illumining the Divine-human Spirit-encounter relationship at the heart of Pentecostal spirituality suggesting that it might be beneficially conceived of as a Spirit-spirit encounter. Through turning to the work of the N.T., in particular the writings of Paul, the potential of such an idea will be further probed as the chapter extends its exegetical investigation of biblical P/pneumatology.

Fee's Work on the Spirit and spirit in Paul

Gordon Fee's anthology, *God's Empowering Presence,* addresses the topic of the Holy Spirit in Paul's letters[54]—giving a thorough exegesis of *every passage* within them that mentions the S/spirit,[55] from which he explicates Paul's pneumatology. As still the leading work on this issue, such a comprehensive approach and work, plus Fee's credentials as a Pentecostal himself, make his N.T. work a valuable counterpart to the preceding discussion of the S/spirit in the O.T. drawn from critical interaction with the pneumatology of Levison.

In *God's Empowering Presence: The Holy Spirit in the Letters of Paul,* Fee makes the case that to really understand the Spirit in Paul, the Spirit must be recognized as an experienced reality and person—a dynamic eschatological experience of the living God. Fee is clear that Paul did not write about the Holy Spirit simply as a doctrinal concept to be systematized, but as a person and power to be experienced—one who is central to Christian life. He comments: "For Paul, the Spirit, as an experienced and living reality, was the absolutely crucial matter for Christian life, from beginning to end."[56]

---

53. Further highlighted by verses such as Gen 6:3; 6:17; 7:22; Job 12:7; 34:14–15; Ps 51:10; 104:29–30 in which the *rūach* spoken of leaves translators with uncertainty as to whether the Holy or human S/spirit is being referred to (see the variety of translations given).

54. Fee's 976-page anthology is the fullest treatment of the topic to date.

55. Fee considers all thirteen of the letters bearing Paul's name to be genuinely Pauline.

56. Fee, *God's Empowering Presence,* 1.

Central to Fee's book are the three words of his title. He relates that God the Holy Spirit is a *person*—the person of the Trinity who, through Christ, makes God known to us, and the person by whom we experience the living God. Linked to this, the person of the Spirit is also God's *presence* with his people; in fulfilment of the O.T. promises, the Holy Spirit is God's personal presence dwelling in and with his new covenant community—they are the N.T. realization of the O.T. tabernacle and temple and the fulfilment of the promises made in Jeremiah and Ezekiel of God's coming to indwell his people. And the Spirit is God's *Empowering* presence among his people—those not left on their own to live out the Christian life but filled with God's power in order to accomplish such a task. So, Fee's key emphases are Person, Presence, and Power.[57] Fee recognizes that the Spirit is not the center of Pauline theology—seeing that more as "salvation in Christ"—but the Spirit of Christ being so integral to making that an experienced reality, the two cannot be separated, underlining again Fee's Trinitarian presuppositions and the essential role the Spirit has in Christian lived experience.[58]

When expounding the relationship of the Holy Spirit to the human spirit in the N.T. texts, Fee makes clear that the vast majority of the (145) occurrences of *pneuma*, appearing in the N.T. writings, refer to the Holy Spirit. Yet he also identifies that there are fourteen references of such which refer to the human spirit (1 Thess 5:23; 1 Cor 2:11; 5:5; 7:34; 14:14; 16:18; 2 Cor 2:13; 7:13; Gal 6:18; Rom 1:9; 8:16; Phlm 25; Phil 4:23; 2 Tim 4:22). Recognizing that some of these fourteen are controversial, and responding in particular to Jewett who thinks many of them are simply referring to the Holy Spirit,[59] Fee convinces his readers of this distinct (human) use by providing an in-depth exegesis of each reference, giving reason to believe that all fourteen refer to the human spirit. In the process, he goes a distance in defining what this human spirit is, stating that this entity "refers to the interior, nonmaterial component of the human personality."[60] In further elaboration, and underlining the relationship between this spirit and the Holy Spirit, he states:

> Those who see this usage [*pneuma* referring to the interior, nonmaterial component of the human personality] as denoting that

---

57. Fee, *God's Empowering Presence*, 5–8.
58. Fee, *God's Empowering Presence*, 896–99.
59. Jewett, *Paul's Anthropological Terms*.
60. Fee, *God's Empowering Presence*, 66.

> part of human existence that serves as the place of intersection between the human and the divine by means of the Holy Spirit are most likely moving in the right direction.[61]

Such "intersection" language is very interesting and draws further attention to the intimate relation of the Holy Spirit to the human spirit in Scripture, one very much emphasized by Pentecostal spirituality. But moving a step further in this direction, Fee then argues that, along with the distinct fourteen verses, there are four further uses of *pneuma* where Paul seems to *deliberately* blur the two (1 Cor 5:3–4; 6:17; 14:14–15; Col 2:5), Fee proposing that the term *pneuma* in these instances could quite happily be translated as S/spirit. He argues that the reason Paul feels content to allow for such fluidity in these instances is that for him "the believer's spirit is the place where, by means of God's own Spirit, the human and the divine interface in the believer's life."[62]

This is interesting and further consistent with the discussion in the previous section surrounding the meaning of the O.T. term *rūach*—both testaments underlining the distinction between the Holy Spirit and the human spirit, yet also the intimate connection between the two. Scriptural exegesis therefore confirms the human "spirit" as the anthropological locus of a human's spirituality, in addition providing legitimacy for conceiving of the encounter at the heart of Pentecostal spirituality as being a Spirit-*spirit* encounter.

Spiritually-Enhancing the Soul

Having drawn from the exegetical work a biblical understanding of the human spirit, the work will now draw upon insight from the philosophy of mind to consider the place and *concept* of the human spirit and its relation to the spiritual soul. To do so, it will return to J. P. Moreland's terminology, employed earlier in the chapter, and a particular suggestion he makes regarding the human spirit. This suggestion will then be taken, modified, and honed, and through further stimulus from Smith's Pentecostal ontology, applied to the model being constructed.

---

61. Fee, *God's Empowering Presence*, 66.
62. Fee, *God's Empowering Presence*, 25.

The spirit *within* the Soul in Engagement with Moreland's Philosophy of Mind

Recalling Moreland's terminology of the soul as having a variety of *faculties*, Moreland suggests that the human *spirit* might itself be viewed as *a* particular faculty of the human soul. In this sense, the spirit is not therefore something ontologically different from the soul,[63] but rather is a compartment or a facility of the soul. Using an everyday analogy, Moreland depicts the soul as being like a chest of drawers[64]—each drawer representing a different faculty of the soul (so one drawer would be the faculty of sensations, another, the faculty of desire, another, that of the will, another, that of the spirit). So, the spirit is part of the soul, but a specific faculty within it. Moreland explicates:

> The *spirit is that faculty of the soul through which the person relates to God* (Ps 51:10; Rom 8:16; Eph 4:23).* Before the new birth, the spirit is real and has certain abilities to be aware of God. But most of the capacities of the unregenerate spirit are dead and inoperative. At the new birth, God activates, makes alive those capacities and implants new capacities in the spirit, such as new desires for God's Word, Christian fellowship, growth in spiritual maturity. These activated and newly implanted potentials are fresh capacities that need to be nourished and developed so they can grow.[65]

This is a creative idea which provides a means of retaining the human spirit—so beloved by Pentecostals—whilst also further addressing the question as to whether it is preferable to employ the term "soul" or

---

63. Pentecostals traditionally appealed to verses such as 1 Thess 5:23 and Heb 4:12, supported then by 1 Cor 14:14–15 to contend that a human is made up of a body, soul, and spirit. That there is a biblical distinction between "soul" and "spirit" is clear from these verses (cf. the list of commentators in the discussion in chapter 1). But given that there is no clear instance of Paul using the term *psuchē* to refer to a spiritual part of a human—in the twelve other times he uses the term (instead tending to use it as a synonym for a person, personal pronoun, or as denoting a "living creature" [cf. Rom 2:9; 11:23; 13:1; 1 Cor 15:45; 2 Cor 1:23; 12:15; Eph 6:5–6; Phil 1:27; 2:29–30; Col 3:23; 1 Thess 2:8.])—it appears there is very little ground for thinking that the "soul" [in Paul's letters] is an immaterial entity (as per the standard trichotomous view). And given that "soul" is used in the book of Hebrews also as more of a synonym for a person/as a personal pronoun (cf. Heb 4:12; 6:19; 10:38; 12:3; 12:17), it appears there is no ground for affirming trichotomy from the passages of Hebrews either.

64. Discovered when hearing an interview given by Moreland for "Closer to Truth," the interview being entitled "Is the Soul Immortal?"

65. Moreland, *What Is the Soul?* 40–41 (emphasis his).

"spirit" in reference to the human (immaterial) spiritual entity (because the terms, on this understanding, are not interchangeable). Moreover, it avoids the having to ground an understanding of the spirit in dubious biblical exegesis (as per the hermeneutics of the trichotomist Pentecostals[66]). In fact, Moreland clarifies this issue (in a footnote marked * in the citation), helpfully stating that the biblical anthropological words for heart, soul, mind, spirit etc. have differing meanings depending on their author and context, and *"no specific use of a biblical term should be read into every occasion of the term."*[67] So (in differentiation from Pentecostals past), this idea of the spirit's being a *faculty* of the soul provides a *philosophical-theological* understanding of the anthropological spirit, one that is consistent with the exegesis above but not an understanding *derived* from scriptural exegesis; it is a philosophical-theological model which gives place for the spirit within the soul.

Whilst an interesting suggestion and model, two issues need to be highlighted and addressed in order to benefit from and apply such an understanding to the model of the soul being developed. First, having defined the spirit as he does, Moreland opts to say no more about the idea.[68] This may not be too surprising given his discipline of philosophy of mind (a discipline that does not commonly welcome theological concepts such as the [anthropological] spirit), however, recognizing the potential in the idea, it appears that more could be said on the issue, and careful consideration of his suggestion would be of benefit in the constructing of the enhanced understanding of the soul and doctrine of

---

66. As was affirmed in chapter 1, commentators are unanimous in thinking that (a) what is of primary emphasis in 1 Thessalonians 5:23 is Paul praying that God would sanctify the Thessalonians *wholly* (linking it back to his exhortations in 3:13 and 4:3–8), and similarly, (b)the main point in Hebrews 4:12 is that the word of God is able to penetrate to the very core of a person's being, and so (c)it would be "precarious" to build a trichotomous doctrine of humanity upon these verses ("precarious" being F. F. Bruce's word—one helpfully summarizing the feelings of wider commentators on this particular issue [see Bruce, *1 and 2 Thessalonians*, 129–30 and Bruce, *Epistle to the Hebrews*, 113]). (For further comment on the relevant issues, see particularly Marshall, *1 and 2 Thessalonians*, 163; Fee, *God's Empowering Presence*, 66, and Fee, *Letters to the Thessalonians*, 230. Further, see Best, *Epistles to the Thessalonians*, 243–44; Morris, *Epistles to the Thessalonians*, 181–82; Malherbe, *Letters to the Thessalonians*, 338–39; Witherington, *1 and 2 Thessalonians*, 173; Ellingworth, *Epistle to the Hebrews*, 263.

67. Expounded as an endnote (22) in Moreland, *What Is the Soul?* 60 (emphasis mine).

68. Other than an even shorter reference to it in his (and Rae's) *Body and Soul*, 204 and a comment in his interview (above) that sees the spirit as "a power of the soul that is capable of being aware of God and the supernatural" (min 1:09–13).

constitution.[69] Second, though being a suggestion that is valuable, it appears that Moreland's conception of the (human) spirit needs modification and refinement for this particular faculty of the soul to more fully cohere with the soul's other faculties and capacities. Moreland's idea of God's (re-)activating the spirit is a helpful contention, as is his proposing that God (re-)enlivens certain capacities, but as the thought currently stands, some of the capacities of this spirit faculty seem to be already the function of other faculties (for example, at regeneration, God implanting new *desires* for his Word.)

In wanting to address these issues to benefit from this suggestion and model, Moreland's idea-with-potential can be constructively modified. If one viewed the human spirit as the *lead* faculty, or indeed *central* faculty of the soul, then the very center/core of the soul would be this faculty of (human) spirit. When this spirit is re-animated by the Holy Spirit, this enables a restored functioning of the other capacities and faculties that are also reduced/damaged by sin, through their being (re-)orientated to God by means of the Spirit's renewing this spirit. Sensations (for instance) of God's presence, or desires to now read his Word, beliefs about new life in Christ, or purposings to live for his kingdom (whilst dormant before new birth) would then be re-fully activated as a result of this renewing of the (S/)spirit; the spirit at the core of the soul being the central and paramount faculty for the correct teleological functioning of the other mental faculties.

To depict this understanding, potentially a more helpful analogy than that of the chest of drawers (and indeed also surpassing the two-dimensional diagrams given in the sections above) would be to picture the soul, instead, as a globe—containing the rich matrix of a person's mental states and capacities. If the spirit were seen as the *core* of the globe, then it might be helpfully depicted that, once Spiritually-renewed, the spirit *illumines* the soul's other faculties and capacities, giving them an enriched degree of capacity than was previously operational before the Spirit's renewal. Whilst careful to underline that this faculty of the soul (like the rest) ordinarily functions in holistic unity with the body, the "spiritual" place of the human—so beloved by the Pentecostal tradition—would, therefore, be retained through this heightened concept of spirit; this gives

---

69. Such a consideration may also commend itself to Pentecostal thinkers given that—in his soul/spirit distinction—Moreland is in line with a view popular (though expressed in differing ways) in the era of the church fathers cf. Irenaeus, *Against Heresies* 2.33.5 and 5.6.1.

(anthropo-) pneumatological resource for the development of Pentecostal spirituality, namely, providing the human spirit as the anthropological means by which the Holy Spirit renews the other capacities of the soul.

This modification of Moreland's suggestion—viewing the spirit faculty as the *lead, central,* and *representative* faculty of the soul—has the additional benefit of meaning that a human being is defined primarily as someone made for the vocation of knowing and serving God. This has implications for understanding of the image of God,[70] but for the purposes of the doctrine of constitution the important factor is that this understanding of the spirit-within-the-soul gives a philosophical-theological *anthropology* to which Smith's Enspirited creation ontology can be applied—the process of which providing a Pentecostal enhancement to this S/spiritual understanding of the soul and so engendering an enhanced Pentecostal doctrine of human constitution.

Pentecostally-Enhancing the Soul

In making the application above and returning to the ontology of Smith (see chapter 4), it can be argued that having the soul's faculty of the spirit renewed by the Holy Spirit is the means and difference between a person participating merely structurally in the Spirit and her participating fully directionally (vocationally) in the Spirit.[71] To make such an application, it would be initially helpful to adapt Smith's terminology and speak of the human spiritual soul (spiritual in a pneumatological sense) as being "Enspiritable" (as opposed to "Enspirited"). This draws attention to the fact that, as fallen people, out of vocational relationship with their creator, humans ordinarily only function with merely a structural participation in the realm of the Spirit. Yet, as per the Pentecostal call to renewal, humans are invited to come and have their spirits renewed by the Holy Spirit, to therefore enjoy directional participation in the Spirit. Of course, once Spiritually renewed, the human spirit is open to Pentecostal *on-going* encounter with the renewing Spirit, but the "structural" spirit only becomes the "directional" spirit by means of the Holy Spirit's renewing work in it.

---

70. See conclusion for further discussion.

71. To remind of Smith's position, the world is Enspirited by the Holy Spirit—creation being dependent on the Spirit for its existence; within that ontology, humans are designed to participate fully in the Spirit in vocational orientation to their creator, but due to the Fall participate merely structurally (maintained merely in existence in the Spirit—unless in receipt of his renewal).

This Pentecostal Enspiritable nature of the spirit-within-the-soul draws attention to the potential and intended orientation that the human soul is designed to have—led by its faculty of spirit—in relational intimacy with the Holy Spirit. In effect, the human spirit serves as the anthropological center/locus and interface of the Spirit-human encounter, and through such S/spiritual encounter, the spirit-hence-soul is made new, transforming the soul from being just potentially Enspiritable, to becoming Enspirited.[72]

When applying this discussion to the doctrine of constitution more fully, it is by means of this Enspiritable spiritual soul that an enhanced Pentecostal doctrine of human constitution can be proposed. Through applying the Enspiritable spiritual soul discussed to the holistic dualist doctrine of constitution—carried over from chapters 4 and 5—this allows for this chapter to propose a Pentecostally-enhanced understanding of the model, proposing that the constitution of a human is an "Enspiritable Holistic Dualism."

Conclusion

This final chapter and part of the book began by initially checking the contemporary (holistic) substance dualist model for "fit" within Pentecostal spirituality and theology through dialogue with Land's *Pentecostal Spirituality*, before progressing from that point to develop a *Pentecostally-*enhanced understanding of the soul.

Through stimulating dialogue with Land's spiritual-theological work, the chapter displayed that the (so-far) constructed soul not only

---

72. Indeed, for a born-again believer—a believer filled with the Holy Spirit—it might be said that her soul is transformed from being a spiritual soul (a soul that is Enspiritable) to being a Spiritual soul (one that is fully Enspirited). Added to the philosophical meaning of "spiritual" (to denote the "immateriality" of the soul), and the theological meaning of "spiritual" (meaning "pertaining to the Spirit"), this usage of the adjective "Spiritual"—this time with a capital "S," to mean "filled with the Holy Spirit"—might validly add a third understanding of the adjective to complement the first two meanings of "spiritual" (with a lowercase "s"). Whilst this uppercase language of "Spiritual" is appropriate for speaking of the soul (and hence "being") of a *believer,* when speaking about the constitution of a human being in general, the language of "spiritual" with a lowercase "s"—in the Enspirit*able* sense of the word—is more appropriate given that the doctrine of constitution applies to *all* humans (created and fallen), some of whom are participating merely in a structural sense in the Spirit. Whilst making this conceptual distinction, the potentiality of being transformed from being a human that is (structurally) spiritual, to being (directionally) Spiritual, is one that all (Enspiritable spiritual) humans are offered in the (Spirit-full) gospel of Christ.

"fits" within Pentecostal spirituality and theology but also offers provision of a better anthropological locus for accommodating the beliefs-affections-practices integral to Pentecostal spirituality. Indeed, proceeding from this spiritual-theological discussion, the chapter then progressed to the point of constructing an enhanced view of the soul—enhanced in a *theological* spiritual sense; this enhanced understanding proffered resource for explicating the anthropological means by which the Holy Spirit renews the human, providing an anthropological locus and interface for the on-going Divine-human encounters at the heart of the spirituality.

By means of considering the concept of the human spirit *within the human soul*, the chapter made a Pentecostal philosophical-theological enhancement of the Swinburnian holistic dualist model drawing upon the sources of biblical studies, philosophy of mind, and Pentecostal pneumatology to make this desired enhancement.

In summary of what was drawn from this tripod of sources, through utilizing the biblical studies of John Levison and Gordon Fee, the chapter identified that, biblically, the spiritual anthropological locus of a human is the (human) spirit. Fuelled by and consistent with this biblical understanding, the chapter proceeded to dialogue with a suggestion from J. P. Moreland, (second,) to contend that the spirit is (not ontologically distinct from the soul [as asserted by the trichotomist view] rather, it is) the *lead faculty* of the soul—its central and representative faculty—and the means by which the Holy Spirit relates to a human. Whilst being careful to maintain that this spirit faculty of the soul (as per the soul's other mental faculties) functions (ordinarily) in holistic union with the body, this philosophical-theological distinction between the soul and spirit was emphasized and, in the latter (the soul's faculty of spirit), an anthropological location identified for the Spirit-spirit encounter at the core of Pentecostal spirituality. Through application of the ontology of Smith, (third,) the chapter further enhanced the model, in a Pentecostal manner, proposing the *Enspiritable* nature of the spirit and hence the spiritual soul.[73]

As such the chapter has proposed a (theologically-) spiritually-enhanced model of the soul to facilitate the proposing of an enhanced Pentecostal doctrine of human constitution—a doctrine the chapter has entitled an *Enspiritable Holistic Dualism*.

---

73. And if employing the additional usage of the adjective, through the Spirit-spirit renewal, the human is transformed from being (lowercase) spiritual to (uppercase) Spiritual.

Conclusion

THE LAST ONE HUNDRED and twenty years have seen the Pentecostal movement burgeoning across the globe. With its core renewal spirituality being that which emphasizes humans' on-going transformative encounter(s) with God, by the Holy Spirit of Christ, in ways that are (more) spontaneous, unexpected, and dramatic—as well as those (more) calm, expected, and formal—the lives and communities of many have been transformed by this renewal spirituality worldwide, with the numbers of Pentecostal believers increasing at an exponential rate.[1]

As the Pentecostal movement has continued to expand, it has attracted scholarly attention and indeed developed its own specific branch of academic theology. Beginning from its distinctive spirituality, from and within which the theology flows, its theology displays four theological emphases in particular—the renewal pneumatological, the eschatological, the holistic anthropological, and the "supernatural" dualistic emphases all being specifically prominent in Pentecostal theology. This

---

1. Compare the figures and trajectory of growth between Burgess, *New International al Dictionary of Pentecostal and Charismatic Movements* (2002), then Johnson, "Global Pentecostal Demographics" (2010), and then Anderson, *Introduction to Pentecostalism* (2nd edition in 2014). Understanding "Pentecostal" in the scholarly sense (as employed in this book) to encompass all Pentecostals(-Charismatics) worldwide, Johnson details there to be 584 million Pentecostals around the world and Anderson suggesting over 600 million—with trajectories of growth indicating that by 2025 30 percent of Christians worldwide will be Pentecostal(-Charismatic). (See further Gabriel, "How Some Pentecostals" [2017]).

discipline of scholarly Pentecostal theology itself is increasing—evident from its (scholarly) journals, conferences, monographs, compendiums, and the centers of Pentecostal-Charismatic studies that are arising in academic institutions around the world. Yet whilst Pentecostal scholarship advances, within that scholarly work there are still certain areas of theology which, to date, have been yet to receive thorough attention—the doctrine of anthropology being one of these areas and a lacuna in Pentecostal theology. With its encompassing specific topics such as the *imago Dei*, sin, and human constitution, these doctrines-within-the doctrine of anthropology have all so far received a dearth of attention in the scholarly sphere, and in particular the doctrine of human constitution has received very limited attention to date. This gap in Pentecostal theology is somewhat surprising given that the doctrine of constitution carries implications for the human aspect of the Divine-human encounter at the core of Pentecostalism, as well as implications for issues such as metaphysics, personhood, ethics, disability, spirits, and personal eschatology. And so, recognizing this lacuna, *The Spiritual Soul* has sought to rectify the issue by giving scrutiny to this topic, giving sustained and focussed attention to the doctrine of human constitution.

In doing so it began with an original historical overview of western Pentecostal thought on the topic over the period of a century (from 1909 through to 2009 [through to 2015 in the subsequent chapter]). From this, a trajectory became apparent, displaying Pentecostals' development of thought on the issue—having moved from strongly trichotomous views in the early twentieth century to more dualistic views at the turn of the twenty-first—to now considering monism at the present and current end of the trajectory. It showed that the most recent contributors to this doctrine of constitution—Yong and then Kärkkäinen[2]—have argued this latter constitutional viewpoint, having potential for ushering the trajectory in this alternative monistic direction. Recognizing its significance and implications, the book then sought to respond—both critically and constructively—to both scholars' work, to propose an enhanced Pentecostal doctrine of human constitution.

In the focus on their work, chapters 2 and 3 highlighted that Yong and Kärkkäinen (helpfully) follow in the footsteps of Pentecostals before

---

2. Whilst theological anthropology remains a field that is under-attended by Pentecostal scholars, footnotes in earlier chapters detail more recent publications on Pentecostal anthropology (to that of Kärkkäinen in 2015) but that are concentrated on other areas of anthropology (and not focussed on the doctrine of constitution).

them who want to ground their anthropology in the (final) authority of Scripture and want to retain a place for the (human) spirit in their theology of constitution. These chapters also revealed that Yong and Kärkkäinen do have good reasons for rejecting the strawmen versions of dualism—Platonist and Classic Cartesian views. Moreover, the appropriateness of a method that values philosophy for constructing a theological doctrine of constitution also became apparent—giving a helpful steer and precedent for the constructive part of the book to proceed in a *philosophical*-theological manner. However, *The Spiritual Soul* has sought to respond specifically to two key contentions made by Yong and Kärkkäinen—namely that dualism of any variety should be rejected (with its immaterial spiritual soul entailed), and that emergent monism is preferable—finding both contentions inadequate. Whilst similar to earlier Pentecostals in being influenced in their theological anthropology by external (theological and philosophical) influences, in the case of Yong and Kärkkäinen these influences have unhelpfully contributed to the shaping of a Pentecostal emergent monist doctrine which is not concordant with some of the articulated Pentecostal theological emphases and is philosophically unpersuasive.

Regarding the first of their key contentions, whilst having grounds for rejecting the strawmen varieties of dualism (the Platonist and Classic Cartesian kinds), it has been seen that Yong and Kärkkäinen's critiques of these strawmen do nothing to rule out dualisms of a more robust variety. Indeed, the following constructive part(s) of the book have given a model of a stronger dualistic variety that surpasses the weaker models critiqued, and indeed proposed an enhanced Pentecostal model of human constitution to Yong and Kärkkäinen's alternative Pentecostal emergent monism.

This enhanced Pentecostal model was constructed by drawing initially upon Cooper to give a *holistic* dualist position drawn from the exegesis of Scripture. In its biblical affirmation of both the physical/material body and the spiritual/immaterial soul, the holistic dualist view showed itself to be concordant with all the Pentecostal emphases—including the eschatological and supernatural/spirit realm emphases with which the emergent monist model was less concordant. Recognizing that this holistic dualist model is biblical but *general* in scope, the following chapter sought to advance within and beyond this understanding to advance a *specific* holistic dualism. Having signposted a number of different (holistic) soul-body dualisms that Pentecostals might be drawn to for additional constructive work on the topic, the chapter identified the model of Swinburne as being particularly philosophically robust, and so expounded his model in detail as a worthy soul-body dualism for continuing to construct an enhanced Pentecostal doctrine of human constitution. (In contrast to Classic Cartesian dualism) Swinburne's contemporary substance dualist model revealed to be a holistic dualist model that is philosophically strong—surpassing the strawmen varieties of dualism and, indeed, Pentecostal emergent monism. So, the final chapter of the book took this contemporary holistic substance dualist model and then renewed it in a Pentecostal manner.

Appreciating this holistic dualism of a contemporary substance dualist variety as being concordant with the Pentecostal emphases (whilst recognizing its being a little under-dynamic as regards the pneumatological Pentecostal emphasis), the final chapter dialogued with Land in order to check that the understanding of the soul on this model comports with Pentecostal theology and spirituality. Finding it to happily comport, and in the process of checking its "fit," the soul was found to have superior capacity for accommodating the anthropology of Pentecostal spirituality. Following this spiritual-theological dialogue, the chapter then pursued the question as to whether this (immaterial) spiritual soul could be (theologically) spiritually enhanced, facilitating not just an enhanced Pentecostal doctrine but giving additional resource (within the model) for expounding the anthropological means of the Holy Spirit's renewal—specifically his renewal of the beliefs-affections-practices integral to Pentecostal spirituality. In the concept of the human spirit—drawn from Pentecostal theological history, engagement with Land, and through dialogue with Levison, Fee, Moreland, and Smith, the chapter provided a theologically-enhanced view of the soul—viewing the spiritual soul, and hence constitutional model, as Enspiritable (by the Holy Spirit) through its faculty of (the human) spirit. This resultant doctrine of human constitution—namely an Enspiritable Holistic Dualism—showed to be concordant with the four Pentecostal emphases, advancing (within but beyond the Cooper-Swinburne model) a model that is also Pentecostally-dynamic in terms of its renewal pneumatological emphasis. As such, through presenting the (immaterial) spiritual soul, enhanced with an (on-goingly) Enspiritable spirit, the goal of the book has been accomplished—proposing an enhanced Pentecostal philosophical-theological doctrine of human constitution.

The Implications and Significance of the Book and Avenues for Further Discussion

The Future of the Pentecostal Trajectory Concerning Human Constitution

In the process of articulating the above, the book has sought to renew the trajectory of Pentecostal thought on the topic of constitution. Contra the monistic direction that might ensue from the work of Yong and Kärkkäinen, through analysis of these scholars' work the potential trichotomy-dualism-monism trajectory—with this possible monistic future direction—has shown to be an unhelpful direction, with a renewed course being preferable. Having scrutinized the fullest versions of the monistic viewpoints that surround Atkinson's article of 2006 (an article in which he proposed a more integrated understanding of the human body and soul), the book has looked at these views but found problems with their monistic outlook. So, instead of allowing these works to lead the trajectory in a monistic direction, the book has proposed a different enhanced next viewpoint to (re)direct the trajectory instead. Having stopped at the monistic viewpoints to observe such landscape in detail, the suggestion for the direction of the trajectory might be that these viewpoints are perceived from a distance, or viewpoints passed through on the journey, but that the journey does not officially "stop" at these vistas or allow them to influence the trajectory's future direction. Following on from the work of Atkinson, then, a preferable next stop on the trajectory would be Enspiritable Holistic Dualism—a stop and a view that espouses an enhanced, holistic, relationship of the human body and soul. As such, this brings renewal of the trajectory—away from trichotomy-dualism-monism—redirecting its course, more suitably, in an enhanced holistic dualist direction.

Philosophical-Theological Approach

Additional implications of the work are entailed in the *approach* the book has taken—having implications for further research done on the topic of human constitution and for the development of the discipline of Pentecostal *philosophical* theology. The pursuing of the doctrine of constitution in a philosophical-theological manner has been carried out in recognition of the degree of philosophy required for adequately handling the topic, and in some ways has been following the approach employed by Yong and Kärkkäinen; however, in recognizing certain missteps in the philosophical work of both of these thinkers, the approach of this present work has been explicitly *philosophical*-theological in nature to ensure the adequate handling of the philosophical issues that are commonly mishandled on the topic of constitution. Recognizing the following four missteps as those that commonly appear in the thinking of anthropological monists—beyond just the work of Yong and Kärkkäinen[3]—it is hoped that exposing these four prevalent errors will enable further research done on the topic of constitution to subsequently avoid these common pitfalls, whilst also displaying to Pentecostals the importance of *philosophical* theology as a requisite discipline within Pentecostal studies.

The four common philosophical missteps that appear in the work of anthropological monists—and which subsequent research on the topic would do well to recognize and avoid—are:

1. The equating of the words "soul" and "dualism" purely with unhelpful Platonist or Classic Cartesian models (as opposed to considering stronger models or understandings of these terms).

As the book has repeated, now on numerous occasions, the best, most biblical, most philosophically defensible understandings of dualism and the soul are quite different from these Platonist and Classic Cartesian caricatures that are regularly (and fashionably) disparaged today. Rather than returning to the strawmen varieties, it is the *best* understandings of dualism and the soul that demand engagement in the present for beneficial discussion of the topic to follow in light of this proper engagement.

2. Making the philosophical category error of equating ontology with function.

Following a trend in biblical studies,[4] this second frequent mistake is to equate a holistic Hebraic worldview with ontological monism; but whilst the biblical Hebraic worldview emphasizes holistic *function*, to mistakenly reduce this concept to (monistic) *ontology* is a philosophical category error. *Functional* (Hebraic) holism also comports very comfortably with

---

3. As has been evident from chapter 3, the following missteps are also evident in the work of Joel B. Green and Nancey Murphy and to an extent, Philip Clayton; they are also evident in monists beyond those considered in this book, such as N. T Wright and M. B. Thompson. See further, Churchouse, "Healthier Anthropology."

4. See Churchouse, "Healthier Anthropology," 111–16.

ontological dualism (indeed being the integrated worldview apparent in the pages of Scripture).

3. Making the category error of equating (certain) issues to do with the mind as being issues in the domain of "science" when actually the discipline being engaged with is philosophy—specifically the philosophy of mind.

Whilst one's understanding needs to be *consistent* with the (neuro)scientific data, the topic of the philosophy of mind is specifically a discipline of *philosophy*, it is not of the domain of science. Supporting one's claim with "science" might add weight to any purported conclusion, but mistakenly considering philosophical viewpoints as the findings of "contemporary science" is an error of category.

4. Treating the topics of the *imago Dei* and the doctrine of human constitution *too* closely, resulting in the blurring of constitution into the topic of the *imago Dei*.

The topic of the *imago Dei* first appears in Gen 1:26–27, verses that are set in a chapter which emphasizes the identity and purpose of humanity; this means that theologically it is accurate to state that humans are relational beings (made for relationship with God, other humans, and the rest of creation). But the ontological question of *constitution* is a distinct and nuanced question, which receives little to no explicit attention in the theological flow of the biblical *imago Dei* texts (even if a certain metaphysical view might be assumed). Within the context of Genesis 1, the topic of the *imago Dei* addresses the questions of the "who" and "why" of humanity—not the "what" (of their constitution).[5] Attempting to address the question of constitution in such close relation to the *imago Dei* means that the categories of the "who" and "why" are confused with the category of the "what"; the question of constitution is unhelpfully blurred into the questions of identity and purpose.

Whilst being reluctant to belabor these errors, exposing these categorical missteps (along with the further critiques in the preceding chapters) is necessary for the avoidance of these (common) mistakes in future handling(s) of the topic of constitution, and further underlines the value of the *philosophical*-theological method for this topic. The method

---

5. Having addressed the topic already, it is worth highlighting that the topic of constitution is not what is being addressed in Gen 2:7 either.

of philosophical theology is one which has seen growth in its employment amongst Pentecostal thinkers in recent times,[6] and one which could further benefit Pentecostal theology in areas such as the Trinity, miracles, the attributes of God, human free will, the atonement, the nature of heaven and hell (to name but a few). But as the section above has displayed, it is particularly important as an approach when addressing the topic of human constitution, given the intricacies of philosophy entailed and the effects which that has on the conclusions one draws.

The Nature of Persons in Light of the Intermediate State and of Angels

Further implications arise due to two pertinent topics that have arisen in the course of this book—those of identity persistence over time (or, applied theologically, the topic of person persistence through the intermediate state) and the topic/nature of angels. Both these pertinent issues carry import for the doctrine of constitution, but in addition they have implications for issues of philosophy and theology more widely. Having seen the difficulty these issues caused for the anthropology of Yong and Kärkkäinen (making their Pentecostal emergent monism less concordant with two of the Pentecostal emphases), these topics of personal identity persistence over time and the nature of angels would likewise cause problems for any monistic position (for similar reasons to those seen in chapters 2 and 3 of this book); but as well as having that impact, these issues carry implications, moreover, for the related and significant topics of *metaphysics* and understanding of *personhood*.

The indicators of Yong and Kärkkäinen's work (and that of Joel Green—their lead dialogue-partner [in biblical studies]) is that they have been influenced by a current trend in theology that wants to move beyond substance metaphysics to a *relational* metaphysics (with Zizioulas's influence being apparent in this potential metaphysical shift); as a result, they are keen to jettison any essentialist view of a person. But as has been seen when articulating Kärkkäinen's handling of the issue of what happens to the person after death, and how the person's identity persists through

---

6. As well as the scholars particularly engaged with in this book, this growing employment of philosophical theology is seen, for example, in the work of Christopher Stephenson ("Should Pentecostal Theology be Analytic Theology?"), Simo Frestadius ("In Search of a 'Pentecostal' Epistemology"), L. William Oliverio Jr. ("Pentecostal Hermeneutics"). See further the (forthcoming) compendium *Analytic Essays in Pentecostal and Charismatic Theology* (Everhart et al., "Analytic Essays").

that time until the final resurrection, if one jettisons an essentialist view, then no sufficient account can be given to ground personal identity persistence through the intermediate state—Zizioulas's relational view being unable to offer an adequate framework for accounting for this issue of personal eschatology.[7] The relational view of persons—which regards them as "beings-in-communion" or "relational beings"—focusses on the trinitarian persons, and so views human persons as relational beings, and, as a result, is helpful to a degree. But unless there is a core (or "kernel") of a person that is able to survive death and exist in the intermediate state—indeed, is the *essence* of the person-that-is-in-relation—then such metaphysics is going to have problems with the issues of identity persistence over time from the point of a person's death through to her resurrection. It is worthy of note on this topic, as well, that the subject of angels rarely receives exposition on a relational view of a person—the preference being to focus just on the Divine and human person(s). But from the biblical and philosophical data given in this book it seems that any metaphysical view of a person needs also to take account of these angelic beings when defining the nature of personhood. Again, because an essentialist view affirms the kernel (or *essence*) of such beings, it can gladly handle the topic of angels in a way that the relational metaphysical view cannot.[8]

Having made these observations, this book might now offer its own definition of a person—one that draws fully upon the (essentialist) understanding of the *soul* as articulated in chapter 5 (recognizing that some kind of essentialism is integral to a cogent definition of personhood) but also upon certain insights of the relational metaphysics above. Chapter 5 defined the soul (in more of an essentialist metaphysical manner) as "a spiritual entity that is the bearer of (a Subject's self-) consciousness,

---

7. Remembering Zizioulas's comment, "[w]hat gives us an identity that does not die is not our nature, but a personal relationship with God" (Zizioulas, "Holy Trinity," 58 cited in Kärkkäinen, "Creation and Humanity," 348) This being an attempt to address the pertinent *philosophical* issue with a *theological* appeal to God that is unsuited and inadequate to address that specifically *philosophical* issue.

8. And indeed, it can bring levels of insight to Pentecostals' understanding of the wider spirit(ual) realm, including insight into the belief of some Pentecostals concerning ancestor spirits/ghosts. (Whilst not able to receive exposition here [and whilst advising a biblical and intellectual cautionary note on such consideration] the ghost of Samuel at Endor, Jesus's apparent acknowledgment of ghosts [Matt 14:26; Luke 24:37–39], the *Holy* Spirit / [traditionally] "Ghost," and the appearance of Moses and Elijah with Jesus at the transfiguration, would appear to give resource for the exploration of such topics as ghostly beings and ancestor spirits.)

which in ordinary (embodied) condition functions in holistic union with the body." In light of the issues of (personal) identity persistence over time and the personhood of angels, such an essentialist view is integral to establishing the definition of a person to follow. Yet whilst this is the dominant ontology at play, the following definition also applies the insights that a relational view has to offer (drawing from the emphases of trinitarian theology and the opening chapters of Genesis). So, drawing from the work of this book, and learning from the relational insights, it seems appropriate to define a person as "a relational being with self-conscious capacities."

Taking account of all the issues highlighted in order to give this full understanding of personhood, this definition carries full implications for the doctrine of the Trinity, of angels, and of humanity—each of whose personhood can be encompassed under such a definition—and of course carrying implications for the related field of ethics.

Ethics

Whilst space allows only for the very beginning of comment and application to the topic of ethics, a few important issues deserve comment here in light of this understanding of personhood arrived at (one derived from the book's exposition of the nature of the human soul). First, with personhood defined in the sense given above, a person is a person due to her essence as a Subject with self-conscious *capacities*. Those capacities do not have to be developed or functioning for the being to be defined as a person. A foetus or someone whose capacities are functionally limited is still unequivocally a person, due to her self-conscious *capacities*—she still has these capacities even if they are not functioning (in part or at all); essential personhood is defined by the (self-conscious) *nature* of her being. But, retaining the nature of personhood being relational, it should be underlined that that person only thrives and finds fullness *in relation to others*. On such an understanding, relationship with God is primary, and indeed relation with humans is vital, but so also are relations to non-persons such as animals and indeed creation more widely—the definition affirms the relational/creational nature of a person, one who finds meaning and flourishing in relation with others.

The *Imago Dei*

On the related anthropological theme, the topic of the *imago Dei* is additionally implicated by the book's work on the spiritual soul. Whilst having made the critique above of those who approach the *imago Dei* too soon (or who even mistakenly equate it with constitution), the book is now in a position to speak into this discussion due to the insights that have been gained in particular from the work of chapter 6. That chapter articulated the model of an Enspiritable spiritual soul—an understanding entailing a *vocational* category for the soul by way of the soul's faculty of *spirit* relating to the Holy Spirit; this, therefore, providing potential and insight for deepening understanding of the nature of the *imago Dei*. Again, whilst full comment is beyond the scope of this conclusion, the understanding of the spiritual soul given might be helpful in contributing to the topic of the *imago Dei* by way of what follows, giving avenues for further exploration for those subsequently addressing the topic.

Whilst a lot of effort, historically, has been poured into trying to identify *ontologically* what the *imago Dei* is, the directional flow of Genesis 1—the original biblical context of the theme—seems to be one much more interested in the topics of *relationship* and *function*, with the emphases of the relevant verses (1:26–28) being the *identity* and *purpose* of humanity.[9] Having proposed in chapter 6 an Enspiritable spiritual soul—an entity of ontological substance but with a theological, vocational purpose—the latter has resonance with the directional flow of Genesis chapter 1 and its interest in the relational-vocation of humans (in vv. 26–28). So, having articulated this theological (relational) purpose in the exposition of the spiritual soul, it might, at this point, be argued that an aspect of what it is to be made in the image of God—and so what it is to be human—is that humans have been created with a self-conscious soul with a leading, central faculty of a human spirit, designed specifically to relate to God. This teleological capacity is one that all humans possess, however, due to the Fall, it needs to be functionally renewed by the Holy Spirit of Christ in order for the human to fully be, and live out, the *imago Dei*.[10] In the person and work of Jesus Christ, and the pouring out of his

---

9. See further Churchouse, "Distinguishing the Imago Dei."

10. This understanding—and definition of the soul given in this book—is one that is gladly able to encompass those with cognitive disabilities (who, it is sometimes feared, might be excluded under certain other views of the *imago Dei*). Remembering that the soul has been defined as "an immaterial entity that is the bearer of (a Subject's self-) consciousness which (in ordinary, embodied, condition) functions in holistic

Pentecostal Spirit, the renewal of this spirit is achieved through reception of this soteriological gift. Drawing the receiver into communion with Christ, the (Holy)Spirit-(human)spirit encounter is the means by which this spiritual soul is renewed, with this Pentecostal Spirit-spirit encounter being an on-going and expected experience in the life of the believer—enabling her to be and carry out the relational-vocation of the *imago Dei*. As such, this Spirit-spirit(ual soul) encounter, so important to Pentecostal spirituality, becomes integral to understanding the God-given human vocation and is the means by which the Spirit of Christ renews a human, and properly enables her to be and live out the *imago Dei*.

Pentecostal Spirituality

Deeply entailed in the exposition of the *imago Dei* detailed above, this book's work on the spiritual soul has implications for Pentecostals' distinctive spirituality itself. The Spirit-spirit(ual soul) encounter, lying at the core of Pentecostal spirituality, gives resource for understanding the anthropological locus (/the anthropological interface or "pole") of the Divine-human encounter, and indeed means of further expounding what is happening in and at that locus *during the experience of* this S/spiritual encounter.

In the anthropology of this Pentecostal S/spiritual encounter (for instance, during times of worship and prayer), the Holy Spirit is enlivening the human spirit—the central faculty of the human soul—so resulting in the whole of the soul being enlivened by this S/spiritual encounter. In alternative Pentecostal language, in such times of S/spiritual encounter, the human spirit is "open" (and furthermore "opened") to the "waters" of the Holy Spirit, so the spirit of the soul being imbued; these life-giving

---

union with the body," this definition has capacity for suggesting how someone suffering from extensive brain damage or malformation might also relate to God (in a way that is consistent with what is articulated in the main text above). With the term "ordinarily" in the definition of the soul above allowing for the potentiality of the soul's disembodiment, it is also a helpful qualification when thinking about the instance of (cognitive) disability—concerning, specifically, how the disabled person's spirit faculty might relate to God (when her brain is limited / inoperative in capacity). For someone with such extensive brain damage or malformation that her spirit faculty of her soul would otherwise be restricted in its relating to God because of the soul's ordinary functional dependence on the brain, this qualification of "ordinarily" would allow for God to relate to such a person's spirit in an extra-ordinary way, (in this particular instance) by way of special, direct relationship with her spirit faculty, so the relationship not being restricted by the brain's limited or inoperative capacity.

Spiritual waters then flow to the rest of the soul, bringing irrigation, fullness, and cleansing to the entirety of the soul's mental faculties. Indeed, additional Pentecostal language—such as the spirit's being "charged" by the Spirit (hence giving energy throughout the soul), or the spirit's being "ignited" by the Spirit (so spreading fire throughout the soul)—bring additional color and insight to this (anthropological) exposition of the Spirit-spirit encounter. And given that the human being is a holistic union of spiritual soul and body, the whole of the person experiences the effects of this S/spiritual encounter (with the topic of healing, for instance, being further implicated by this Spirit-spiritual soul encounter.) So, the anthropological locus of the Divine-human encounter is itself illumined by the work on the spiritual soul, bringing deeper and fuller understanding of what is happening in the Spirit-spirit encounter that lies at the very core and center of Pentecostal spirituality.

Epilogue

PENTECOSTALS LONG FOR AND passionately pray that people might hear and respond to God's invite to come and know life in its fullness through faith in the Lord Jesus Christ. Enjoying his Holy Spirit as the gift of the (heavenly) Father, and as the life-giving Spiritual rivers poured out by the resurrected and ascended Christ, Pentecostals participate in these Spiritual rivers in a joyful, vocational way, and indeed pray for his on-going renewal in the lives of themselves and of others. This enjoyment of the Spirit's renewing and longing for others to experience him likewise might be furthered by a deepening knowledge of the anthropology entailed in this encounter. Indeed, recognizing, from the work of this book, that in this (Divine-human) Spirit-spirit encounter, one's spiritual soul is being renewed by Christ's (life-giving, transformative) Spirit, (it is hoped that) this might fuel Pentecostal longing for the Spirit's on-going renewal(s) and indeed a genuine and loving desire to extend the invite to others. Moreover, in understanding that through such an encounter one's spiritual soul is being renewed by the life-giving Holy Spirit, this might appeal more widely to others who may similarly desire this renewal.

This increasing of Pentecostals' longing, and opportunity for others who desire this renewal, are those that a Pentecostal worship gathering would seek to nurture and facilitate, and with such S/spiritual transformation being the goal of Pentecostal theology as well as its spirituality, such seems an apt place to finish this book on theological anthropology.

So, in light of these longings and desires, the book will end with the lyrics of an invocational song. In language of imploration—calling the Spirit of Christ to come and to fill one's spiritual soul (now with deeper meaning entailed)—the words of this worshipful song provide a means of S/spiritual reflection on the thought expressed in this book, and words of prayer and desire for those wanting to experience this S/spiritual renewal. So, bringing the book to a close with these words of this song to the Spirit—words of reflection and invocation (read, ideally, at an even pace):

> Come, Holy Ghost, Creator blest,
> And in my soul take up your rest;
> Come with your grace and heavenly aid
> To fill the heart which you have made.
>
> O comforter, to you I cry,
> O heavenly gift of God Most High,
> O fount of life and fire of love,
> and sweet anointing from above.
>
> O may your grace on me bestow
> The Father and the Son to know;
> And You, through endless times confessed,
> Of both the eternal Spirit blest.
>
> Now to the Father and the Son,
> Who rose from death, be glory given,
> With You, O Holy Comforter,
> From now by all in earth and heaven.[1]

---

1. Maurus, *Veni Creator Spiritus*.

Bibliography

Albrecht, Daniel E., and Ervin B. Howard. "Pentecostal Spirituality." In *The Cambridge Companion to Pentecostalism,* edited by Cecil M. Robeck Jr. and Amos Yong, 235–53. New York: Cambridge University Press, 2014.
Allen, David L. *Hebrews: The New American Commentary.* Nashville: B&H, 2010.
Alston, William P., and Thomas W. Smythe. "Swinburne's Argument for Dualism." *Faith and Philosophy* 11 (1994) 127–33.
Anderson, Allan H. *An Introduction to Pentecostalism: Global Charismatic Christianity.* 2nd ed. Cambridge: Cambridge University Press, 2014.
———. *Spirit-Filled World: Religious Dis-Continuity in African Pentecostalism.* London: Palgrave Macmillan, 2018.
———. "Varieties, Taxonomies, and Definitions." In *Studying Global Pentecostalism: Theories and Methods,* edited by Allan H. Anderson et al., 13–29. Berkeley: University of California Press, 2010.
Anderson, Robert M. *Vision of the Disinherited: Lessons from American Pentecostalism.* Peabody: Hendrickson, 1979.
Aquinas, Thomas. *Summa Contra Gentiles.* Translated by Anton C. Pegis et al. Notre Dame, IN: University of Notre Dame Press, 1975.
———. *Summa Theologiae.* Translated by English Dominican Fathers. 61 vols. London: Burns, Oates, and Washbourne, 1911.
Arnold, Bill. "Soul-Searching Questions about 1 Samuel 28: Samuel's Appearance at Endor and Christian Anthropology." In *What About the Soul? Neuroscience and Christian Anthropology,* edited by Joel B. Green, 75–84. Nashville: Abingdon, 2004.
Arrington, French L. *Christian Doctrine: A Pentecostal Perspective.* Cleveland, TN: Pathway, 1992.
Astuti, Rita. "Are We All Natural Dualists? A Cognitive Development Approach." *Journal of the Royal Anthropological Institute* 7 (2001) 429–47.
Atkinson, William. "Spirit, Soul and Body: The Trichotomy of Kenyon, Hagin and Copeland." *Refleks* 5 (2006) 98–118.

Augustine, Daniela C. *The Spirit and the Common Good: Shared Flourishing in the Image of God*. Grand Rapids: Eerdmans, 2019.

Augustine, Daniela C., and Chris E. Green, eds. *The Politics of the Spirit: Pentecostal Reflections on Public Responsibility and the Common Good*. Lanham: Seymour, 2023.

Ayala, Francisco J. *Darwin's Gift to Science and Religion*. Washington, DC: Joseph Henry Press, 2007.

Badham, Paul. *Christian Beliefs about Life after Death*. London: Macmillan, 1976.

Baker, C. D., and Frank D. Macchia. "Created Spirit Beings." In *Systematic Theology*, edited by Stanley Horton, 179–213. Springfield: Logion, 1994.

Baker, Mark C., and Goetz, Stewart, eds. *The Soul Hypothesis: Investigations into the Existence of the Soul*. New York: Continuum, 2011.

Barnett, David. "You Are Simple." In *The Waning of Materialism*, edited by Robert C. Koons, and George Bealer, 161–74. Oxford: Oxford University Press, 2010.

Barr, James. *The Semantics of Biblical Language*. Oxford: Oxford University Press, 1961.

Barth, Karl. *Church Dogmatics*. Edited by Thomas F. Torrance and Geoffrey W. Bromiley. Edinburgh: T. & T. Clark, 1956–1981.

Berkhof, Louis. *Systematic Theology*. Edinburgh: Banner of Truth, 1939.

Best, Ernest. *The First and Second Epistles to the Thessalonians*. Exeter: Blacks, 1972.

Biola University. "'Panel 2' Question and Response Panel at Biola University's Conference 'Neuroscience and the Soul.'" July 12, 2013. https://www.youtube.com/watch?v=7_0JliALgIo.

Block, Ned. "Troubles with Functionalism." In *Readings in Philosophy of Psychology*, edited by Ned Block, 268–305. Cambridge, MA: Harvard University Press, 1980.

Bloom, Paul. *Descartes' Baby: How the Science of Childhood Development Explains what makes us Human*. New York: Basic, 2004.

Boddy, Alexander. "The Holy Trinity in Us." *Confidence* no. 141 (1926) 171–73.

———. "The Indwelling and Abiding Trinity." *Confidence* 5 no. 6 (1912) 123–25.

Boddy, John T. "Divine Rationality." *Pentecostal Evangel* (1921) 1, 3.

———. "Self—Its Authorship and What It Really Is." *Pentecostal Evangel* (1917) 5.

Boethius. "A Treatise Against Eutychus and Nestorius." In *The Theological Tractates*, translated by H. F. Stewart, 73–127. London: Heinemann, 1918.

Bonsirven, Joseph, SJ. *Palestinian Judaism in the Time of Jesus Christ*. Translated by W. Wolf. New York: Holt, Rinehart, and Winston, 1964.

Braine, David. *The Human Person: Animal and Spirit*. Notre Dame, IN: University of Notre Dame Press, 1992.

Broad, C. D. *The Mind and its Place in Nature*. London: Kegan Paul, 1925.

Broughton, Janet, and John Carniero, eds. *A Companion to Descartes*. Oxford: Blackwell, 1992.

Brown, Warren S., et al., eds. *Whatever Happened to the Soul? Scientific and Theological Portraits of Human Nature*. Minneapolis: Fortress, 1998.

Bruce, F. F. *1 and 2 Thessalonians: Word Biblical Commentary*. Nashville: Thomas Nelson, 1982.

———. *The Epistle to the Hebrews*. Grand Rapids: Eerdmans, 1990.

———. "Paul on Immortality." *Scottish Journal of Theology* 24 (1971) 457–72.

Burgess, Stanley, ed. *The New International Dictionary of Pentecostal and Charismatic Movements*. Grand Rapids: Zondervan, 2002.

Cartledge, Mark J. *Encountering the Spirit: The Charismatic Tradition*. London: Darton, Longman and Todd Ltd, 2006.

———. *The Mediation of the Spirit: Interventions in Practical Theology*. Grand Rapids: Eerdmans, 2015.

———. "Text-Community-Spirit: The Challenges Posed by Pentecostal Method to Evangelical Theology." In *Spirit and Scripture: Exploring a Pneumatic Hermeneutic*, edited by Kevin L. Spawn and Archie T. Wright, 130–42. London: T. & T. Clark, 2011.

Cartledge, Mark J., and Swoboda, A.J., eds. *Scripting Pentecost: A Study of Pentecostals, Worship and Liturgy*. Grand Rapids: Eerdmans, 2016.

Cavallin, H. C. C. *Life After Death: Paul's Argument for the Resurrection of the Dead in 1 Corinthians; Part 1: An Enquiry into the Jewish Background*. Lund: Gleerup, 1974.

Chalmers, David J. *The Character of Consciousness*. Oxford: Oxford University Press, 2010.

———. *The Conscious Mind: In Search of a Fundamental Theory*. New York: Oxford University Press, 1996.

Chan, Simon. *Pentecostal Theology and the Christian Spiritual Tradition*. Eugene, OR: Wipf & Stock, 2000.

Chen, C. Elmer. "The Pentecostal Doctrine of Spirit Baptism: A Theodramatic model with special reference to the concept of the imago Dei." PhD diss., University of Birmingham, 2017.

Chomsky, Noam. *Language and Mind*. New York: Harcourt, Brace & World, 1968.

Churchouse, Matthew J. "Angels and what they could Bring." *Journal of Pentecostal Theology* 31 (2022) 97–113.

———. "Distinguishing the imago Dei from the Soul." *The Heythrop Journal* 62 (2021) 270–77.

———. "A Healthier Anthropology with a Richer View of the Soul: A Response to the Theological Anthropology of N.T. Wright and M.B. Thompson." *Journal of Anglican Studies* 21 (2023) 106–27.

———. "How Could (Some) Pentecostal Theology be Analytic Theology? A Proposal, Proto-exemplar, and an example in the Doctrine of God." In *Analytic Essays in Pentecostal and Charismatic Theology*, edited by Drew T. Everhart et al. Eugene, OR: Cascade, forthcoming.

———. "Renewing the Soul: Towards an Enhanced Pentecostal Philosophical Theological Doctrine of Human Constitution." PhD diss., University of Birmingham, 2017.

Clayton, Philip. *Mind and Emergence: From Quantum to Consciousness*. Oxford: Oxford University Press, 2004.

———. "Neuroscience, the Person, and God: An Emergentist Account." In *Neuroscience and the Person: Scientific Perspectives on Divine Action*, edited by Robert J. Russell et al., 181–214. Vatican City State: Vatican Observatory, 2004.

Cohen, Emma, et al. "Cross-Cultural Similarities and Differences in Person-Body Reasoning: Experimental Evidence from the UK and Brazilian Amazon." *Cognitive Science* 35 (2011) 1282–1304.

Collins, Robin. "The Energy of the Soul." In *The Soul Hypothesis: Investigations into the Existence of the Soul*, edited by Mark C. Baker and Stewart Goetz, 123–37. New York: Continuum, 2011.

Cooper, John W. *Body, Soul and Life Everlasting: Biblical Anthropology and the Monism-Dualism Debate*. Repr. Grand Rapids: Eerdmans, 2000.

———. *Panentheism: The Other God of the Philosophers—from Plato to the Present*. Grand Rapids: Baker Academic, 2006.

Copeland, Kenneth. "Part 1." *Believer's Voice of Victory* n.d. (2005) 2–5.
Costello, Daniel, "Tarrying on the Lord: Affections, Virtues and Theological Ethics in Pentecostal Perspective." *Journal of Pentecostal Theology* 13 (2004) 31–56.
Cottingham, John. "Cartesian Dualism: Theology, Metaphysics and Science." In *The Cambridge Companion to Descartes*, edited by John Cottingham, 236–57. Cambridge: Cambridge University Press, 2006.
Coulter, Dale M. "The Whole Gospel for the Whole Person: Ontology, Affectivity, and Sacramentality." *Pneuma* 35 (2013) 157–61.
Coulter, Dale M. and Amos Yong, eds. *The Spirit, the Affections and the Christian Tradition*. Notre Dame, IN: University of Notre Dame Press, 2016.
Cox, Harvey. *Fire From Heaven: The Rise of Pentecostal Spirituality and the Reshaping of Religion in the Twenty-First Century*. Reading, MA: Addison Wesley Longman, 1994.
Craig, William Lane. "Omnipresence of God." Reasonable Faith Ministry, April 22, 2015. http://www.reasonablefaith.org/defenders-2-podcast/transcript/s3-8.
Crisp, Oliver D. "Analytic Theology." *Expository Times* 122 (2011) 469–77.
Crisp, Oliver D., and Michael C. Rea, eds. *Analytic Theology: New Essays in the Philosophy of Theology*. Oxford: Oxford University Press, 2009.
Cross, F. L., and Livingstone, E. A., eds. *Oxford Dictionary of the Christian Church*. 3rd ed. Oxford: Oxford University Press, 2005.
Cross, Terry. "The Rich Feast of Theology: Can Pentecostals Bring the Main Course or Only the Relish?" *Journal of Pentecostal Theology* 16 (2000) 27–47.
Cullmann, Oscar. "Immortality of the Soul or Resurrection of the Dead: The Witness of the New Testament". 1955 lectures, First published as "Unsterblichkeit der Seele und Auferstehung der Toten." *Theologische Zeitschrift* 12 (1956) 126–56.
Dahl, Murdoch E. *The Resurrection of the Body: A Study of 1 Corinthians 15*. Studies in Biblical Theology 36. London: SCM, 1962.
Davies, Brian, ed. *Thomas Aquinas: Contemporary Philosophical Perspectives*. Oxford: Oxford University Press, 2002.
Davies, Brian, and Stump, Eleanore, eds. *The Oxford Handbook of Thomas Aquinas*. Oxford: Oxford University Press, 2012.
Dennett, Daniel. *Explaining Consciousness*. Boston: Little, Brown, 1991.
Descartes, René. *Meditations on First Philosophy*. Translated and edited by Elizabeth S. Haldane et al. London: Routledge, 1993.
———. *The Philosophical Writings of Descartes*. 3 vols. Translated by John Cottingham et al. Cambridge: Cambridge University Press, 1984–1991.
Dew, James K. "Swinburne's New Soul: A Response to Mind, Brain and Free Will." *European Journal for Philosophy of Religion* 6 (2014) 29–37.
Donaldson, A. M., and Buchanan, A. T. "Filled with the Spirit: A Synopsis and Explication." *Pneuma* 33 (2011) 25–34.
Duffield, Guy P., and Van Cleave N. M. *Foundations of Pentecostal Theology*. Los Angeles: L.I.F.E. Bible College, 1983.
Dunn, James. *The Theology of Paul the Apostle*. Edinburgh: T. & T. Clark, 1998.
Dunstan, G. R. "The Moral Status of the Human Embryo: A Tradition Recalled." *Journal of Medical Ethics* 1 (1984) 38–44.
Dyrness, William A. *Themes in Old Testament Theology*. Exeter: Paternoster, 1979.
Editorial. "The Spirit of Man and the Spirit of God." *Pentecostal Evangel* (1924).
Edwards, Denis. *Breath of Life: A Theology of the Creator Spirit*. Mary Knoll, NY: Orbis, 2004.

Ellingworth, Paul. *The Epistle to the Hebrews: A Commentary on the Greek Text.* Grand Rapids: Eerdmans, 1993.

Evans, C. Stephen. "Swinburne, Mind, Brain and Free Will" [Book Review.] *Faith and Philosophy* 31 (2014) 105–8.

Everhart, Drew T., et al., eds. *Analytic Essays in Pentecostal and Charismatic Theology.* Eugene, OR: Cascade, forthcoming.

Everitt, Nicholas. "Substance Dualism and Disembodied Existence." *Faith and Philosophy* 17 (2000) 331–47.

Everts, Janet M. "Filled with the Spirit from the Old Testament to the Apostle Paul: A Conversation with John Levison." *Pneuma* 33 (2011) 63–68.

Faupel, William D. *Everlasting Gospel: The Significance of Eschatology in the Development of Pentecostal Thought.* Sheffield: Sheffield Academic Press, 1996.

Fee, Gordon D. *The First Epistle to the Corinthians.* Grand Rapids: Eerdmans, 1987.

———. *The First and Second Letters to the Thessalonians: The New International Commentary on the New Testament.* Grand Rapids: Eerdmans, 2009.

———. *God's Empowering Presence: The Holy Spirit in the Letters of Paul.* Peabody, MA: Hendrickson, 1994.

———. "Hermeneutics and historical precedent: A major problem in Pentecostal Hermeneutics." In *Perspectives on the New Pentecostalism,* edited by Russell P. Spittler, 118–32. Grand Rapids: Baker, 1976.

Fisher, H. E. "Does the Bible Teach Physical Immortality?" *Foursquare Magazine* 30 (1957) 8–9.

Foster, John. *The Immaterial Self: A Defence of the Cartesian Dualist Conception of the Mind.* London and New York: Routledge, 1991.

Frestadius, Simo. "In Search of a 'Pentecostal' Epistemology." *Pneuma* 38 (2016) 93–114.

Gabriel, Andrew K. "How Some Pentecostals Misrepresent Their Global Size." Exploring Theology, Scripture and Ministry, September 26, 2017. https://www.andrewkgabriel.com/2017/09/26/how-many-pentecostals/.

———. "The Intensity of the Spirit in a Spirit-Filled World: Spirit Baptism, Subsequence, and the Spirit of Creation." *Pneuma* 34 (2012) 365–82.

Gage, Warren. *The Gospel of Genesis: Studies in Protology and Eschatology.* Winona Lake, IN: Carpenter, 1984.

Green, Chris E. *Towards a Pentecostal Theology of the Lord's Supper: Foretasting the Kingdom.* Cleveland, TN: CPT, 2012.

Green, Joel B. "'Bodies—That Is, Human Lives': A Re-examination of Human Nature in the Bible." In *Whatever Happened to the Soul? Scientific and Theological Portraits of Human Nature,* edited by Warren S. Brown et al., 149–73. Minneapolis: Fortress, 1998.

———. *Body, Soul, and Human Life: The Nature of Humanity in the Bible.* Grand Rapids: Baker Academic, 2008.

———. "On Doing Without a Soul: A New Testament Perspective." July 12, 2013. www.youtube.com/watch?v=SDqm9rCq2MO.

———. "Out-of-Body Experiences: What do they mean?' *Signs of the Times,* June 2009. http://signstimes.com/?p=article&a=40027604761.645.

———. "A Response, by author Joel B. Green, to Scott B. Rae's review of *Body, Soul, and Human Life: The Nature of Humanity in the Bible.*" *Perspectives on Science and Christian Faith* 61 (2009) 194–96.

———. "Sacred and Neural? Minds, Souls, and Humans." February 28, 2016. www.youtube.com/watch?v=9twS0Fp3fpl.

———. "What Are Human Beings?" *Theology, News and Notes.* http://cms.fuller.edu/TNN/Issues/Spring_2013/What_Are_Human_Beings_/.

———. "What Does It Mean To Be Human? Another Chapter in the On-Going Interaction of Science and Scripture." In *From Cells to Souls—and Beyond: Changing Portraits of Human Nature,* edited by Malcolm Jeeves, 179–98. Grand Rapids: Eerdmans, 2004.

Green, Joel B., ed. *What About the Soul? Neuroscience and Christian Anthropology.* Nashville: Abingdon, 2004.

Grenz, Stanley J. *The Social God and the Relational Self.* Louisville, KY: Westminster John Knox, 2007.

———. *Theology for the Community of God.* Grand Rapids: Eerdmans, 2000.

Grudem, Wayne. *Systematic Theology: An Introduction to Bible Doctrine.* Leicester: InterVarsity, 1994.

Gunkel, Hermann, *Die Wirkungen des heiligen Geistes.* Göttingen: Vandenhoeck & Ruprechts Verlag, 1888.

Guthrie, Donald. *Hebrews: An Introduction and Commentary.* Downers Grove, IL: IVP Academic, 1983.

Habermas, Gary. "Evidential Near-Death Experiences." In *The Blackwell Companion to Substance Dualism,* edited by Jonathan Loose et al., 227–46. Hoboken, NJ: John Wiley & Sons, 2018.

Hagin, Kenneth. *In Him.* Tulsa: Faith Library, 1975.

Hart, Larry D. *Truth Aflame: Theology for the Church in Renewal.* Repr. Grand Rapids: Zondervan, 2005.

Hasker, William. "The Dialectic of Soul and Body." *American Catholic Philosophical Quarterly* 87 (2013) 495–509.

———. "The Dialectic of Soul and Body." August 1, 2013. www.youtube.com/watch?XwUMBIlkRXk.

———. "Emergent Dualism: Challenge to a Materialist Consensus." In *What About the Soul? Neuroscience and Christian Anthropology,* edited by Joel B. Green, 101–16. Nashville: Abingdon, 2004.

———. *The Emergent Self.* New York: Cornell University Press, 1999.

———. "Persons and the Unity of Consciousness." In *The Waning of Materialism,* edited by Robert C. Koons and George Bealer, 175–90. New York: Oxford University Press, 2010.

———. "Souls, Beastly and Human." In *The Soul Hypothesis: Investigations into the Existence of the Soul,* edited by Mark C. Baker and Stewart Goetz, 202–19. New York: Continuum, 2011.

———. "Swinburne's Modal Argument for Dualism: Epistemically Circular." *Faith and Philosophy* 15 (1998) 366–72.

Hatfield, Gary. *Descartes and the Meditations.* London and New York: Routledge, 2003.

———. "Rene Descartes." *The Stanford Encyclopaedia of Philosophy.* http://plato.stanford.edu/archives/spr2014/entries/descartes.academia.

Hollenweger, Walter J. *The Pentecostals.* London: SCM, 1972.

Horton, Stanley. "The Last Things." In *Systematic Theology,* edited by Stanley Horton, 597–638. Springfield: Logion, 1994.

Howespian, A. A. "Who or What Are We?" *Review of Metaphysics* 45 (1992) 483–502.

Huttinga, Wolter. "Participation and Communicability: Herman Bavinck and John Milbank on the Relation between God and the World." http://www.academia.edu/11252500/Participation_and_Communicability_Herman_Bavinck_and_John_Milbank_on_the_Relation_between_God_and_the_World.

Irenaeus. *Against Heresies.* Translated by Dominic J. Unger. New York: Paulist, 1992.

Jaworski, William. *Structure and the Metaphysics of Mind: How Hylomorphism Solves the Mind-Body Problem.* Oxford: Oxford University Press, 2016.

Jewett, Robert. *Paul's Anthropological Terms: A Study of Their Use in Conflict Settings.* Arbeiten zur Geschichte des antiken Judentums und des Urchristentums 10. Leiden: Brill, 1971.

Johnson, Todd M. "Global Pentecostal Demographics." In *Spirit and Power: The Growth and Global Impact of Pentecostalism,* edited by Donald E. Miller et al., 320–21. Oxford: Oxford University Press, 2013)

Johnston, Mark. "Hylomorphism." *Journal of Philosophy* 103 (2006) 652–98.

Kaiser, Otto. *Death and Life.* Nashville: Abingdon, 1981.

Kärkkäinen, Veli-Matti. *Christ and Reconciliation.* Vol. 1, *A Constructive Christian Theology for the Pluralistic World.* Grand Rapids: Eerdmans, 2013.

———. *Creation and Humanity.* Vol. 3, *A Constructive Christian Theology for the Church in the Pluralistic World.* Grand Rapids: Eerdmans, 2015.

———. "The Holy Spirit and Justification: The Ecumenical Significance of Luther's Doctrine of Justification." *Pneuma: The Journal of the Society for Pentecostal Studies* 24 (2002) 26–39.

———. "Pentecostal Pneumatology of Religions: The Contribution of Pentecostalism to Our Understanding of the Work of God's Spirit in the World." In *The Spirit in the World: Emerging Pentecostal Theologies in Global Contexts,* edited by Veli-Matti Kärkkäinen, 155–80. Grand Rapids: Eerdmans, 2009.

———. "The Pentecostal Understanding of Mission." In *Pentecostal Mission and Global Christianity,* edited by Wonsuk Ma et al., 26–44. Oxford: Regnum, 2013.

———. "'Surveying the Land and Charting the Territory of the Spirit': A Biographical Footnote to Clark Pinnock's Review of My Pneumatology." *Journal of Pentecostal Theology* 12 (2003) 9–13.

———. "Toward a Pneumatological Theology of Religions: A Pentecostal-Charismatic Inquiry." *International Review of Mission* 91 (2009) 187–98.

———. "'Trinity as Communion in the Spirit': *Koinonia,* Trinity, and *Filioque* in the Roman Catholic-Pentecostal Dialogue." *Pneuma* 22 (2000) 209–30.

Kärkkäinen, Veli-Matti, et al., eds. *Loosing the Spirits: Interdisciplinary and Religio-Cultural Discourses on a Spirit-Filled World.* New York: Palgrave Macmillan, 2013.

Kenyon, Esseck W. *The Bible in the Light of Our Redemption.* 3rd ed. Lynnwood, TX: Kenyon's Gospel Publishing Society, 1969.

Kim, Jaegwon. "Causality and Dualism." Lecture given at the University of Notre Dame, March 7, 1998.

Land, Steven J. *Pentecostal Spirituality: A Passion for the Kingdom.* Journal of Pentecostal Theology Supplement 1. Sheffield: Sheffield Academic, 1993.

Leftow, Brian. "Souls Dipped in Dust." In *Soul, Body, and Survival,* edited by Kevin Corcoran, 120–38. Ithaca: Cornell University Press, 2001.

———. "Soul, Mind and Brain." In *The Waning of Materialism,* edited by Robert C. Koons, and George Bealer, 395–416. New York: Oxford University Press, 2010.

Levison, John R. *Filled with the Spirit.* Grand Rapids: Eerdmans, 2009.

———. "*Filled With the Spirit*: A Conversation with Pentecostal and Charismatic Scholars." *Journal of Pentecostal Theology* 20 (2011) 213–31.

———. "Recommendations for the Future of Pneumatology." *Pneuma* 33 (2011) 79–93.

Lycan, William. "Giving Dualism its Due." *Australian Journal of Philosophy* 87 (2009) 551–63.

Macchia, Frank D. *Baptized in the Spirit: A Global Pentecostal Theology.* Grand Rapids: Eerdmans, 2006.

———. *Jesus the Spirit Baptizer: Christology in Light of Pentecost.* Grand Rapids: Eerdmans, 2018.

———. "The Spirit of Life and the Spirit of Immortality: An Appreciative Review of Levison's *Filled with the Spirit.*" *Pneuma* 33 (2011) 69–78.

Malherbe, Abraham J. *The Letters to the Thessalonians.* New York: Doubleday, 2000.

Mann, Mark. "Traditionalist or Reformist: Amos Yong, Pentecostalism, and the Future of Evangelical Theology." In *The Theology of Amos Yong and the New Face of Pentecostal Scholarship*, edited by Wolfgang Vondey, and Martin W. Mittelstadt, 199–220. Leiden: Brill, 2013.

Marshall, Ian Howard, *1 and 2 Thessalonians: The New Century Bible Commentary.* Grand Rapids: Eerdmans, 1983.

Mathers, Hannah. *The Interpreting Spirit: Spirit, Scripture, and Interpretation in the Renewal Tradition.* Eugene, OR: Pickwick Publications, 2020.

Maurus Rhabanus. *Veni Creator Spiritus, Mentus tuorum visita.* Translated by Richard Mant, *Ancient Hymns* 1837 (modified for individual use in the contemporary, Churchouse). https://reginacaeliparish.org/documents/Veni%20Creator%20Spirtus.pdf.

McDaniel, J. "Where is the Holy Spirit Anyway? Response to a Sceptic Environmentalist." *Ecumenical Review* 42 (1990) 162–74

McGee. Gary B. "'More than Evangelical': The Challenge of the Evolving Theological Identity of the Assemblies of God." *Pneuma* 25 (2003) 289–300.

McGinn, Colin. "Can We Solve the Mind-Body Problem?" *Mind* 98 (1989) 349–66.

———. *The Problem of Consciousness.* Oxford: Blackwell, 1991.

McKinnon, Allan. "Response to Michael Wilkinson's lecture 'Pentecostalism, the Body and Embodiment.'" The Hollenweger Lecture, University of Birmingham, June 14, 2016.

Menuge, Angus. "Critique of Christian Physicalism." March 2, 2015. https://www.youtube.com/watch?v=ObNtUcBZ3Hw.

Menzies, William. *Anointed to Serve: The Story of the Assemblies of God.* Springfield, MI: Gospel Publishing House, 1971.

Menzies, William, and Stanley Horton, eds. *Bible Doctrines: A Pentecostal Perspective.* Springfield: Logion, 1993.

Moore, Andrew. "Philosophy of Religion or Philosophical Theology?" *International Journal of Systematic Theology* 3 (2001) 309–28.

Moreland, J. P. *Consciousness and the Existence of God.* New York: Routledge, 2008.

———. "A Critique of and Alternative to Nancey Murphy's Christian Physicalism." Unpublished paper received in personal correspondence, February 2015.

———. "Is the Soul Immortal?" Closer to Truth, September 14, 2022. https://closertotruth.com/video/morjp-011/?referrer=7871.

———. "Mental vs Top-Down Causation: Sic et Non: Why Top-Down Causation Does not Support Mental Causation." *Philosophia Christi* 15 (2013) 133–48.

———. "The Origin of the Soul in Light of Twinning, Cloning and Frozen Embryos." *Journal of the International Society of Christian Apologetics* 3 (2010) 1–12.

———. *What Is the Soul? Recovering Human Personhood in a Scientific Age*. Norcross, GA: RZIM, 2002.

Moreland, J. P., and Scott B. Rae. *Body and Soul: Human Nature and the Crisis of Ethics*. Downers Grove, IL: InterVarsity, 2000.

Morowitz, Harold J. *The Emergence of Everything: How the World Became Complex*. New York: Oxford University Press, 2002.

Morris, Leon. *The First and Second Epistles to the Thessalonians: The New International Commentary on the New Testament*. Grand Rapids: Eerdmans, 1991.

Moser, Paul and Arnold Vander Nat. "Surviving Souls." *Canadian Journal of Philosophy* 23 (1993) 101–6.

Munyon, Tim. "The Creation of the Universe and Humankind." In *Systematic Theology*, edited by Stanley Horton, 215–53. Springfield: Logion, 1994.

Murphy, Nancey. "Human Nature: Historical, Scientific, and Religious Issues." In *Whatever Happened to the Soul? Scientific and Theological Portraits of Human Nature*, edited by Warren S. Brown et al., 1–29. Minneapolis: Fortress, 1998.

———. "Immortality Versus Resurrection in the Christian Tradition." *Annals of the New York Academy of Sciences* 1234 (2011) 76–82.

———. "Nonreductive Physicalism: Philosophical Issues." In *Whatever Happened to the Soul? Scientific and Theological Portraits of Human Nature*, edited by Warren S. Brown et al., 127–48. Minneapolis: Fortress, 1998.

Murray, Michael J., and Michael C. Rea. "Philosophy and Christian Theology." *The Stanford Encyclopaedia of Philosophy*. https://plato.stanford.edu/archives/win2016/entries/christiantheology-philosophy/.

Nagasawa, Yujin, "Review of the Evolution of the Soul," The Secular Web, June 23, 2005. https://infidels.org/library/modern/yujin-nagasawa-soul/.

Nagel, Thomas. *Mind and Cosmos: Why the Materialist Neo-Darwinian Conception of Nature is Almost Certainly False*. New York: Oxford University Press, 2012.

———. "What Is It Like to Be a Bat?" *The Philosophical Review* 83 (1974) 433–50.

Nee, Watchman. *The Spiritual Man*. Repr. New York: Christian Fellowship Publishers, 1977.

Notre Dame Centre for Advanced Study. "Mind, Soul, World: Conclusions and Discussion of Closing Thoughts and Comments." https://www.youtube.com/watch?v=pZ5yQ7t6oUQ.

———. "Mind, Soul, World: Introduction." https://www.youtube.com/watch?v=MUWMvhZyqoo.

O'Brien, Peter T. *The Letter to the Hebrews*. Grand Rapids: Eerdmans, 2010.

Oliverio, L. William, Jr. "The Theological Hermeneutic of Amos Yong, In the Prime of His Theological Career." *Australian Pentecostal Studies* 21 (2020) 4–28.

———. "The One and the Many: Amos Yong and the Pluralism and Dissolution of Late Modernity." In *The Theology of Amos Yong and the New Face of Pentecostal Scholarship*, edited by Wolfgang Vondey and Martin W. Mittelstadt, 45–61. Leiden: Brill, 2013.

———. *Pentecostal Hermeneutics in the Late Modern World: Essays on the Condition of our Interpretation*. Eugene, OR: Pickwick, 2022.

Orwig, A. W. "Jesus as Saviour of the Soul and Healer of the Body." *Pentecostal Evangel* (1925) 9.

Pannenberg, Wolfhart. *Systematic Theology*. Grand Rapids: Eerdmans, 1994.

———. *Toward a Theology of Nature: Essays on Science and Faith.* Louisville, KY: Westminster John Knox, 1993.

———. "Philosophy of Mind and Human Nature." In *The Oxford Handbook of Thomas Aquinas,* edited by Brian Davies and Eleanore Stump, 348–65. Oxford: Oxford University Press, 2012.

Peacocke, Arthur, and Philip Clayton, eds. *In Whom We Live, Move, and Have our Being.* Grand Rapids: Eerdmans, 2004.

Pearlman, Myers. *Knowing the Doctrines of the Bible.* Springfield: Gospel Publishing House, 1937.

Pelikan, Jaroslav, ed. *Luther's Works.* St. Louis: Concordia, 1956.

Penfield, Wilder. *The Mystery of the Mind.* Princeton: Princeton University Press, 1975.

Peterson, Gregory R. *Minding God: Theology and the Cognitive Sciences.* Minneapolis: Fortress, 2003.

Pinnock, Clark. *Flame of Love.* Downers Grove, IL: InterVarsity, 1996.

———. "A Review of Veli-Matti Kärkkäinen's *Pneumatology: The Holy Spirit in Ecumenical, International, and Contextual Perspective.*" *Journal of Pentecostal Theology* 12 (2003) 3–8.

Plantinga, Alvin. "Augustinian Christian Philosophy." *The Monist* 75 (1992) 291–320.

———. "Methodological Naturalism?" *Perspectives on Science and Christian Faith* 49 (1997) 143–54.

Plato. *Meno.* In *Plato: Complete Works,* edited by John Cooper, translated by G. M. A. Grube, 870–97. Indianapolis: Hackett, 1997.

Plato. *Phaedo.* In *Plato: Complete Works,* edited by John Cooper, translated by G. M. A. Grube, 49–100. Indianapolis: Hackett, 1997.

Plato. *Phaedrus.* In *Plato: Complete Works,* edited by John Cooper, translated by G. M. A. Grube, 506–56. Indianapolis: Hackett, 1997.

Polkinghorne, John. *Sciences and the Trinity: The Christian Encounter with Reality.* New Haven, CT: Yale University Press, 2004.

———. "Anthropology in an Evolutionary Context." In *God and Human Dignity,* edited by R. Kendall Soulen and Linda Woodhead, 89–103. Grand Rapids: Eerdmans, 2006.

Popper, Karl, and John C. Eccles. *The Self and Its Brain: An Argument for Interactionism.* London: Routledge, 1977.

Rahner, Karl. *Theological Investigations,* Vol. 21. Edited by Paul Imhof, translated by Hugh M. Riley. New York: Crossroad, 1988.

Richert, R. A., and P. L. Harris. "The Ghost in My Body: Children's Developing Concept of the Soul." *Journal of Cognition and Culture* 6 (2006) 409–27.

Robinson, Daniel N. "Minds, Brains, and Brains in a Vat." In *The Soul Hypothesis: Investigations into the Existence of the Soul,* edited by Mark C. Baker and Stewart Goetz, 46–72. New York: Continuum, 2011.

Rozemond, Marleen. "Descartes's Dualism." In *A Companion to Descartes,* edited by Janet Broughton and John Carniero, John, 372–39. Oxford, Blackwell, 1992.

Russell, D. S. *The Message and Method of Jewish Apocalyptic.* Philadelphia: Westminster, 1964.

Schwöbel, Christoph. "Rational Theology in Trinitarian Perspective: Wolfhart Pannenberg's Systematic Theology." *Journal of Theological Studies* 47 (1996) 498–527.

Searle, John. *The Rediscovery of the Mind.* Cambridge, MA: MIT Press, 1992.

Shelton, James B. "Delphi and Jerusalem: Two Spirits or Holy Spirit? A Review of John R. Levison's *Filled with the Spirit.*" *Pneuma* 33 (2011) 47–58.

Shoemaker, Sydney, and Richard Swinburne. *Personal Identity*. Oxford: Basil Blackwell, 1984.

Shrier, Paul, and Cahleen Shrier. "Wesley's Sanctification Narrative: A Tool for Understanding the Holy Spirit's Work in a More Physical Soul." *Pneuma* 31 (2009) 225–41.

Smith, James K. A. *Introducing Radical Orthodoxy: Mapping a Post-Secular Theology*. Grand Rapids: Baker Academic, 2004.

———. "The Spirit, Religions and the World as Sacrament: A Response to Amos Yong's Pneumatological Assist." *Journal of Pentecostal Theology* 15 (2007) 251–61.

———. *Thinking in Tongues: Pentecostal Contributions to Christian Philosophy*. Grand Rapids: Eerdmans, 2010.

Smith, James K. A., and Amos Yong, eds. *Science and the Spirit: A Pentecostal engagement with the Sciences*. Bloomington: Indiana University Press, 2010.

Sperry, Roger W. "Mind-Brain Interaction: Mentalism, Yes; Dualism, No." *Neuroscience* 5 (1980) 195–206.

———. "A Modified Concept of Consciousness." *Psychological Review* 76 (1969) 532–36.

Spittler, R. P., ed. *Perspectives on the New Pentecostalism*. Grand Rapids: Baker, 1976.

Stedman, Ray C. *Hebrews*. Downers Grove, IL: InterVarsity, 1992.

Stephenson, Christopher A., ed. *An Amos Yong Reader: The Pentecostal Spirit*. Eugene, OR: Cascade, 2020.

———. "Reality, Knowledge and Life in Community: Metaphysics, Epistemology and Hermeneutics in the Work of Amos Yong." In *The Theology of Amos Yong and the New Face of Pentecostal Scholarship*, edited by Wolfgang Vondey and Martin W. Mittelstadt, 63–82. Leiden: Brill, 2013.

———. "Should Pentecostal Theology be Analytic Theology?" *Pneuma* 36 (2014) 246–64.

Stephenson, Lisa. *Dismantling the Dualisms for American Pentecostal Women in Ministry: A Feminist-Pneumatological Approach*. Leiden: Brill, 2011.

Stone, Selina R. "Holy Spirit, Holy Bodies? Pentecostal Spirituality, Pneumatology and the Politics of Embodiment." PhD diss., University of Birmingham, 2021.

Stott, John W. R. *I Believe in Preaching*. London: Hodder and Stoughton, 1982.

Stump, Eleanore. *Aquinas*. London and New York: Routledge, 2003.

———. "God's Simplicity." In *The Oxford Handbook of Thomas Aquinas*, edited by Brian Davies, and Eleanore Stump, 135–43. Oxford: Oxford University Press, 2012.

———. "Non-Cartesian Substance Dualism and Materialism without Reductionism." *Faith and Philosophy* 12 (1995) 505–31.

Stump, Eleanore, and Norman Kretzmann. "An Objection to Swinburne's Argument for Dualism." *Faith and Philosophy* 13 (1996) 405–12.

Swinburne, Richard. *Are We Bodies or Souls?* Oxford: Oxford University Press, 2019.

———. "The Argument from Consciousness." March 4, 2015. https://www.youtube.com/watch?v=cD3agKZZLVA.

———. "Dualism Intact." *Faith and Philosophy* 13 (1996) 68–77.

———. *The Evolution of the Soul*. Repr. Oxford: Oxford University Press, 1997.

———. *Mind, Brain and Free Will*. Oxford: Oxford University Press, 2013.

———. "The Modal Argument In Not Circular." *Faith and Philosophy* 15 (1999) 371–72.

———. "Personal Identity." *Proceedings of the Aristotelian Society* 74 (1973) 231–47.
———. "Precis of Mind, Brain and Free Will." *European Journal of Philosophy of Religion* 6 (2014) 1–3.
———. "Reply to Stump and Kretzmann." *Faith and Philosophy* 13 (1996) 413–14.
———. "Substance Dualism." Lecture given at University of Birmingham, April 25, 2012.
———. "Summary of Are We Bodies or Souls?" *Roczniki Filozoficzne* 69 (2021) 7–10.
Taliaferro, Charles. *Consciousness and the Mind of God*. Cambridge: Cambridge University Press, 1994.
Titterington, E.J. G. "What Genesis 1–3 Teaches About Man." *Pentecostal Evangel*, June 24, 1956.
Turner, Max. "Levison's *Filled with the Spirit*: A Brief Appreciation and Response." *Journal of Pentecostal Theology* 20 (2011) 193–200.
Vanhoozer, Kevin J. *The Drama of Doctrine: A Canonical-Linguistic Approach to Christian Theology*. Louisville, KY: Westminster John Knox, 2005.
Van Lommel, Pim. *Consciousness Beyond Life: The Science of the Near-Death Experience*. London: Harper Collins, 2011.
Vondey, Wolfgang. "Between This and That: Reality and Sacramentality in the Pentecostal Worldview." *Journal of Pentecostal Theology* 19 (2010) 243–64.
———. *Beyond Pentecostalism: The Crisis of Global Christianity and the Renewal of the Theological Agenda*. Grand Rapids: Eerdmans, 2010.
———. "Does God Have a Place in the Universe? Physics and the Quest for the Holy Spirit." In *Science and the Spirit: A Pentecostal Engagement with the Sciences*, edited by James K. A. Smith and Amos Yong, 75–91. Bloomington: Indiana University Press, 2010.
———. "Pentecostalism and the Possibility of Global Theology." *Pneuma* 28 (2006) 289–312.
———. *Pentecostal Theology: Living the Full Gospel*. London and New York: Bloomsbury T. & T. Clark, 2017.
———. "Prolegomena to Global Pentecostal Theology." Lecture to the Society for Pentecostal Studies, Lakeland, United States, January 1, 2015.
———. "The Theology of the Altar and Pentecostal Sacramentality." In *Scripting Pentecost: A Study of Pentecostals, Worship and Liturgy*, edited by Mark J. Cartledge and A. J. Swoboda, 94–107. Grand Rapids: Eerdmans, 2016.
Vondey, Wolfgang, and Martin W., Mittelstadt, eds. *The Theology of Amos Yong and the New Face of Pentecostal Scholarship*. Leiden: Brill, 2013.
Wagner, C. Peter. *Territorial Spirits: Insights into Strategic Level Spiritual Warfare & Intercession*. Ventura, CA: Gospel Light Publications, 1991.
Walton, John H. *The Lost World of Genesis One*. Downers Grove, IL: InterVarsity, 2009.
Warrington, Keith. *Pentecostal Theology: Theology of Encounter*. London: T. & T. Clark, 2008.
Wellman, H. M. *The Child's Theory of Mind*. Cambridge, MA: MIT Press, 1990.
Wellman, H. M., and C. N. Johnson. "Developing Dualism: From Intuitive Understanding to Transcendental Ideas." In *Psycho-Physical Dualism Today: An Inter-disciplinary Approach*, edited by Alessandro Antonietti, Antonella Corradini, and E. Jonathan Lowe, 3–36. New York: Lexington, 2008.
Wenham, Gordon J. *Genesis 1–15: Word Biblical Commentary*. Waco, TX: Word, 1987.
Westermann, Claus. *Genesis 1–11: A Commentary*. Translated by J. J. Scullion. Minneapolis: Augsburg, 1984.

Bibliography

Williams, E. S. *Systematic Theology*. Springfield, MS: Gospel Publishing House, 1953.
Williams, J. Rodman. *Renewal Theology*. Grand Rapids: Zondervan, 1988.
Wimber John, and Kevin Springer. *Power Evangelism*. San Francisco: Harper & Row, 1986.
Witherington, Ben, III. *1 and 2 Thessalonians: A Socio-Rhetorical Commentary*. Grand Rapids: Eerdmans, 2006.
Wolff, Hans-Walter. *Anthropology of the Old Testament*. Translated by Margaret Kohl. Philadelphia: Fortress, 1974.
Wood, William. "Analytic Theology as a way of life." *Journal of Analytic Theology* 2 (2014) 43–60.
Wright, Archie T. "The Spirit in Early Jewish Biblical Interpretation: Examining John R. Levison's *Filled with the Spirit*." *Pneuma* 33 (2011) 35–46.
Wright, N. T. "Mind, Spirit, Soul and Body: All for One and One for All, Reflections on Paul's Anthropology in his Complex Contexts." March 18, 2011. http://ntwrightpage.com/Wright_SCP_MindSpiritSoulBody.htm.
———. *The New Testament and the People of God*. Minneapolis: Fortress, 1992.
Yong, Amos. "Christian and Buddhist Perspectives on Neuropsychology and the Human Person: *Pneuma* and *Pratityasamutpada*." *Zygon* 40 (2005) 143–65.
———. *The Dialogical Spirit: Christian Reason and Theological Method in the Third Millennium*. Eugene, OR: Cascade, 2014.
———. *Discerning the Spirit(s): A Pentecostal-Charismatic Contribution to Christian Theology of Religions*. Sheffield: Sheffield Academic Press, 2000.
———. "Radically Orthodox, Reformed, and Pentecostal: Rethinking the Intersection of Post/modernity and the Religions in Conversation with James K.A. Smith." *Journal of Pentecostal Theology* 15 (2007) 233–50.
———. *The Spirit of Creation: Modern Science and Divine Action in the Pentecostal-Charismatic Imagination*. Grand Rapids: Eerdmans, 2011.
———. *Spirit-Word-Community: Theological Hermeneutics in Trinitarian Perspective*. Aldershot: Ashgate, 2002.
———. *Theology and Down Syndrome: Re-imagining Disability in Late Modernity*. Waco, TX: Baylor University Press, 2007.
———. "Whither Evangelical Theology: The Work of Veli-Matti Kärkkäinen as a case study of Contemporary Trajectories." *Evangelical Review of Theology* 30 (2006) 60–85.
Yong, Amos, with Jonathan A. Anderson. *Renewing Christian Theology*. Waco, TX: Baylor University Press, 2014.
Yong, Amos, and Steven M. Studebaker, eds. *Pentecostal Theology and Jonathan Edwards*. London: Bloomsbury T. & T. Clark, 2019.
Zimmerman, Dean W. "Two Cartesian Arguments for the Simplicity of the Soul," *American Philosophical Quarterly* 28 (1991) 217–26.
Zizioulas, John D. *Being as Communion*. New York: St. Vladimir's Seminary Press, 1985.
———. "The Doctrine of the Holy Trinity: The Significance of the Cappadocian Contribution." In *Trinitarian Theology Today: Essays on Divine Being and Acts*, edited by Christoph Schwöbel, 44–60. Edinburgh: T. & T. Clark, 1995.

Subject Index

Affections, 29, 199–203, 206–9, 211, 224, 228
Afterlife (the), 8, 103, 147–48, 154, 158 (*see also* Eschatology)
Angels, xi, 7–9, 21, 104–5, 135, 140–41, 143, 148, 160, 162, 215, 232–34
"Animal spirits," 123
Animals, 27–30, 32, 42, 66, 85, 89, 108, 123–25, 174–76, 178, 189, 234

Bāsār, 144, 149 (*see also* Body; Sōma)
Beliefs, 15, 35, 145, 156, 169, 176–78, 189, 199, 201, 207–11, 221, 224, 228
    Memory beliefs, 28, 169, 175
    Second order (/ beliefs about beliefs), 178
Body / Bodies, ix-x, 9, 14–15, 21–24, 26, 28–29, 31–34, 37, 42, 44, 49, 53–58, 61–63, 67–68, 72–75, 77, 83, 87, 91, 93–98, 100, 102–3, 105, 108–10, 119–26, 131, 137, 143–49, 151, 153–55, 160, 162–67, 169–73, 178–83, 186–94, 197, 221, 224, 227–29, 234, 237 (*see also* Bāsār; Sōma; Embodied / Embodiment)

Brain
    Events / States, 56–57, 62, 94–95, 165, 168 (*see also* Mental Events / States)
    Hemispheres, 169–70
    (the) Human, 9, 35, 56–59, 61, 73–76, 94–98, 103, 106, 108–9, 123, 165, 167–75, 178–81, 184–86, 189
    Neurons, 73–74, 94, 168
Breath of God, 28, 86, 213–14 (*see also* Rūach)

C-fibres, 96
Character, xi, xiii-xiv, 88, 169–70, 176–78, 207, 213–14,
Charismatic, ix, 2–3, 30, 74, 214, 226
Christ, 5–6, 15, 37, 151, 154–55, 191, 214, 217, 221, 235–36, 239–40
Christology, 8
Church
    History, 2, 37–38, 70, 86, 141, 144
    Pentecostal / Charismatic churches, ix, 30
    The, 33, 69, 86, 135, 137

Classical Pentecostal
  Believers, 1–2, 30, 200
  Heritage, 68, 199
  Theology, 200
Conscious
  Awareness, 41, 207, 210
  Beings, 96
  Capacities, 234
  Existence, 145–46
  Experience, 109, 168, 204
  Life, 30–31
Consciousness
  God-, 23
  Human / self-, 24, 33, 59, 61, 66, 72–73, 91, 96, 105–8, 141–42, 148–49, 162–64, 172–73, 175–76, 178, 190–92, 194, 233–35 (*see also* Mind)
  Reality of, 76, 94
  World-, 23
Creation
  Doctrine of, 27, 63, 69, 85–86, 90, 120, 134, 136, 138, 190, 192, 214, 231, 234
  Enchanted / Enspirited, 134–40, 162, 222 (*see also* Ontology—Pentecostal / Enspirited)
  Genesis accounts of, 27, 54, 64–67, 83
  New / Renewed, 21, 103–4, 110, 120, 190, 209–10 (*see also* Eschatology)
  Spirit of, 52, 60, 63, 65

Death
  Human survival of, 25, 32, 55, 91, 100, 102, 111, 144–45, 148, 153, 155, 163, 178, 180, 193, 233 (*see also* Hades; Personal Identity persistence over time; Near-death experiences; *Sheol*)
  Jesus's, 154
  Life-after-, 8, 25, 29, 145–47, 154, 157, 178–79, 180, 191, 193 (*see also* Afterlife)
  Physical, 86–87, 91, 103, 110–11, 143–45, 147–48, 153–56, 159, 163, 165, 169, 178, 186, 188, 194, 232–33, 240

Demons, 7, 87–88, 104, 134, 140–41, 162, 215
Desires, 96, 119, 169, 176–78, 189, 201, 204, 206–10, 219, 221, 240
  Second order (/ desires about desires), 178
Dichotomy (/ Bipartite anthropology), 22, 25–26, 28–29, 32–34, 38–39, 42, 49, 146 (*see also* Dualism)
Disability, 52, 226
Dualism / Dualist(ic) anthropology
  Aristotelian-Thomistic, 56, 75, 122–23, 164–66, 187–88
  Classic Cartesian, 73, 75, 92, 94–96, 99, 112–13, 117–18, 120–26, 131, 166, 174–78, 190, 227–28, 230
  Contemporary forms of, 92, 95–97, 99–100, 126, 132, 166, 191, 227, 230
  Emergent, 164–66
  Enspiritable Holistic, viii, 10, 15–16, 197, 223–24, 228–29
  Holistic / Psychosomatic, vii, 14, 34, 93, 99, 112, 131, 134, 143–44, 146, 155–56, 158–61, 162–65, 197, 227–28
  More "Physical," 34–35, 49, 79
  Platonist, 89, 92, 96, 99, 112–13, 117–20, 126, 131, 166, 190, 227–28, 230
  Soul-body (all varieties of), 9, 13–15, 31, 37–40, 49, 52–53, 55–57, 62, 72–73, 75–76, 79–80, 83–84, 87–89, 92–94, 97, 99–100, 103, 106, 111–12, 117, 122, 131, 144, 147, 151–53, 159, 163–64, 166, 173, 193, 226–29
  Swinburne's Contemporary Cartesian (holistic) substance, 14–15, 95, 162, 165–78, 180–94, 197–98, 223–24, 228
Dualism / Dualist(ic) macro ontology (/ whole of reality)
  Pentecostal, 7, 142, 230–31 (*see also* Pentecostal theological emphases—"Supernatural" dualistic)
  Platonist, 120

Subject Index

Embodied / Embodiment, 7, 29, 50, 53–55, 61, 63, 78, 83–84, 88–89, 92, 94, 102, 110, 119–20, 146, 157, 163–65, 178–79, 189–94, 234
Emergence
  Strong / sui generis, 58, 106–7
  Theory of, 61, 65–67, 103, 105, 107–8, 110–11
  Weak / structural, 107
  Emergent
  Angels, 9
  Minds, 58–62, 67, 95–96, 98, 107, 109, 116,
  Properties / Mental activities, 57, 61–62, 96, 106–7, 134
  Universe, 65, 67, 104
Emotions, 30–31, 56, 71, 73–74, 83, 169, 200, 202, 210
Empowering
  The Holy Spirit's, 6, 24, 102, 216–17
Encounter
  Divine-human, x–xi, 1, 5, 7–8, 87, 133, 201, 203, 211, 216, 218, 222–26, 236–37, 239
  Human-human, 201
  Necromantic, 157
Epistemology, 70, 97–98, 120, 134
Eschatology
  Lukan, 154–55, 158
  Personal, 10, 28, 91, 102, 104–5, 145–46, 149–50, 153–56, 161, 226, 233
  Renewed Creation, 102, 110, 120, 161, 165
Eschaton, 70, 110–11, 120, 165
Ethics, 8, 70, 175, 226, 234
Evangelical
  Believers, 38–39
  Influence, 39–40
  Theology, 3, 33, 40
  Tradition, 27, 33–34, 39, 145
Evolutionary history and science, 41, 58, 61, 106, 165, 174

Full Gospel (the), 5

Gehenna, 158 (*see also* Hades; Sheol)

Ghosts, 8, 145, 162, 240 (*see also* spirits—ancestral)
God, 1, 23–25, 30–31, 37, 51, 55, 65–66, 71, 74, 77–78, 85–87, 98, 104, 110, 120, 133–38, 141, 162, 178–79, 191, 199, 213–17, 221–22, 225, 231–33, 236, 240 (*see also* Breath of God; God-consciousness; Image of God; Kingdom of God; Spirit of God)
  Relation to (/ Relationship with), 26–27, 44, 54, 85–86, 89–90, 135–38, 231, 234 (*see also* Divine-Human Encounter; Encounter with the Holy Spirit)
  Greek thought, 37–38, 86–87, 148–49 (*see also* Hellenistic Culture)

Hades, 149–50, 158 (*see also* Death; Sheol)
Healing, 7, 139, 237
Heart, 29, 55, 77, 144, 199, 200–203, 206, 208, 210, 215–16, 220, 240 (*see also Lēb*; *Kardia*)
Hellenistic Culture, 87, 147, 150, (*see also* Greek thought)
Hermeneutics
  Pentecostal, 36, 39–41, 43, 220
  Theological 51, 63
Holistic / Hebraic Holism, 53–55, 61, 63, 67, 71–72, 76, 83–84, 87–90, 92, 126, 131, 142–49, 152, 155–56, 159, 188, 191, 230 (*see also* Dualism—Holistic)
Holy Spirit 3, 11–12, 23, 51–52, 63, 65–66, 69, 101–2, 134–42, 211, 215–18, 221–22, 236–37, 239,
  Distinction and relationship between the human spirit and the, 11–12, 23, 212, 215–18, 223–24, 229, 235–36
  Encounter(s) with the, x–xi, 1, 4, 7, 133, 225–26
  Eschatological, 6, 216
  Experience of the, 5–6, 69 (*see also* Divine-human encounter)
  Filled with the, 3
  In Paul's letters, 216

Subject Index

Holy Spirit (*cont.*)
    Outpouring of the, 6
    Person of the, 2, 5, 134, 217
    "Radical openness to the," 4 (*see also*
        Pentecostal social imaginary /
        pneumatological imaginary /
        worldview)
    Renewing work of the, 1–2, 5, 15,
        34, 203, 211, 222, 228, 235, 239
    Spirit baptism, 1, 4
    Spirit-filled world, vii, 4, 104,
        139–43, 212 (*see also* Creation—
        Enchanted / Enspirited;
        Ontology—Pentecostal /
        Enspirited)
    Spirit of Christ, xiv, 1, 15, 133, 217,
        225, 235–36, 240
    Spirit of God, 12, 138, 213–15
    Spirit of / in creation, 64, 134
    Trinitarian, 21
Human Constitution, vii–viii, 8–16, 19–
    21, 23–24, 27, 29–30, 33–36, 39–
    43, 45, 49–51, 53, 57, 65, 68–69,
    71, 79–80, 82, 92–93, 96, 112–13,
    117, 127, 129, 131–33, 142–44,
    146, 156, 160–62, 193–95, 198,
    211, 221–24, 226–32, 235
Hylomorphism, 75, 165 (*see also*
    Aristotelian-Thomistic
    Metaphysics)

Identity
    Human, ix, 53–54, 61, 73, 88, 92–93,
        103, 187, 189–90, 231, 235
    Leibniz's law of non-, 108
    Personal, 56, 125, 170–71
    Personal identity persistence over
        time, 91, 102–4, 110–12, 232–34
    Rūach Elōhīm, 64
Image of God (/ *imago Dei*), 27–30,
    54–55, 66, 71, 83, 85–86, 88–90,
    92, 222, 226, 231, 235–36
    Functional view of the, 66, 235–36
    Relational view of the, 54, 88,
        235–36
    Structural view of the, 54, 235–36
Incarnation, 120, 136, 190, 192
"Inner parts," 144 (*see also Qereb*)

Interaction
    God-world, 63, 98
    "Problem" of 56, 75, 94, 96–97, 99,
        124–25
    Soul-body, 56, 75, 95–96, 98–99,
        122–23, 165, 174
    Intermediate state, 91, 102–4, 111,
        144, 147–50, 153–55, 157–59,
        163, 232–33 (*see also* Personal
        eschatology)
    Paradise, 155, 158
Intertestamental period (/ I.P.), 144,
    146–47, 149–50, 158–59, 214

Judgment (Final), 102, 146–48, 150,
    155, 159 (*see also* Eschatology)

Kardia, 149, 151 (*see also Lēb*; Heart)
Kingdom of God, 6–7, 102, 110,
    199–200

Language
    Human capacity for, 58, 124, 175
Lēb, 144, 149 (*see also* Heart; *Kardia*)
Luke
    Eschatology of, 154–55, 158
    Gospel of, 6, 87–88
    Holistic soteriology of, 90
    Pneumatology of, 214–15
Lutherans, 68, 70

Materialism / Physicalism, 93, 192
    Nonreductive, 76
Materiality, 30, 54–55, 61, 63, 76, 83,
    134, 136, 191
Mental
    Activity, 57, 63, 94–96
    Causation, 56, 75
    Events / States, 57, 62, 76, 95–96,
        165, 168–69, 173, 176, 179, 204,
        206–8, 210
    Life, 56, 94, 169, 175, 179–80, 204
    Properties, 106, 187, 221
Metaphysics, 8, 70–71, 226, 232
    Aristotelian-Thomistic, 166 (*see also*
        Hylomorphism)
    Corpuscularian, 166
    Platonist, 151

Subject Index

Relational 232–33
Substance 72, 232
Methodology, 35–36, 52, 105, 159
Mind, ix, 9, 29–30, 55, 58–59, 63, 66, 70, 75–77, 85, 91, 94, 96–98, 103, 106–9, 121–25, 141–42, 147, 164–66, 168–73, 176, 180–81, 184, 186, 192, 200, 202–3, 205, 215, 219–20, 231 (*see also* Consciousness—Human / self-consciousness)
   Emergent theory of, 60, 62, 96, 109, 165
   Mind-body question / relation, 42, 56, 58, 61–62, 67–68, 76, 93–96, 98, 105–8, 124, 143,182–83
   Philosophy of, 11, 15, 42, 52, 56–57, 59, 64, 76–78, 82, 93–95, 105, 107, 109, 112, 126, 163–64, 166, 170, 180, 185, 189, 194, 205, 211–12, 218–19, 224, 231
Miracles / The Miraculous, 1,3, 134–36, 139, 232
Monism / Monist(ic)
   Anthropological, 7 fn. 23, 10, 16, 34, 50, 56, 58, 72, 75, 79, 84, 87–88, 92, 113, 144–45, 152–53, 159, 161, 226, 229–30, 232
   Emergent, 9–10, 13, 58–62, 64, 67, 76–81, 96, 100–107, 109–12, 131–32, 197, 227–28, 232
   Macro ontology (whole of reality), 60–62, 106
   Multidimensional, 69, 76, 78–79

Naturalism, 60, 139
Near-death experiences (/ NDEs), 108, 178, 185–86
Necromancy, 145–46, 157
Neo-Pentecostal / Neo-Charismatic, 2, 30
Nephesh, 86, 144, 149, 213 (*see also* *Psuchē*; Soul)

Ontology
   Human, 53–55, 72, 92, 100, 106, 108, 126, 144, 152, 155, 159, 162, 165, 194, 219, 224, 230–33, 235

Pentecostal / Enspirited (Spirit-enchanted participatory), 14–15, 132–42, 162, 212, 218, 222, 224 (*see also* Creation—Enchanted / Enspirited)

Passions
   Human, 15, 73, 83, 199, 200–201
Pentecostal movement, 3, 225 (*see also* Spirituality—Pentecostal)
Pentecostal social imaginary / pneumatological imaginary / worldview, 4, 132–33, 160
Pentecostal theological emphases, 5–10, 13–15, 80, 100–101, 104–5, 112, 161, 197, 225, 227–28
   Renewal pneumatological, 4–7, 100–102, 112, 194, 197, 228
   Eschatological (kingdom), 6–8, 100, 102–5, 112, 132, 194, 199. 225, 227
   Holistic Embodied, 7, 100–102, 113, 167, 191, 194
   "Supernatural" dualistic, 14, 100, 104–5, 142–43, 194, 225
Pentecostal trajectory of anthropological thought, 8, 10–13, 16, 20, 36, 39, 45, 49–50, 68, 79, 113, 131, 226, 229
Person,
   Angelic, 234
   Core / "essential," 108, 155, 159, 169–73, 187–90, 192–94
   Divine, 233–35
   First-person perspective, 58, 123, 168–69
   Human, 24–26, 34–35, 44–45, 52, 55, 67, 74, 77–78, 84–85, 89–90, 94, 96, 102–3, 110, 118–19, 122, 138, 145–48, 152–54, 157, 159, 168–74, 176–78, 182, 187–89, 200, 202–5, 207, 209–10, 213–16, 219, 221–22, 232–34, 237
Personhood, 8, 85, 87–88, 91, 103, 170, 226, 232–34
   Essentialist view, 8, 85, 87, 89–90, 232, 234
   Relational view, 8, 85, 87, 90–92, 233–34

Subject Index

Pharisees, 148, 150
Pineal Gland, 123, 125
Pneuma (see also Holy Spirit; spirit—human)
   (Holy), 217–18
   (Human), 149, 151, 217–18
   Journal 215
Pneumatology, 6-8, 11, 13–14, 19, 64, 100–101, 132, 137, 139–40, 161–63, 165, 194, 197–98, 211–16, 222, 224–25 (see also Holy Spirit; Pentecostal theological emphases—Renewal pneumatological emphasis)
Possibility (Modal)
   Logical, 170–72, 178, 180
   Metaphysical, 172, 178
Post / Late-modern ideology, 191
Psuchē, 149, 151 (see also *Nephesh*; Soul)
Purposings (/ volitions / intentions / willings), 31, 169, 176, 178, 204–5, 209–10, 213, 221

Qereb, 144 (see also "Inner parts")
Quantum physics, 63, 69

Rationality, 58, 71, 83, 121, 175
Relationality, 55, 61, 66, 83, 88–89, 92
Renewal Tradition, 2
Rephaîm, 145–46, 157
Resurrection (See also Eschatology)
   Final, 56, 61, 91, 102–3, 110–11, 120, 146–48, 153–55, 158, 163, 165, 191, 233
   Jesus's (own) 6, 191
Rūach
   Divine, 64–65, 73, 212–13, 215, 218 (see also Breath of God)
   Human, 144, 149, 212–13, 215, 218
   Levison's view of the, 213–16

Sadducees, 147, 150
Science, 41, 52, 60–61, 63–64, 68, 75–77, 83, 93–94, 96–97, 99, 106–7, 110, 125–27, 138–39, 167–68, 174, 231
   Neuroscience, xi, 35, 56–57, 60, 62, 73, 75–77, 83, 93–96, 168–69

Scripture (authority of), 4–5, 12, 35–37, 49–50, 131, 142–43, 197, 227
Self (the human), 29, 71, 145, 165 (see also Human / self-consciousness)
Sensations, 76, 96, 123, 168–69, 176, 178, 204, 210, 219, 221
Sheol, 145–47, 149 (see also Death; Hades)
Sōma, 151 (see also *Bāsār*; Body)
Soul
   Animal, 175
   Capacities of the human, 189, 204–6, 208, 210–11, 219, 221–22, 234
   Faculties of the human, 28–29, 32, 85, 90–91, 182, 189, 204–5, 308, 219, 221, 224, 237
   The human spiritual (immaterial), ix-x, 9, 11, 14–15, 21–22, 24–29, 31, 33–35, 37, 43–45, 53–57, 59, 67, 72–73, 75, 77–78, 83, 86, 93–96, 98, 100, 103, 108, 111, 118–20, 122–26, 140, 142, 144, 146–47, 151–55, 160, 162–67, 171–76, 178–80, 184, 186–94, 197, 203–6, 208, 210–12, 215, 218–22, 227–30, 234
   The human spiritual (pertaining to the Spirit), i, iii, v, viii, x-xi, xiii-xiv, 11–12, 15–16, 118, 194, 197, 211–12, 222–24, 226–28, 235–37, 239–40
   The Enspiritable spiritual, 222–24, 228, 235
Spirit, the (see Holy Spirit)
spirit
   (the) Human, 11–12, 15, 21–26, 28–35, 37, 43–45, 49–50, 55, 59, 66, 72, 77–78, 104, 131, 140, 144, 146–49, 151, 153–55, 161, 192, 198, 211–12, 214–24, 227–28, 235–37 (see also *Pneuma*—(Human)
   Levison's view of the, 212–16
   Realm / World, 7–8, 14, 100, 104, 140, 142–43, 162, 192, 227

spirits (other), 134–36, 139–40, 142, 226
  Ancestral, 7–8, 162
  Angel, 104, 141
  Animal, 29
Spiritual gifts, 4
Spirituality, x, 57, 102, 198–99, 201, 218
  Pentecostal, x, 1–5, 8, 11, 15, 30, 33, 102, 132–33, 135, 137, 139, 142, 190, 194, 198–205, 208, 210–12, 216, 218, 222–25, 228, 236–37, 239–40
"Subject" (the First-Person), 76, 109, 123, 125, 163, 168–70, 176, 180, 182, 233–34
Supernatural realm, 7, 104, 135, 227 (see also spirit—Realm)
Supervenience, 9, 59, 61, 97, 165, 207 (see also Emergence)

Teleology (/ Teleological Functioning), 123–24, 221, 235

Thoughts, 123, 169, 176, 178, 204–5
Transformation (Spiritual), ix, 1, 87, 110, 133, 147–48, 201, 223, 225, 239
Trichotomy (Tripartite Anthropology), 3, 21–26, 28, 31–34, 37–40, 42–44, 49, 79, 151–52, 220, 224, 226, 229
Trinity, 8, 21, 217, 232, 234

Vocation (Human), 66, 85, 88–89, 92–93, 213, 222, 235–36, 239

Worship (Practices), ix, 1, 4, 7, 28–29, 133–34, 139, 141, 210, 236, 239–40
Will, 31, 35, 202–3, 205, 219 (see also Purposings)
  (Human) Free Will, 59, 85, 91, 167, 171–72, 175, 181, 184–86, 232

Author Index

Anderson, Allan, 2
Aquinas, Thomas, 38, 189
Arnauld, Antoine, 124
Arnold, Bill, 157
Arrington, French, 32
Atkinson, William, 34, 39, 42, 229

Barnett, David, 107
Barth, Karl, 85, 88, 90–91
Berkhof, Louis, 37–38
Brown, Warren, 34, 58, 76

Cartledge, Mark, 2
Clayton, Philip, 57–58, 60–67, 76–78, 81, 101, 105–7, 109, 111–12
Collins, Robin, 98
Cooper, John, 14, 34, 39, 142–61, 193, 197, 227–28
Cottingham, John, 125

Descartes, René, 97–98, 117–18, 120–26, 167, 174, 180, 187, 191–92
Duffield, Guy, and VanCleave, N.M., 28–31, 39

Eccles, John, 96
Elizabeth, (Princess), 125

Evans, C. Stephen, 186, 192

Fee, Gordon, 15, 40, 44–45
Foster, John, 165

Green, Joel, 34, 67, 77, 83–93, 98, 105, 110–12, 155–59, 232
Grudem, Wayne, 32–33, 39, 42, 141

Habermas, Gary, 185–86
Hart, Larry, 32–33, 39, 42
Hasker, William, 98, 165–66, 183–84
Hatfield, Gary, 125, 180

Jeeves, Malcolm, 34, 58

Kärkkäinen, Veli-Matti, iv, vii, 8–12, 33, 45, 47, 49–50, 60–84, 88, 91–94, 96–107, 109–13, 117, 126, 131, 142, 161, 164, 186, 190, 197, 226–27
Land, Steven, 4, 15, 198–207, 210–11, 223, 228
Leftow, Brian, 165
Levison, John, 15, 212–16, 224, 228
Locke, John, 91
Luther, Martin, 37–38

Macchia, Frank, 141
Mathers, Hannah, 2
McDaniel, Jay, 65
Moreland, J.P., 15, 107, 165, 186–88, 204, 212, 218–22, 224, 228
Morowitz, Harold, 61–62
Munyon, Tim, 32, 39
Murphy, Nancey, 34, 58, 60, 62, 67, 76, 81, 93–96, 98, 101, 105–6, 112

Nee, Watchman, 22–26, 31, 38, 40

Pannenberg, Wolfhart, 68, 70, 72
Pasnau, Robert, 165
Pearlman, Myer, 24–28, 31, 38
Peterson, Gregory, 57–58,
Plato, 118–20

Robinson, Daniel, 97

Shrier, Paul, and Shier, Cahleen, 34, 49
Smith, James K.A., 4, 14–15, 132–42, 160, 212, 218, 222, 224, 228

Stump, Eleanore, 165
Stump, Eleanore, and Kretzmann, Norman, 183
Swinburne, Richard, 14, 165–94, 197, 207–8

Taliaferro, Charles, 165

Vondey, Wolfgang, 201

Williams, E.S., 27–28,
Williams, J. Rodman, 28–33, 39
Wolff, Hans Walter, 145, 213
Wright, N.T., 77–78

Yong, Amos, iv, vii, 2, 4, 8–12, 33, 45, 47, 49–68, 72–73, 75–76, 78–84, 88, 91–94, 96–107, 109–13, 117, 126, 131, 136–37, 140, 142, 157, 161, 164, 186, 190, 197, 226–27, 229–30, 232

Zizioulas, John, 103

Scripture Index

OLD TESTAMENT

Genesis

1:1	27, 101
1:2	64–65
1:21	27
1:26–27	27, 54, 66, 84–86, 89, 91–92, 231
1:26–28	65, 235
1:30	65, 86
2:3	27
2:7	23, 25, 28, 31, 65–66, 73, 92, 101

Numbers

16:22	215

Nehemiah

9:6	141

Job

7:17–18	84, 88–89

Psalms

8	84, 89
32:2	215
51:10	219
104:25–30	219
144	84, 88–89

Ecclesiastes

3:21	29

Isaiah

26:14	146

Daniel

12:1–2	146

Joel

2:28	6

NEW TESTAMENT

Matthew
10:28	45, 151, 154
22:32	154
28:18–20	6

Mark
1:15	6
12:30	29

Luke
1:46–47	23, 40, 43
8:26–39	87
16:19–31	155, 158
20:35	154
23:42–43	158
23:46	154

Acts
2:17	6
23:6–8	154

Romans
1:9	217
8:16	217, 219

1 Corinthians
2:11	217
5:3–4	218
5:5	217
6:17	218
7:34	217
14:14	151, 217
14:14–15	218
15:50	110
16:18	217

2 Corinthians
2:13	217
5:1–10	29, 154
7:13	217

Galatians
6:18	217

Ephesians
4:23	219

Philippians
1:21–23	154
3:20–21	154
4:23	217

Colossians
2:5	218

1 Thessalonians
3:13	43
4:3–8	43
4:13–18	154
5:23	23, 25, 40, 43–44, 151, 217

2 Timothy
4:22	217

Philemon
25	217

Hebrews
4:12	23, 25, 40, 43–44, 151
12:23	153

1 Peter
3:19–20	154

Revelation
6:9–11	32, 154

www.ingramcontent.com/pod-product-compliance
Lightning Source LLC
Chambersburg PA
CBHW051631230426
43669CB00013B/2263